前 言
Preface

"国际贸易实务"是我国经管类专业的核心课程之一，也是商务英语专业的骨干支撑课程。它以商品的进出口为研究对象，重点介绍商品进出口业务的基本理论、基本知识和基本技能。通过本课程的学习，学生将熟悉国际贸易惯例，掌握进出口的基本流程和国际货物买卖合同的主要条款及操作技巧，为从事进出口贸易工作打下良好的基础。

本教材中英文对照，兼顾英语专业和非英语专业学生的需求，用英语作为媒介语来讲授专业知识，帮助学生在特定的英语语言环境中直接、系统地学习国际贸易操作实务，中文译文可以使学生加深理解，用已掌握的英语来系统地学习专业知识，掌握国际贸易中的英语术语、语言特点和文体特征，使学生既具有扎实的国际贸易专业知识，又拥有娴熟的英语语言技能。

在编写中，我们注重以下三点：

1. 以"必需、够用"为原则，突出实用性。全书以国际货物买卖合同内容为核心，以合同的签订和履行的业务操作程序为主线，广泛取材于当代国内外商务活动，材料新颖、内容充实，阐明了商品进出口业务的基本理论和基本知识。

2. 注重实际操作技能的培养。教材中融进了大量的案例分析和课后练习，体现了知识性、技能性的有机结合，使学生毕业后可达到与用人单位的"无缝链接"，实现零距离上岗。

3. 援引最新国际贸易惯例，注重新颖性。注重国际贸易知识的更新，采用最新的国际贸易惯例，对 2011 年 1 月 1 日生效的《2010 年国际贸易术语解释通则》即 INCOTERMS2010 的有关内容进行了详尽的介绍和解释。

本教材可以作为高等院校经管类和商务英语类专业的教材，也可作为外贸行业的各类培训参考书以及相关专业学生或从事国际贸易工作者的自学参考书。

本教材由王珍(浙江长征职业技术学院)、董建民(浙江纺织服装职业技术学院)任主编，高伟(浙江外国语大学)、袁清(浙江万向职业技术学院)、吕孟荣(浙江商业职业技术学院)任副主编，于越杭（宁波诺丁汉大学）参编。具体分工如下：王珍编写第3、10、11、12章及第6、7、8、9章的译文部分，高伟编写第1章和第9章的英语和练习部分，袁清编写第2章和第6章的英语和练习部分。董建民编写第4、5章的英语和练习部分，吕孟荣编写第7、8章的英语和练习部分，于越杭负责第4、5章的中文译文部分。由王珍负责大纲编写和统稿，并对全书进行定稿。

教材中难免存在纰漏之处，敬请各相关院校和读者在使用过程中给予指正，并将改进意见及时反馈给我们，以便在修订时完善。

编　者

2012 年 8 月

CONTENTS 目录

Chapter 3

Chapter 4

Chapter 5

Chapter 6

Chapter 7

Chapter 8

International Payment & Settlement (II)　国际支付和结算(二)………......**116**

Chapter 9

Inspection, Claims, Force Majeure & Arbitration 检验、索赔、不可抗力和仲裁…**132**

Chapter 10

Business Negotiation & Contract Conclusion　交易的磋商和合同的签订…...**144**

Chapter 11

Chapter 12

CHAPTER 1

Introduction
导　论

Focus

In this chapter, you will learn:

✧ What is international trade;

✧ Classification of international trade;

✧ Some other basic concepts of international trade;

✧ Parties involved in international trade;

✧ Organizations involved in international trade.

1.1　What Is International Trade?　什么是国际贸易？

International trade is the exchange of goods or services between two or more countries (regions), involving the use of one or more currencies. International trade is also known as foreign trade, world trade or global trade.

Foreign Trade Law of the People's Republic of China defines international trade as foreign trade, that is, import & export of goods and technologies and international trade in services. According to Organization for Economic Cooperation & Development (OECD), world trade includes imports & exports of goods and services. The World Trade Organization (WTO) covers global trade on such topics as goods, services and intellectual property rights. Nations like the United Kingdom and Japan also call international trade as overseas trade because they are island countries which have to ship goods to other nations over the seas.

Countries in the world participate in international trade because of different reasons. Absolute advantage, comparative advantage, factor endowment and the Leontief paradox are some of the international trade theories put forward by famous economists at different times. International trade increases competition, prevents monopoly and provides stimulus to economic growth, technical development and rising in living standards in different countries. In most countries, it represents a significant share of its Gross Domestic Product.

In a broad sense, international trade involves the exchange of goods, and services across international borders or territories. International trade is also a branch of economics, which, together with international finance, forms the larger branch of international economics. In a narrow sense, international trade involves only commodity trade. This textbook, *International Trade Practice* mainly refers to the practical exercises in procedures for handling import & export of commodity products.

国际贸易是两个或两个以上的国家（地区）进行货物和服务交换，涉及一种或多种货币。国际贸易又称为对外贸易、世界贸易或全球贸易。

《中华人民共和国对外贸易法》把国际贸易定义为对外贸易，即货物与技术的进出口，以及国际间的服务贸易。按照"经济合作与发展组织"的解释，世界贸易包含货物与服务的进出口。"世界贸易组织"将全球贸易划分为货物、服务和知识产权等方面。同样，英国和日本也将国际贸易称作海外贸易，因为二者为岛国，两国的货物需通过海运往其他国家。

世界各国因不同原因参与国际贸易。绝对优势、比较优势、要素禀赋和里昂惕夫反论等是部分不同时期著名经济学家提出的国际贸易理论。国际贸易加剧竞争，防止垄断，刺激经济发展、技术进步和各国生活水平的提高。在大多数国家，国际贸易在国内生产总值中占有显著的份额。

从广义上来说，国际贸易包含货物和服务跨国界的交换。国际贸易也是经济学的一个分支，它和国际金融一起构成国际经济学这一更大的分支。从狭义上来说，国际贸易仅仅涉及货物贸易。本教材《国际贸易实务》主要是指进行进出口货物操作程序中的实际业务。

1.2　Classification of International Trade 国际贸易的种类

According to the direction of commodity movement, international trade can be classified into export trade, import trade and transit trade.

Export is any goods or commodity that is transported from one country to another country through the Customs. China was once famous for the export of silk products and is still known for its export of garments and textile products. Export goods are provided to foreign markets by domestic producers.

Import is any goods or commodity that is brought into one country from another country through the Customs. Import goods are provided to domestic markets by foreign producers. China used to import cars and now it mostly imports foreign luxuries and advanced machinery and technology.

Transit trade refers to the transportation of goods from an exporting country to an importing country through a third country or region, which has no direct involvement in the deal.

Regarding form and content, international trade can also be classified into goods trade, tangible or visible trade and service trade, intangible or invisible trade.

Visible trade relates to goods traded while invisible trade relates to services provided for the buyers. According to the WTO, these invisible services mainly include business, communication, construction, distribution, finance and tourism services. For example, the United Kingdom used to be powerful in visible trade and is now very strong in invisible trade because of its worldwide services in insurance and stock exchange markets. Trade in services normally does not need customs declaration.

As trade relation is concerned, international trade can sometimes be classified into direct trade, indirect trade and entrepot trade or intermediary trade.

When a manufacturing country trades directly with a consuming country, it is called direct trade. When a

根据货物的流向，国际贸易可以划分为出口贸易、进口贸易和过境贸易。

出口是指经海关通关，由一国运往另一国的货物。中国曾经以出口丝绸产品而著称，现在仍然以出口服装和纺织品闻名。出口货物是由国内的生产者提供给国外的市场。

进口是指经海关通关，由一国进入另一国的货物。进口货物是由国外的生产者提供给国内的市场。中国过去进口轿车，现在主要进口奢侈品、先进的机械和技术。

过境贸易是指货物从出口国运往进口国，途经第三国或地区，该国或地区不直接涉及该项交易。

从形式和内容来看，国际贸易可分为货物贸易或有形贸易和服务贸易或无形贸易。

有形贸易针对的是交易的货物，而无形贸易针对的是给买方提供的服务。根据"世界贸易组织"的定义，这些无形的服务主要包括商务、通信、建筑、分销、金融和旅游服务。例如，英国的有形贸易过去很强盛，现在无形贸易由于提供全球保险和股票市交易场服务而强大。服务贸易通常不需向海关申报。

就贸易关系而言，国际贸易有时也可划分为直接贸易、间接贸易和转口或中转贸易。

生产国与消费国直接进行贸易，称为直接贸易。生产国与消费

manufacturing country trades indirectly with a consuming country through a third country, it is called indirect trade.

Entrepot trade is one kind of indirect trade. If a trade is concluded not directly between a manufacturing country and a consuming country, but conducted by a third country, it is called entrepot trade. In other words, the third country imports from the manufacturing country, then it exports to the consuming country. Country or region engaged in entrepot trade usually has a good location or favourable trade conditions. For example, as a free trade zone, Hong Kong, China has a good location and is an ideal area for entrepot trade. It can import directly from other countries and export into mainland China; the other way round, it can import from mainland China and export to other countries in the world.

国通过第三国进行间接贸易, 称为间接贸易。

转口贸易是间接贸易的一种形式。如果生产国与消费国不直接进行贸易, 而是通过第三国, 称为转口贸易。换言之, 第三国从生产国进口, 然后出口到消费国。从事转口贸易的国家或地区通常有着良好的地理位置或有利的贸易环境。例如, 作为贸易自由区, 中国香港有着良好的地理优势, 是从事转口贸易的理想地。香港地区可以从其他国家直接进口, 然后出口到中国内地。反之, 香港地区可以从中国内地进口, 然后出口到世界各国。

1.3 Some Other Basic Concepts of International Trade
国际贸易中一些其他基本概念

There are two commonly used trade systems by which international commodity trade statistics are compiled: general trade system and special trade system. The United Nations recommendations advise using the general trade system that provides a more comprehensive recording of external trade flows than does the special system. The general trade system is also adopted in China. General trade includes all goods that cross the national frontier and goods which are imported into and exported from custom-bonded warehouses and free zones. The general trade system is in use when the statistical territory of a country coincides with its economic territory so that imports include all goods entering the economic territory of a compiling country and exports include all goods leaving the economic territory of a compiling country.

The balance of trade, which is also an important concept in international trade, is the difference between the value of imports & exports in an economy over a certain period of time. A positive

国际货物贸易统计数据收集依据两种常用的贸易体系: 总贸易体系和专门贸易体系。联合国推荐使用总贸易体系, 总贸易体系比专门贸易体系提供更详细的外部贸易流入记录。中国也采用总贸易体系。总贸易包括所有越过边界的货物, 以及通过海关监管的仓库和自由贸易区进口与出口的货物。当一国的统计版图与其经济版图相同时, 使用总贸易体系, 这时, 进口包括所有进入统计国经济版图的货物。出口包括所有离开统计国经济版图的货物。

贸易差额, 在国际贸易中是一个同样的重要概念, 是指一个经济体在某段时间内进口与出口

balance of trade is known as a trade surplus and consists of exporting more than is imported; a negative balance of trade is known as a trade gap or, formally, a trade deficit. The balance of trade is sometimes divided into goods and service balance; especially in the United Kingdom the terms visible and invisible balance are used. China has had a trade surplus for the past few years. However，it is always difficult for every country to keep a perfect balance in international trade.

Standard International Trade Classification (SITC) is the classification system kept by the United Nations to classify the exports and imports of a country to enable comparing different countries and years. The SITC classification is used for comparing the composition of foreign trade and the composition of international trade. Its purpose is for compiling international trade statistics on all merchandise entering international trade, and to promote international comparability of international trade statistics. The commodity groupings of SITC reflect:

★ The materials used in production;

★ The processing stage;

★ Market practices and uses of the products;

★ The importance of the commodities in terms of world trade, and technological changes.

The composition of foreign trade shows the standard of economic, industrial developments of a country while the composition of international trade shows the standard of economic, industrial developments of the world.

额的差值。贸易顺差是指贸易盈余，即出口多于进口。贸易逆差是指贸易缺口，更正式地称为贸易赤字。贸易差额有时分为货物和服务差额。特别是英国使用有形和无形差额这些术语。过去几年里，中国一直保持贸易盈余。但是，要使每个国家在国际贸易中都保持完美的平衡是很困难的。

《联合国国际贸易标准分类》是联合国对一国的出口和进口分类的方法，以便对不同的国家和年份进行比较。它是用来比较对外贸易和国际贸易的结构。其目的是编制国际贸易所有商品的贸易统计数据，并促进国际贸易统计数据的国际可比性。其商品分类反映：

★ 生产使用的材料；

★ 处理阶段；

★ 市场实践和产品的使用；

★ 世界贸易中商品的重要性，以及技术的变化。

对外贸易的构成显示了一个国家的经济水平和工业发展，而国际贸易的构成显示了世界经济水平和工业的发展。

1.4 Parties Involved in International Transaction
国际贸易中的基本当事人

There are many parties involved in the process for the fulfillment of an import or export contract. Foreign trade operators are referred to as the legal persons or other organizations engaged in handling the import and export of

完成进口和出口合同的过程中涉及很多当事方。外贸经营者被称做国际贸易中处理进出口货物与服务的法人或组织。国际贸

goods or services in international trade. Major parties involved in international trade are the seller (exporter) and buyer (importer). The seller is the party that provides the products or services and the buyer is the party that purchases the goods or services. Sometimes a seller or buyer can be a manufacturer or a trading company. Sometimes an importer or exporter may appoint an agent. An agent is normally a commission earner.

Apart from import & export operators, many other parties are involved in an international transaction. One important party is the Customs that is in charge of import & export declarations. Another important party is the carrier that transports goods from one country into another. Then there is the insurer or insurance company, the party that arranges an insurance to indemnify for importer or exporter's losses. Next party is the banks that act as opening bank, advising bank, negotiating bank and reimbursing bank. Inspection agency is also an important party that examines the commodities under import & export contracts. If there is a dispute between the buyer and the seller, an arbitration institution or a law court will be another party involved.

易主要的当事方为卖方（出口方）和买方（进口方）。卖方是提供产品或服务的一方，而买方是购买货物与服务的一方。有时，卖方或买方可以是生产商或贸易公司。有时，进口商或出口商可能会指定一个代理商。代理商通常收取佣金。

除了进口商和出口商，国际交易还有很多其他当事方。一个重要的当事方就是海关。海关负责进口和出口的报关。另一个当事方是承运人，负责货物从一国到另一国的运输。然后，还有承保人或保险公司负责保险，对进口商或出口商的损失进行赔偿。下一个当事方是银行，充当开证行、通知行、议付行和偿付行。检验机构也是一个重要的当事方，负责检验进出口合同项下的货物。如果买方和卖方有了争议，仲裁机构或法庭将成为另一个当事方。

1.5 Organizations Involved in International Trade
国际贸易中的组织

1.5.1 International Chamber of Commerce (ICC)
国际商会

International Chamber of Commerce (ICC) is the global organization of world business for economic growth, job creation and prosperity. It was founded in Paris in 1919 with an aim that remains unchanged: to serve world business by promoting trade and investment,

国际商会是有关世界贸易的全球性组织，它的宗旨是促进经济发展、创造就业和繁荣。国际商会成立于1919年。它自始至终致力于促进贸易和投资，开放货

open markets for goods and services, and the free flow of capital. ICC sets rules and standards for international trade, for example, INCOTERMS 2010. Today, ICC has 16 commissions of experts from the private sector covering every specialized field of concern to international business and thousands of member companies and associations in around 130 countries. Members include many of the world's most influential companies and represent every major industrial and service sector. The ICC International Court of Arbitration is the world's leading body for resolving international trade disputes by arbitration.

物与服务市场，鼓励资本自由流动，从而服务于世界贸易。国际商会为国际贸易制订规则和标准。例如，《2010年国际贸易术语解释通则》。如今，国际商会有16个专家委员会，他们来自国际商务各个专业领域的私营部门，以及分布在130个国家的成千上万的会员公司和协会。成员包括世界上许多最有影响力的公司，代表每一个主要的工业和服务部门。国际商会国际仲裁会是世界上通过仲裁解决国际贸易争端的重要机构。

1.5.2 ICC China
国际商会中国分会

ICC China is the ICC China national committee. This national body was founded on January 1st, 1995. ICC China's members, state-owned, private or foreign-invested, come from a full range of sectors such as manufacture, trade, finance, transport, insurance and commerce. It represents the interest of businesses operating in China and speaks on their behalf with the Chinese government and intergovernmental organizations, and facilitates members' participation in international business activities as well as the discussion and formulation of business practices, usages, rules at international levels.

国际商会中国分会是国际商会中国国家分会，成立于1995年1月1日。国际商会中国分会的会员有国企、私企和外企，来自于制造、贸易、金融、运输、保险和商业等各个行业。国际商会中国分会代表了在华商界的利益，并替它们与中国政府和政府间组织对话，并促进成员参与国际商务活动以及讨论和制定国际商业习惯、惯例和规则。

1.5.3 China Council for the Promotion of International Trade (CCPIT)
中国国际贸易促进委员会

Established in May 1952, China Council for the Promotion of International Trade (CCPIT) comprises VIPs, enterprises and organizations representing the economic and trade sectors in China. It is the most important and the

中国国际贸易促进委员会成立于1952年5月，包括贵宾、企业和组织，代表中国经济和贸易等行业。它是最重要和最大的促

largest institution for the promotion of foreign trade in China. With the approval of the Chinese government, the CCPIT adopted in 1988 a separate name China Chamber of International Commerce (CCOIC), which is used simultaneously with the CCPIT.

进中国对外贸易的机构。由中国政府批准，中国国际贸易促进委员会于 1988 年采用另一个名称：中国国际商会，用来与中国国际贸易促进委员会并称。

1.5.4 The World Trade Organization (WTO)
世界贸易组织

The World Trade Organization (WTO) deals with the rules of trade between nations at a global level. It's an organization for liberalizing trade. It's a forum for governments to negotiate trade agreements. It's a place for them to settle trade disputes. The WTO was established in Geneva on January 1st, 1995 and was the successor to the General Agreement on Tariffs and Trade (GATT), which was created in 1948. The last and largest GATT round, was the Uruguay Round which lasted from 1986 to 1994 and led to the WTO's creation. Whereas the GATT had mainly dealt with trade in goods, the WTO and its agreements now cover trade in services, and in traded inventions, creations and designs of intellectual property. The WTO agreements are complex because they are legal texts covering a wide range of activities. They deal with: agriculture, textiles and clothing, banking, telecommunications, government purchases, industrial standards and product safety, food sanitation regulations, intellectual property. However, there are a number of simple, fundamental principles which are the foundation of the multilateral trading system. These are:

★ Trade without discrimination

    A. Most-Favoured-Nation (MFN): treating other people equally;

    B. National Treatment: Treating foreigners and locals equally;

世界贸易组织（世贸组织）在全球处理国家之间的贸易规则。它是负责贸易自由化的组织。它是一个政府商谈贸易协定的论坛，也是一个解决贸易争端的地方。世贸组织于 1995 年 1 月 1 日在日内瓦成立，前身是 1948 年成立的"关税与贸易总协定"（关贸总协定）。最近和最大的关贸总协定谈判是乌拉圭回合，从 1986 年持续至 1994 年，并导致了世贸组织的创立。关贸总协定主要处理货物贸易协议、世贸组织及其协定，包括服务贸易以及拥有知识产权的发明、创造和设计的交易。世贸组织协议是复杂的，因为这些法律文本涵盖范围广泛。它们涉及：农业、纺织品和服装、金融、电信、政府采购、行业标准和产品的安全、食品卫生法规、知识产权。然而，有一些简单的基本原则，它们是多边贸易体系的基础。它们是：

★ 非歧视性贸易原则

    A. 最惠国待遇：同等对待他国人；

    B. 国民待遇：对待外国人和本地人一视同仁；

★ Freer trade: gradually, through negotiation;

★ Predictability: through binding and transparency;

★ Promoting fair competition;

★ Encouraging development and economic reform.

Most of the issues that the WTO focuses on derive from previous trade negotiations, especially from the Uruguay Round. The organization is currently working with its members on a new trade negotiation called the Doha Development Agenda (Doha Round), launched in 2001. The WTO has nearly 150 members, which is over 97% of world trade. It is responsible for negotiating and implementing new trade agreements, and is in charge of policing member countries' adherence to all the WTO agreements, signed by the majority of the world's trading nations and ratified in their parliaments.

Dispute settlement is regarded by the WTO as the central pillar of the multilateral trading system, and as a unique contribution to the stability of the global economy. WTO members have agreed that, if they believe fellow-members are violating trade rules, they will use the multilateral system of settling disputes instead of taking action unilaterally. That means abiding by the agreed procedures, and respecting judgments. This system is based on clearly-defined rules, with timetables for completing a case. First rulings are made by a panel. Appeals based on points of law are possible. Ultimate responsibility for settling disputes lies with member governments, through the Dispute Settlement Body. Although much of the procedure does resemble a court, the preferred solution is for the countries concerned to discuss their problems and settle the dispute by themselves. The first stage is therefore consultations between the governments concerned, and even when the case has progressed to other stages, consultation and mediation are still possible.

★ 自由贸易原则：逐步通过谈判实现；

★ 可预测性：通过政策的约束力和透明性来达到；

★ 促进公平竞争；

★ 鼓励发展和经济改革。

世贸组织关注的大多数议题来自于以前的贸易谈判，特别是乌拉圭回合。该组织目前正在与它的成员进行一轮新的贸易谈判。该谈判开始于 2001 年，称为多哈发展议程（多哈回合）。世贸组织成员近 150 个，贸易额超过世界贸易的 97%。世贸组织负责谈判和实施新的贸易协定，并负责监管各国遵守所有协定的情况。世界上大多数的贸易国都签署了世界组织的这些协定，并且这些协定得到他们的议会批准。

争端裁决被世贸组织视为多边贸易体系的支柱，并对全球经济的稳定作出了独特的贡献。世贸组织成员同意，如果他们认为其他成员违反贸易规则，他们将利用多边贸易体系解决争端，而不是单方面采取行动。这意味着遵守既定的程序，并尊重裁决。这一机制是基于明了的规则，且有案件完成的时间表。第一次裁决由小组做出。基于法律的上诉是可能的。争端的最终解决责任在于成员国的政府，经由争端解决机构处理。虽然大部分的过程类似于一个法庭，首选的解决方案还是有关国家讨论自己的问题，自己解决争端。第一阶段是有关政府之间的协商，甚至在案件进展到其他阶段，咨询和调解仍然是可能的。

The WTO Secretariat has around 600 staff and is headed by a director-general who is appointed by the Ministerial Conference, which is its highest and decisive body. The WTO's headquarters is in Geneva, Switzerland.

China's accession to the WTO was on Dec. 11th, 2001.

世贸组织秘书处有 600 人左右,由一名最高决定机构——部长级会议任命的总干事负责。世界贸易组织的总部在瑞士日内瓦。

中国于 2001 年 12 月 11 日加入世界贸易组织。

1.5.5　Laws & Regulations Applicable to International Trade
　　　　国际贸易中适用的法律和条例

Laws & regulations applicable to international trade include the following:

1. Domestic Trade Laws

Different domestic laws are adopted in different nations and international trade should first of all conform to national trade laws. In China, business contracts should abide by Contract Law of the People's Republic of China. In its Article 126, it states that the parties to a contract involving foreign interest may choose the law applicable to the settlement of their contract disputes, except as otherwise stipulated by law. If the parties to a contract involving foreign interest have not made a choice, the law of the country to which the contract is most closely connected shall be applied.

2. International Trade Practices

International trade practices are one of the major sources of international business law. They are not enforceable unless agreed upon by both parties in the contract. Customary international trade practices are INCOTERMS 2010, Uniform Customs and Practice for Documentary Credits 600 (UCP 600) and Uniform Rules for Collections (URC 522). According to General Principles of the Civil Law of the PRC, inter-national practices may be applied to matters for which neither the law of the People's Republic of China nor any international treaty concluded or acceded to by the PRC has any provisions.

3. International Trade Onventions

International trade conventions include bilateral or multilateral agreements on international trade, transportation

适用于国际贸易的法律法规包括:

1. 国内贸易法律

不同的国家采用了不同的国内法律,跨国贸易首先要符合国家贸易法律。在中国,商务合同应当遵守《中华人民共和国合同法》。其第 126 条规定,合同当事人的涉外利益方可以选择适用的法律处理合同争议,法律另有规定的除外。如果涉及外国利益方的合同当事人没有选择,应采用与合同有最密切联系国的法律。

2. 国际贸易惯例

国际贸易惯例是国际商法的一个主要来源。它们不具约束力,除非当事人双方在合同中约定。国际贸易惯例有《2010 年国际贸易术语解释通则》、《跟单信用证统一惯例 600》和《托收统一规则 522》。根据《中华人民共和国民法通则》的规定,在中华人民共和国法律和中国参加或缔约的国际条约没有规定的情况下,可以适用国际贸易惯例。

3. 国际贸易公约

国际贸易公约包括双边或多边的国际贸易、海运、陆运或空运、

by sea, land or air, intellectual properties and arbitration. The most important international trade convention is United Nations Convention on Contracts for the International Sale of Goods. This convention establishes a comprehensive code of legal rules governing the formation of contracts for the international sale of goods, the obligations of the buyer and seller, remedies for breach of contract and other aspects of the contract. The convention was adopted in Vienna on April 11th, 1980 and entered into force on January 1st, 1988. This convention consists of the following four parts:

★ Sphere of application and general provisions;

★ Formation of the contract;

★ Sale of the goods;

★ Final provisions.

However, when quoting this convention we should remember that if any international treaty concluded or acceded to by the PRC contains provisions differing from those in the civil laws of the PRC, the provisions of the international treaty shall apply, unless the provisions are ones on which the PRC has announced reservations.

知识产权和仲裁的协议。最重要的国际贸易公约是《联合国国际货物销售合同》。该公约建立了一个全面的法律规则准则,规范了国际货物销售合同、买方和卖方的义务、违反合同的补救措施等合同的方方面面。该公约于 1980 年 4 月 11 日在维也纳通过,并于 1988 年 1 月 1 日生效。该公约由以下四部分组成:

★ 适用范围和总则;

★ 合同的订立;

★ 货物销售;

★ 最终条款。

然而,引用该公约时应记住,如果任何中华人民共和国参加和缔约的国际条约与中华人民共和国的民法不同时,采用国际条约,除非该条约属于中华人民共和国声明保留条款。

Exercises

I. 术语翻译

国际贸易	贸易差额
出口	进口
有形贸易	无形贸易
总贸易体系	专门贸易体系
过境贸易	转口贸易
买方	卖方
国际商会	2010 年国际贸易术语解释通则
世界贸易组织	关贸总协定
跟单信用证统一惯例	联合国国际货物销售合同公约

II. 英译汉

1. Import and export are two sides of the same coin, and both can have beneficial effects on the home market. Imports create competition for home-produced goods; exports give a manufacturer a larger market for his products and help to reduce the unit cost.

2. Upon accession, China shall eliminate or bring into conformity with the WTO Agreement all special trade arrangements, including barter trade arrangements with third countries and separate customs territories, which are not in conformity with the WTO Agreement.

3. INCOTERMS, the official ICC rules for the interpretation of trade terms, facilitate the conduct of international trade, define clearly the parties' respective obligations in a sales contract and reduce the risk of legal implications.

4. This convention applies to contracts of sale of goods between parties whose places of business are in different states. It governs only the formation of the contract of sale and the rights and obligations of the seller and the buyer arising from such a contract.

III. 单项选择

1. 对外贸易是指一国(地区)同别国(地区)进行货物和服务交换的活动。从一个国家来看，这种交换活动为对外贸易；从国际范围来看，称为(   )。
   A. 国际贸易   B. 转口贸易   C. 货物贸易   D. 服务贸易

2. 如英国和日本这样的海岛国家又把对外贸易称为(   )。
   A. 国外贸易   B. 商业贸易   C. 海外贸易   D. 外国贸易

3. 实物商品的进出口称为(   )。
   A. 有形贸易   B. 无形贸易   C. 直接贸易   D. 转口贸易

4. 商品生产国与消费国之间的贸易称为(   )。
   A. 转口贸易   B. 过境贸易   C. 直接贸易   D. 间接贸易

5. 我国内地某公司出口一批货物给香港某公司，该香港公司又将这批货物转卖给美国某公司，这个贸易现象对于香港而言称为(   )。
   A. 间接进口   B. 间接出口   C. 转口贸易   D. 易货贸易

6. 下列关于总贸易体系的表述中，正确的是(   )。
   A. 总贸易体系是国际服务贸易的统计方法
   B. 总贸易体系是以一国关境作为统计界限
   C. 总贸易体系是以一国的国境作为统计界限
   D. 我国采用的不是总贸易体系

7. 专门贸易体系是指以(   )作为统计界限。
   A. 关境   B. 国境   C. 货物进出口   D. 服务进出口

8. 当一定时期内一国出口总额超过进口总额时称为(   )。
   A. 贸易平衡   B. 贸易失衡   C. 贸易逆差   D. 贸易顺差

9. 全球最大的贸易商会是(   )。

    A. WTO   B. IMF   C. APEC   D. ICC

10. 国际商会在中国的机构是中国国际商会，即(   )。

    A. 商务部   B. 中国贸促会   C. 商检局   D. 进出口银行

11. 世界贸易组织的英文缩写是(   )。

    A. APEC   B. GATT   C. WTO   D. OECD

12. "乌拉圭回合"多边贸易谈判正式发起于(   )。

    A. 1986 年   B. 1988 年   C. 1992 年   D. 1995 年

13. 世界贸易组织成立于(   )。

    A. 1945 年   B. 1985 年   C. 1995 年   D. 2000 年

14. 世界贸易组织的最高权力机构是(   )。

    A. 总理事会   B. 秘书处   C. 专门委员会   D. 部长级会议

15. 世界贸易组织的最惠国待遇条款和国民待遇条款体现了其(   )。

    A. 非歧视原则   B. 公平竞争原则

    C. 一般禁止数量原则   D. 对发展中国家的优惠待遇原则

16. 在有关贸易术语的国际贸易惯例中，使用最广的是(   )。

    A. 《1932 年华沙—牛津规则》   B. 《美国对外贸易定义 1941 年修订本》

    C. 《托收统一规则》   D. 《2010 年国际贸易术语解释通则》

17. 与我国进行进出口贸易关系最大，也是最重要的一项国际公约是(   )。

    A. 《联合国国际货物销售合同公约》   B. 《跟单信用证统一惯例》

    C. 《托收统一规则》   D. 《2010 年国际贸易术语解释通则》

Ⅳ. 判断题

(   ) 1. In a broad sense, international trade is the exchange of goods between two or more countries (regions), involving the use of one or more currencies.

(   ) 2. Transit trade is entirely the same as entrepot trade.

(   ) 3. Trade in services normally does not need customs declaration.

(   ) 4. The special trade system is adopted in China.

(   ) 5. It is always good for every country to keep a perfect balance in international trade.

(   ) 6. An arbitration institution or a law court might be a party that can not be avoided in international trade.

(   ) 7. The GATT is the successor of the WTO.

(   ) 8. The Ministerial Conference is its highest and decisive body of the WTO.

(   ) 9. International trade contracts should follow international trade practices and conventions and should not consider national trade laws.

(   ) 10. International trade practices are not international business laws. They are not enforceable.

CHAPTER 2

Trade Terms
贸易术语

Focus

In this chapter, you will learn:

✧ Introduction to trade terms;
✧ Four trade terms for sea and inland waterway transport in INCOTERMS 2010;
✧ Seven trade terms for any mode or modes of transport in INCOTERMS 2010;
✧ INCOTERMS & contracts.

Sending goods from one country to another, as part of a commercial transaction, can be a risky business. If they are lost or damaged, or if delivery does not take place for some other reason, the climate of confidence between parties may degenerate to the point where a law suit is brought. However, above all, the seller and buyer in international contracts want their deals to be successfully completed.

If, when drawing up their contracts, the buyer and seller have some commonly understood rules to specifically refer to, they can be sure of defining their respective responsibilities simply and safely. In so doing they eliminate any possibility of misunderstanding and subsequent dispute.

The purpose of INCOTERMS is to provide a set of international rules for the interpretation of the most commonly used trade terms in foreign trade. Thus, the uncertainties of different interpretations of such terms in different countries can be avoided or at least reduced by a considerable degree.

作为商业交易的一部分,将货物从一国运送到另一国的过程充满着风险。如果货物被丢失或损坏,或由于一些其他原因,使得货物无法交付,买卖双方之间就可能因失信而诉诸法律。然而,国际合同中的买卖双方首先都希望他们能成功完成交易。

如果在签约时,买卖双方能对某些规则的具体含义达成共识,既简单又安全地明确各自的责任,这样,双方就能消除任何可能的误解以及随之而来的争端。

《国际贸易术语解释通则》的目的就是提供一套国际规则以解释对外贸易中最常用的贸易术语。这样可以避免或至少相当程度地减少因不同国家对贸易术语的不同解释而产生的不确定性。

2.1   Introduction to Trade Terms 贸易术语概述

Price is the core of the negotiation and key problem for the buyer and seller which results in their economic profits. The two parties should firstly reach an agreement on the price otherwise the contract could not be concluded.

In international trade, as the buyer and seller are from different nations or regions, the pricing problems the seller tackles are more complicated than those in domestic trade. In addition to the cost of the goods included in the calculation of the export price, the price quotations are invariably accompanied by an indication as to which party is to pay the cost of shipment, insurance, customs duties, and other incidental charges, and to bear the risks during transportation and formalities to be carried out in transit. All these and many

价格是买卖双方谈判的核心和关键问题,直接关系到其经济利益。买卖双方应首先在价格上达成协议,否则合同就无法订立。

在国际贸易中,由于买卖双方来自不同的国家或地区,双方需处理的价格问题要比国内贸易更为复杂。在出口货物的成本计算中,出口报价中一定包含着哪一方支付运费、保险、关税以及其他附属费用,哪一方承担运输途中的风险以及清关手续。所有这些及其他事情都说明双方合同

other things are referred to as responsibilities of the parties to a contract. However, it is difficult to stipulate all the details of responsibilities in contracts, hence the necessity of the trade terms arises.

中的责任。但是，要在合同中详细规定双方的具体责任并不容易，因此有必要使用贸易术语。

2.1.1 What Are Trade Terms?
什么是贸易术语？

Trade terms refer to the division of responsibilities between parties to a contract(buyer and seller in a sale), by using abbreviation of three English letters, including the selling prices, the payment of costs such as shipping, insurance and customs; the arrangement of the performance of these activities; and the determination of the transfer of title to goods. In a word, the use of trade terms considerably facilitates negotiation and signing of contracts.

贸易术语是指用三个缩写的英文字母来划分合同中买卖双方的责任，包括销售价格、费用的支付，如运费、保险费和关税；由谁负责办理这些手续；货物所有权如何转移等。总之，贸易术语的使用大大便利了谈判和合同的签订过程。

2.1.2 International Conventions on Trade Terms
有关贸易术语的国际贸易惯例

Trade terms have been developed in practice over many years to fit particular circumstances. In order to avoid the uncertainties of different interpretations of trade terms in different countries or at least reduce by a considerable degree, three influential international trade practices appear as follows:

贸易术语是在多年的贸易实践中为适应贸易中的具体情况而产生的。为了避免或至少相当程度地减少贸易术语在不同国家的不同解释而产生的不确定性，三个有影响力的国际贸易惯例应运而生。具体如下：

◆ *Warsaw-Oxford Rules 1932* 1932 年华沙—牛津规则

In 1928, the International Law Association held a meeting in Warsaw, and worked out the Uniform Rules for CIF Sales Contracts, which was called Warsaw Rules 1928, and renamed Warsaw-Oxford Rules 1932 at the Oxford Convention and includes 21 clauses. It is mainly used to indicate the nature and characteristic of the CIF contract and also to stipulate the responsibilities of the two parties under CIF terms.

1928 年，国际法协会在华沙举行会议，为解释 CIF 合同而制定了统一规则，即《1928 年华沙规则》。在 1932 年的牛津会议上，该规则被重新命名为《1932 年华沙—牛津规则》，共 21 条。该规则主要对 CIF 合同的性质和特点作了解释，并规定了 CIF 术语下买卖双方的责任。

◆ *Revised American Foreign Trade Definitions 1990* 1990 年美国对外贸易定义修正本

In 1919, nine American commercial groups drew up the U.S. Export Quotations and Abbreviations, then revised it in 1941 and renamed as Revised American Foreign Trade Definitions 1941. It was adopted by the American Chamber of Commerce, the National Importers Association and the American Foreign Trade Association in the same year and revised again in 1990.It defines six trade terms, i.e. Ex (point of origin), FOB, FAS, C&F, CIF and Ex Dock. Among them, FOB is explained quite differently from that in INCOTERMS. We must pay more attention. These trade terms are often adopted in the United States of America, Canada and some other countries in America.

1919 年，九个美国商业团体制定了《美国出口报价及其缩写》，然后在 1941 年修正，更名为《1941 年美国对外贸易定义修正本》。同年，它被美国商会、美国国家进口商协会和美国对外贸易协会通过。在 1990 年又再次进行了修改。该惯例对六个贸易术语进行了解释，即 Ex (point of origin)、FOB、FAS、C&F、CIF 和 Ex Dock。其中，FOB 术语的解释与 INCOTERMS 中的解释有相当大的不同。我们必须高度关注。这些贸易术语常常被美国、加拿大和美洲的一些其他国家使用。

◆ *International Rules for the Interpretation of Trade Terms* 国际贸易术语解释通则

Frequently parties to a contract are unaware of the different trading practices in their respective countries. This can give rise to misunderstanding, disputes and litigation with all the waste of time and money that entails. In order to remedy these problems, the International Chamber of Commerce first published in 1936 a set of international rules for the interpretation of trade terms. These rules were known as INCOTERMS 1936. Amendments and additions were later made in 1953, 1967, 1976, 1980, 1990，2000 and presently 2010 in order to bring the rules in line with current international trade practices.

In the present 2010 version of INCOTERMS, there are 11 trade terms which have been grouped into two different categories (see Table 2.1): those for any mode or modes of transport and those for sea and inland waterway transport. The following is a chart setting out the new classification of INCOTERMS 2010.

合同双方常常不了解对方国家的贸易习惯从而引起误解、争议和诉讼，浪费时间和金钱。为了纠正这些问题，国际商会于 1936 年首次出版了一套解释贸易术语的国际规则。这些规则被称为 INCOTERMS 1936。随后，于 1953 年、1967 年、1976 年、1980 年、1990 年、2000 年和 2010 年对 INCOTERMS 作了修订和补充，以使其符合当前的国际贸易实践。

目前使用的 2010 年版本的《国际贸易术语解释通则》中，有 11 个贸易术语，分成不同的两类 (请参见表 2.1)：适用于任一或多种运输方式的贸易术语和只适用于海运及内河运输的贸易术语。下面是 INCOTERMS 2010。

Table 2.1   Structure of INCOTERMS 2010

EXW	EX Works 工厂交货	
FCA	Free Carrier 货交承运人	
CPT	Carriage Paid to 运费付至	Suit to Any Mode or Modes of Transportation
CIP	Carriage and Insurance Paid to 运费、保险费付至	适用于各种运输方式
DAT	Delivered at Terminal 运输终端交货	
DAP	Delivered at Place 目的地交货	
DDP	Delivered Duty Paid 完税后交货	
FAS	Free Alongside Ship 船边交货	
FOB	Free on Board 船上交货	Suit to Sea and Inland Waterway Transportation Mode
CFR	Cost and Freight 成本加运费	适用于海运和内河运输方式
CIF	Cost, Insurance and Freight 成本、保险费加运费	

2.2 Four Trade Terms For Sea and Inland Waterway Transport in INCOTERMS 2010
INCOTERMS 2010 中适用于水上运输方式的 4 种贸易术语

There are four trade terms for sea and inland waterway transport in INCOTERMS 2010 which are FAS, FOB, CFR, and CIF.

在《2010 年国际贸易术语解释通则》中，有 4 个只适用于海上或内河运输方式的贸易术语，即 FAS、FOB、CFR 及 CIF。

2.2.1 FAS / Free Alongside Ship (…named port of shipment)
启运港船边交货(……指定的装运港)

"Free Alongside Ship" means that the seller delivers when the goods are placed alongside the vessel at the named port of shipment. This means that the buyer has to bear all the costs and risks of loss or damage to the goods from that moment.

The FAS term requires the seller to clear the goods for export.

However, if the parties wish the buyer to clear the goods for export, this should be made clear by adding explicit wording to this effect in the contract of sale.

This term can be used only for sea or inland waterway transport.

"船边交货"指卖方在指定的装运港将货物放置在船边，即完成其交货义务。这意味着买方必须自该时刻起，承担一切费用和货物灭失或损坏的风险。

该术语要求卖方办理出口清关手续。

但是，如果希望买方办理出口清关手续，应在合同中用文字明确规定。

该术语仅限于海上运输或内河运输。

2.2.2 FOB / Free on Board (…named port of shipment)
船上交货(……指定装运港)

"Free on Board" means that the seller delivers the goods on board the vessel nominated by the buyer at the named port of shipment or procures the goods already so delivered. This means that the buyer has to bear all costs and risks of loss of or damage to the goods when the goods are on board the vessel.

The FOB term requires the seller to clear the goods for export. This term can be used only for sea or inland waterway transport.

"船上交货"指卖方在指定的装运港将货物交到买方指派的船上，即完成其交货义务。买方必须承担自货物装上船后的一切费用和货物灭失或损坏的风险。

该术语要求卖方办理出口清关手续。该术语仅限于海上或内河运输。

FOB may not be appropriate where goods are handed over to the carrier before they are on board the vessel, for example goods in containers, which are typically delivered at a terminal. In such situations, the FCA rule should be used.

When adopting the FOB term, the link-up of vessel and goods becomes more important otherwise dead freight or demurrage will occur. Therefore details of linking-up of vessel and goods should be made clear by adding explicit wording in the contract of sale and the two parties should closely contact each other to avoid any additional losses or dispute.

In order to make it clear who is responsible for the loading of the goods, the buyer and the seller may add some additional conditions, which become the variations under FOB. These variations concern only problems relating to different kinds of charges, they do not affect the separation of risk and the property transfer in the goods.

★　**FOB Liner Terms**

It means that the buyer will be responsible for loading and the seller doesn't have to pay loading expenses.

★　**FOB Under Tackle**

This term only requires the seller to send and place the goods on the wharf or within the reach of the ship's tackle. Loading expenses incurred thereafter will be borne by the buyer.

★　**FOB Stowed**

Under this term, the seller loads the goods into the ship's hold and pays the loading expenses including stowing expenses.

★　**FOB Trimmed**

The seller pays all the loading expenses including trimming expenses (which actually also includes stowing expense).

FOB 不适用于货物在装船前移交给承运人的情形。比如，货物通过集装箱运输，并通常在目的地交付。在这些情形下，应使用 FCA 术语。

在使用 FOB 术语时，船货衔接问题就非常重要，否则会产生空舱费或滞期费。因此，买卖双方应在合同中对船货衔接事项作明确规定，并应密切联系，以防产生额外的损失或纠纷。

为分清由谁负担装船费用，买卖双方可以在 FOB 术语后加列字句或缩写，即 FOB 术语的变形。这些变形只用于解决装船费用问题，并不改变货物的风险点和所有权的转移。

★　**FOB 班轮条件**

指由买方承担装船费用，卖方不负担装船费用。

★　**FOB 吊钩下交货**

该术语要求卖方将货物置于轮船吊钩可及之处，从货物起吊开始的装货费用由买方负担。

★　**FOB 包括理舱**

该术语要求卖方将货物装入船舱并负担包括理舱费在内的装船费用。

★　**FOB 包括平舱**

卖方支付包括平舱费在内的装船费用（也包括理舱费在内）。

Case Study

某中国公司欲从美国进口 4000 件瓷器，单价为 US$10.00/PC FOB Vessel New York。买方根据合同按期开出以卖方为受益人的总金额为 US$40,000.00 的不可撤销即期信用证。但是,卖方来电要求买方将信用证金额增至 US$40,800.00，否则，买方须另行电汇卖方相关的出口报关费用及出口许可证费用。

请问：卖方的要求合理吗？

2.2.3　CFR / Cost and Freight (…named port of destination)　成本加运费(……指定目的港)

"Cost and Freight" means that the seller delivers the goods on board the vessel at the named port of shipment or procures the goods already so delivered.

The seller must pay the costs and freight necessary to bring the goods to the named port of destination. But the risk of loss of or damage to the goods, as well as any additional costs due to events occurring after the time of delivery, are transferred from the seller to the buyer when the goods are on board the vessel.

The CFR term requires the seller to clear the goods for export.

This term may not be appropriate where goods are handed over to the carrier before they are on board the vessel, for example goods in containers, which are typically delivered at a terminal. In such circumstances, the CPT rule should be used.

When adopting the CFR term, the seller is responsible for booking the space or chartering. Also, it is very important for the seller to send without any delay the shipping advice to the buyer after finishing the loading. Otherwise all the risks and losses thereafter will be borne by the seller.

To specify clearly the responsibility and cost of unloading, the variations under CFR can also be used:

★　CFR Liner Terms

It means that the unloading expenses are borne by the party who pays the freight, i.e. the seller.

"成本加运费"指卖方在指定的装运港将货物交到自己安排的船上，即完成其交货义务。

卖方必须支付货物运至指定目的港所必需的费用和运费，但自卖方将货装上船后，货物灭失或损坏的风险，以及交货后由于发生事件而引起的任何额外费用由卖方转移至买方。

该术语要求卖方办理出口清关手续。

该术语不适用于货物在装船前移交给承运人的情形。比如，货物通过集装箱运输，并通常在目的地交付。在这样的情况下，应当适用 CPT 术语。

当采用 CFR 术语时，由卖方负责租船或订舱。另外，货物装船后，卖方及时向买方发出装运通知非常重要。否则卖方将承担货物装船后的所有风险及损失。

为明确由谁负担卸货责任和费用，可用 CFR 术语的变形。

★　CFR 班轮条件

指卸货费用由支付运费的一方，即卖方承担。

★ CFR Landed

It means that the seller shall bear the expenses for unloading/ landing the goods from the ship onto the dock or wharf or land at the port of destination, including the expenses of lighterage and dockage.

★ CFR Ex Ship's Hold

It means that the buyer shall bear the expenses for slinging up the goods from the hold to the dock. The discharging charges shall be borne by the buyer.

These variations concern only problems relating to different kinds of charges, they do not affect the separation of risk and the property transfer in the goods.

★ CFR 卸至岸上

指卖方须承担将货物卸到目的港岸上的费用，包括驳船费和码头费。

★ CFR 舱底交货

指买方承担将货物从舱底起吊卸到码头的费用。卸货费由买方承担。

这些变形只是用以解决相关各类费用问题，并不改变货物的风险点和所有权的转移。

2.2.4 CIF / Cost, Insurance and Freight (…named port of destination) 成本、保险费加运费(……指定目的港)

"Cost, Insurance and Freight" means that the seller delivers the goods on board the vessel at the named port of shipment or procures the goods already so delivered.

The seller must pay the costs and freight necessary to bring the goods to the named port of destination. But the risk of loss of or damage to the goods, as well as any additional costs due to events occurring after the time of delivery, are transferred from the seller to the buyer when the goods are on board the vessel. However, in CIF the seller also has to procure marine insurance on the goods during the carriage.

Consequently, the seller contracts for insurance and pays the insurance premium. The buyer should note that under the CIF term the seller is required to obtain insurance only on minimum cover. Should the buyer wish to have the protection of greater cover, he would either need to agree expressly with the seller or to make his own extra insurance arrangements.

The CFR term requires the seller to clear the goods for export.

This term may not be appropriate where goods are handed over to the carrier before they are on board the vessel, for example goods in containers, which are typically

"成本、保险费加运费"指卖方在指定的装运港将货物交到自己安排的船上，即完成其交货义务。

卖方必须支付货物运至指定目的港所必需的费用和运费，但自卖方交货后，货物灭失或损坏的风险，以及交货后由于发生事件而引起的任何额外费用由卖方转移至买方。不过，CIF 术语要求卖方办理货物运输途中的海上保险。

因此，卖方应订立保险合同，支付保险费。买方应知道，CIF 术语下卖方只需投保最低责任的保险险别。如果买方希望有更高的保险险别的保障，应与卖方明确达成协议，或者自行作出额外的保险安排。

该术语要求卖方办理出口清关手续。

该术语不适用于货物在装船前移交给承运人的情形。比如，货物通过集装箱运输，并通常在目的

delivered at a terminal. In such circumstances, the CIP rule should be used.

To specify clearly the responsibility and cost of unloading, as CFR, the variations under CIF can also be used:

★　CIF Liner Terms

★　CIF Landed

★　CIF Ex Ship's Hold

These variations concern only problems relating to different kinds of charges; they do not affect the separation of risk and the property transfer in the goods.

When adopting the CIF terms, the following points should draw our attention:

★　Duty of insurance

INCOTERMS 2010 stipulates that the seller shall effect insurance on minimum cover of the Institute Cargo Clause or any similar set of clauses if no specific agreement in the contract appears.

★　A sale of the documents

The CIF contract is a special type of contract—a sale of the documents. As long as the seller presents a full set of documents in conformity with the contract, the buyer shall fulfill the duty of payment. Even if the goods delivered are lost or damaged in transit, the buyer is not entitled to reject payment. So the CIF contract is a typical "symbolic delivery".

地交付。在这样的情况下，应当适用 CIP 术语。

为明确由谁负担卸货责任和费用，如同 CFR 术语一样，可用 CIF 术语的变形。

★　CIF 班轮条件

★　CIF 卸至岸上

★　CIF 舱底交货

这些变形只用以解决相关各类费用问题，并不改变货物的风险点和所有权的转移。

当采用 CIF 术语时，要注意以下几点：

★　保险责任

INCOTERMS 2010 规定，如果合同中没有特别说明，卖方只需投保协会货物条款中的最低险别，或者任何类似的保险条款。

★　单据买卖

CIF 合同是一种特殊类型的合同——单据买卖。只要卖方提交了全套与合同规定相符的单据，买方就应当履行付款义务。即使交付的货物在运输途中丢失或损坏，买方无权拒绝付款。所以 CIF 合同是典型的"象征性交货"。

Case Study

某中国公司以 CIF New York, U.S.A. 向美国进口商出口一批圣诞灯，由于该商品为季节性商品，双方同意在合同中规定如下：

信用证开证时间：9 月底。

到货时间：不迟于 12 月 2 日。否则买方有权取消合同。如已支付货款，该货款将退回至买方。

请问：该案例有什么问题吗？该合同是 CIF 合同吗？

2.3 Seven Trade Terms For Any Mode or Modes of Transport in INCOTERMS 2010
INCOTERMS 2010 中适用于各种运输方式的 7 种贸易术语

There are other seven trade terms in INCOTERMS 2010 which are EXW, FCA, CPT, CIP, DAT, DAP and DDP.

在《2010 年国际贸易术语解释通则》中还有另七种贸易术语：EXW、FCA、CPT、CIP、DAT、DAP 及 DDP。

2.3.1 EXW / Ex Works (...named place)
工厂交货(⋯⋯指定地点)

"Ex Works" means that the seller delivers when he places the goods at the disposal of the buyer at the seller's premises or another named place (i.e. works, factory, warehouse, etc.) and not cleared for export and not loaded on any collecting vehicle.

This term thus represents the minimum obligation for the seller, and the buyer has to bear all the costs and risks involved in taking the goods from the seller's premises.

However, if the parties wish the seller to be responsible for the loading of the goods on departure and to bear the risks and all the costs of such loading, this should be made clear by adding explicit wording to this effect in the contract of sale. This term should not be used when the buyer cannot carry out the export formalities directly or indirectly unless the seller agrees that he will load at his cost and risk.

"工厂交货"是指卖方在其处所（工厂、仓库等）将货物置于买方处置之下时，即完成了交货。卖方不负责出口清关，也不负责将货物装上买方备妥的车辆。

该术语是卖方负担义务最少的术语，买方须承担自卖方所在处所提取货物至目的地所需的一切费用和风险。

然而，如果买卖双方希望卖方负责装货，并承担装货的所有风险和费用，应在合同中就此意思用文字明确规定。如买方不能直接或间接办理出口手续，就不应使用该术语，除非卖方同意负责装货并承担装货的所有风险和费用。

2.3.2 FCA / Free Carrier (...named place)
货交承运人(⋯⋯指定地点)

"Free Carrier" means that the seller delivers the goods, cleared for export, to the carrier nominated by the buyer at the named place. It should be noted that the chosen place of

"货交承运人"是指卖方在指定地将经出口清关的货物交给买方指定的承运人，即完成了交

delivery has an impact on the obligations of loading and unloading of the goods at that place. If delivery occurs at the seller's premises, the seller is responsible for loading. If delivery occurs at any other place, the seller is not responsible for unloading.

This term may be used irrespective of the mode of transport, including multimodal transport.

"Carrier" means any person who, in a contract of carriage, undertakes to perform or to procure the performance of transport by rail, road, air, sea, inland waterway or by a combination of such modes.

If the buyer nominates a person other than a carrier to receive the goods, the seller is deemed to have fulfilled his obligation to deliver the goods when they are delivered to that person.

货。应注意，选定的交货地对在该地装货和卸货的义务有影响。如在卖方所在处所，卖方负责装货。如在任何其他地方交货，卖方不负责卸货。

该术语可用于各种运输方式，包括多式联运。

"承运人"指在运输合同中承担履行铁路、公路、航空、海运、内河运输或多式运输的承运人。

如买方指定一个非承运人的人收取货物，当货物被交给该人时，应认为卖方已履行了交货义务。

2.3.3　CPT / Carriage Paid to (...named place of destination) 运费付至(……指定目的地)

"Carriage Paid to..." means that the seller delivers the goods to the carrier nominated by himself and pay the cost of carriage necessary to bring the goods to the named destination. This means that the buyer bears all risks and any other costs occurring after the goods have been so delivered.

If subsequent carriers are used for the carriage to the agreed destination, the risk passes when the goods have been delivered to the first carrier.

The CPT term requires the seller to clear the goods for export.

This term may be used irrespective of the mode of transport, including multimodal transport.

"运费付至……"是指当货物已被交给由卖方指定的承运人时，卖方即完成了交货，并且，卖方必须支付将货物运至指定目的地所需的运费。这意味着买方将承担交货后所有的风险及发生的任何额外费用。

如果为了将货物运至指定的目的地需要利用后续承运人，风险也自货物交付给第一承运人时转移。

CPT 术语要求卖方办理出口清关手续。

该术语适用于任何运输方式，包括多式运输。

2.3.4 CIP / Carriage and Insurance Paid to (...named place of destination) 运费和保险费付至(......指定目的地)

"Carriage and Insurance Paid to..." means that the seller delivers the goods to the carrier nominated by him, but the seller must in addition pay the cost of carriage necessary to bring the goods to the named destination. This means that the buyer bears all risks and any additional costs occurring after the goods have been delivered. However, in CIP the seller also has to procure insurance on the goods during the carriage. Consequently, the seller contracts for insurance and pays the insurance premium.

The buyer should note that under the CIP term the seller is required to obtain insurance only on minimum cover. Should the buyer wish to have the protection of greater cover, he would either need to agree as much expressly with the seller or to make his own extra insurance arrangements.

If subsequent carriers are used for the carriage to the agreed destination, the risk passes when the goods have been delivered to the first carrier.

The CIP term requires the seller to clear the goods for export.

This term may be used irrespective of the mode of transport, including multimodal transport.

"运费、保险费付至......"是指卖方将货物交至卖方指定的承运人时，即完成了交货，但卖方必须另外支付将货物运至指定目的地所需的运费。这意味着买方将承担交货后所有的风险及发生的任何额外费用。但是，CIP术语要求卖方取得运输过程中的货物保险。因此，卖方需订立保险合同，并支付保险费。

买方应注意，CIP术语下卖方只需按最低责任的保险险别取得保险。如买方希望获得更大责任的保险险别，应与卖方明确商定或自己额外办理保险。

如果为了将货物运至指定的目的地需要利用后续承运人，风险也自货物交付给第一承运人时转移。

CIP术语要求卖方办理出口清关手续。

该术语适用于任何运输方式，包括多式运输。

2.3.5 DAT / Delivered at Terminal (...named terminal at port or place of destination) 运输终端交货(......指定目的港或目的地)

"Delivered at Terminal" means that the seller delivers when the goods, once unloaded from the arriving means of transport, are placed at the disposal of the buyer at a named terminal at the named port or place of destination. "Terminal" includes any place, whether covered or not, such as a quay, warehouse, container yard or road, rail or air

"运输终端交货"是指卖方在指定的目的港或目的地的指定终端卸货后将货物交给买方处置，即完成交货。"终端"包括任何地方，无论约定或者不约定，包括码头、仓库、集装箱堆场或

cargo terminal.

The seller bears all risks involved in bringing the goods to and unloading them at the terminal at the named port or place of destination. The parties are well advised to specify as clearly as possible the terminal and, if possible, a specific point within the terminal at the agreed port or place of destination, as the risks to that point are for the account of the seller. The seller is advised to procure a contract of carriage that matches this choice precisely.

Moreover, if the parties intend the seller to bear the risks and costs involved in transporting and handling the goods from the terminal to another place, then the DAP or DDP rules should be used.

DAT requires the seller to clear the goods for export, where applicable.

However, the seller has no obligation to clear the goods for import, pay any import duty or carry out any import customs formalities.

This rule may be used irrespective of the mode of transport.

公路、铁路、空运货站。

卖方应承担将货物运至指定目的地和卸货所产生的一切风险和费用。建议买卖双方尽量明确指定终端，如可能，应指定在约定的目的港或目的地的终端内的一个特定地点，因为（货物）到达这一地点的风险是由卖方承担。建议卖方签订一份与这种选择准确契合的运输合同。

此外，若买卖双方希望卖方承担从终端到另一地点的运输及管理货物所产生的风险和费用，则应使用 DAP 或 DDP 术语。

在通常实施时，DAT 术语要求卖方办理货物出口清关手续。

但是，卖方没有义务办理货物进口清关手续并支付任何进口税或办理任何进口报关手续。

此术语可用于各种运输方式。

2.3.6　DAP / Delivered at Place (…named place of destination) 目的地交货（……指定目的地）

"Delivered at Place" means that the seller delivers when the goods are placed at the disposal of the buyer on the arriving means of transport ready for unloading at the named place of destination. The seller bears all risks involved in bringing the goods to the named place.

The parties are well advised to specify as clearly as possible the point within the agreed place of destination, as the risks to that point are for the account of the seller. The seller is advised to procure contracts of carriage that match this choice precisely. If the seller incurs costs under its contract of carriage related to unloading at the place of destination, the seller is not entitled to recover such costs from the buyer unless otherwise agreed between the parties.

"目的地交货"是指卖方在指定的交货地点，将仍处于运输工具上尚未卸下的货物交给买方处置，即完成交货。卖方须承担货物运至指定目的地的一切风险。

尽管卖方承担货物到达目的地前的风险，该术语仍建议双方尽量明确指定交货目的地。建议卖方签订恰好匹配这种选择的运输合同。如果卖方按照运输合同承担了货物在目的地的卸货费用，那么除非双方达成一致，卖方无权向买方追讨该笔费用。

DAP requires the seller to clear the goods for export, where applicable.

However, the seller has no obligation to clear the goods for import, pay any import duty or carry out any import customs formalities. If the parties wish the seller to clear the goods for import, pay any import duty and carry out any import customs formalities, the DDP term should be used.

This rule may be used irrespective of the mode of transport.

在通常实施时，DAP 术语要求卖方办理货物的出口清关手续。

但卖方没有义务办理货物的进口清关手续，支付任何进口税或者办理任何进口海关手续，如果当事人希望卖方办理货物进口清关手续，支付任何进口税和办理任何进口海关手续，则应使用 DDP 术语。

该术语可用于各种运输方式。

2.3.7 DDP / Delivered Duty Paid (…named place of destination) 完税后交货(……指定目的地)

"Delivered Duty Paid" means that the seller delivers the goods when the goods are placed at the disposal of the buyer, cleared for import on the arriving means of transport ready for unloading at the named place of destination. The seller bears all the costs and risks involved in bringing the goods to the place of destination and has an obligation to clear the goods not only for export but also for import, to pay any duty for both export and import and to carry out all customs formalities.

DDP represents the maximum obligation for the seller. The parties are well advised to specify as clearly as possible the point within the agreed place of destination, as the costs and risks to that point are for the account of the seller. If the seller incurs costs under its contract of carriage related to unloading at the place of destination, the seller is not entitled to recover such costs from the buyer unless otherwise agreed between the parties.

The parties are well advised not to use DDP if the seller is unable directly or indirectly to obtain import clearance.

If the parties wish the buyer to bear all risks and costs of import clearance, the DAP rule should be used.

Any VAT or other taxes payable upon import are for the seller's account unless expressly agreed otherwise in the sales contract.

This term may be used irrespective of the mode of transport.

"完税后交货"是指卖方在指定的目的地，将在交货运输工具上的货物交给买方处置，并办理进口清关手续。卖方承担将货物运至指定目的地的一切风险和费用，并有义务办理出口与进口清关手续，支付出口及进口税费，以及办理一切海关手续。

DDP 术语下卖方承担最大责任。因为到达指定地点过程中的费用和风险都由卖方承担，建议买卖双方尽可能明确指定目的地。如果卖方承担在目的地卸货费用，则其无权向买方收取，除非双方另有约定。

如果卖方不能直接或间接地取得进口许可，不建议买卖双方使用 DDP 术语。

如果买卖双方希望买方承担进口的所有风险和费用，应使用 DAP 术语。

任何增值税或其他进口税费由卖方承担，除非合同另有约定。

该术语可用于各种运输方式。

2.3.8 Differences between FOB, CFR, CIF and FCA, CPT, CIP
FOB, CFR, CIF 和 FCA, CPT, CIP 的区别

Table 2.2 Differences between FOB, CFR, CIF and FCA, CPT, CIP

	FOB, CFR, CIF	FCA, CPT, CIP
Who bears the risks and charges for export formalities 谁承担出口清关风险及费用	the seller 卖方	the seller 卖方
Who bears the risks and charges for import formalities 谁承担进口清关风险及费用	the buyer 买方	the buyer 买方
Contract under trade terms 贸易术语下的合同性质	Shipment contract 装运合同	Shipment contract 装运合同
Mode of transport suitable 适用的运输方式	Ocean transport and inland waterway transport 海运及内河航运	Various transportation mode 各种运输方式
The seller's place of delivery 卖方交货地点	Port of loading 装运港	Inland or port of the exporter's country 内地或出口国港口
Point for division of risk between the buyer and seller 买卖双方的风险划分点	When goods on board the vessel at the named port of shipment 当货物在装运港装上船时	When goods at the disposal of the carrier 当货物交由买方指定的承运人处置时

2.4 INCOTERMS & Contracts INCOTERMS 与合同

Since INCOTERMS are standard definitions, they are used in contracts to reduce confusion and prevent traders having difficulty understanding the import requirements and shipping practice used in other countries.

Using the correct INCOTERMS clarifies the contracts you have with your suppliers or customers. You should use the current version, INCOTERMS 2010, and note this in the contract. These terms should also be used on any paperwork linked to the contract, such as invoices

由于《国际贸易术语解释通则》标准化定义了买卖双方的权利和义务，在合同中使用之，能减少双方的困惑，防止对其他国家有关进口要求及运输手续理解上的困难。

正确使用《国际贸易术语解释通则》可以分清买卖双方合同中的权利和义务。建议使用当前

or statements. Failing to state that you are using INCOTERMS 2010 could result in a dispute.

Most contracts from January 1st, 2011 will refer to INCOTERMS 2010, unless the seller and the buyer agree to use an earlier version. Contracts dated before 1 January, 2011 are still bound under INCOTERMS 2010.

The sales contract between the buyer and seller should also state which country's legal system will be used in case of a dispute. If both parties' countries are signed up to the UN Convention, this will provide the legal framework for settling the dispute. INCOTERMS will provide the legal backbone to settle the dispute.

版本，即《2010 年国际贸易术语解释通则》，并在合同中注明。贸易术语还应用在任何与合同有关的文本里，如发票或声明中加以使用。不注明使用《2010 年国际贸易术语解释通则》，可能会导致双方发生争执。

从 2011 年 1 月 1 日起，大多数合同将适用《2010 年国际贸易术语解释通则》，除非双方同意使用较早版本。2011 年 1 月 1 日前的合同仍适用于《2000 年国际贸易易术语解释通则》。

买卖双方应在合同中明确，如出现争议，将使用哪国的法律解决争端。如果双方均已签署了联合国公约，就为解决争端提供了法律框架。《国际贸易术语解释通则》将为解决争端提供法律支柱。

Exercises

I. 术语翻译

FOB 班轮条件	FOB 吊钩下交货
平舱	理舱
CFR 卸至岸上	CFR 舱底交货
国际贸易术语解释通则	船舷
多式联运	内河航运
清关	投保
单据买卖	象征性交货

II. 填空

1. FOB, CFR, CIF 与 FCA, CPT, CIP 两组术语的主要区别是，前一组适用于(   )运输方式，而后一组适用于任何一种运输方式。

2. 在 11 个术语中最常用的三种术语分别是(   )、(   )和(   )。

3. 如果按照 CFR 术语成交，需要特别注意的问题是，当卖方在完成发货任务以后必须及时向买主发出(　　　　)。

4. FOB 术语的变形规定买卖双方由谁承担(　　　　)的问题，CIF 和 CFR 术语的三种变形规定了买卖双方之间由谁承担(　　　　)的问题，它们并不改变这些术语的交货地点和风险划分的界限。

5. 把下列术语翻译成中文: FOB(　　　　), CFR(　　　　), EXW(　　　　), DAT(　　　　), CPT(　　　　), DDP(　　　　)。

6. 在《美国对外贸易定义》所解释的 6 个贸易术语中，(　　　　)术语的解释与《通则》的解释区别最大。

7. FOB 术语常用的变形有(　　　　), (　　　　), (　　　　), (　　　　)。

8. (　　　　)贸易术语的含义为在 FOB 条件下，卖方承担包括理舱费和平舱费在内的各项装船费用。

III. 单项选择题

1. 国际贸易惯例的适用是以当事人的意思自治为基础的，因为(　　　　)。
   A. 惯例即是行业内的法律　　　　　　　　B. 惯例有强制性
   C. 当事人有权在合同中作不符合惯例的规定　D. 法院会维护惯例的有效性

2. 《1932 年华沙—牛津规则》是国际法协会专门为解释(　　　　)术语合同而制定的。
   A. FOB　　　　　　B. CFR　　　　　　C. CIF　　　　　　D. CIP

3. 在交货地点上，《1990 年美国对外贸易定义修订本》中对(　　　　)的解释与 INCOTERMS 2010 中对 FOB 的解释相同。
   A. FOB Under Tackle　B. FOB　　　　C. FOB Vessel　　　D. FOB Liner Terms

4. 在 INCOTERMS 2010 中解释的 11 个术语中，按照卖方交货责任大小依次排列，其中卖方责任最大的是(　　　　)。
   A. EXW　　　　　　B. FOB　　　　　　C. DDP　　　　　　D. DAT

5. FOB 班轮条件下，买卖双方的风险划分点是在(　　　　)。
   A. 装运港的班轮边上 B. 装运港的班轮上 C. 装运港的船上　　D. 装运港的码头

6. 下列术语中卖方不负责办理出口手续及支付相关费用的是(　　　　)。
   A. FCA　　　　　　B. FAS　　　　　　C. FOB　　　　　　D. EXW

7. 在下列术语中，只有(　　　　)需要由卖方办理进口报关并承担有关费用。
   A. EXW　　　　　　B. DAT　　　　　　C. DDP　　　　　　D. FOB

8. 在一般情况下，按 CFR 贸易术语成交的合同中，不应计入货物价格的是(　　　　)。
   A. 货物成本　　　B. 运费　　　　　C. 保险费　　　　　D. 各项出口税费

9. 象征性交货意指卖方的交货义务是(　　　　)。
   A. 不交货　　　　　　　　　　　　B. 既交单又实际性交货
   C. 凭单交货　　　　　　　　　　　D. 实际性交货

10. 从交货方式上看，CIF 是一种典型的象征性交货。这句话的含义是(　　)。

　　A. 卖方以态度明确的函电表示交货

　　B. 卖方以提交全套合格单据来履行交货义务

　　C. 卖方无须实际准备足货，只要少量样品即可代表

　　D. 买方对不符合合同要求的货物，只要单据合格，无权索赔

11. 在以 CIF 和 CFR 术语成交的条件下，货物运输保险分别由卖方和买方办理，运输途中货物灭失和损坏的风险(　　)。

　　A. 前者由卖方承担，后者由买方承担　　B. 均由卖方承担

　　C. 均由买方承担　　D. 前者由买方承担，后者由卖方承担

12. CFR 合同下，如果卖方装船后未及时向买方发出装船通知，致使买方未能办理货运保险，则运输途中的风险由(　　)。

　　A. 买方承担　　B. 卖方承担　　C. 承运人承担　　D. 买卖双方各承担一半

13. 在使用下列何种贸易术语进行交易时，卖方及时向买方发出"已装船通知"至关重要，因为它将直接影响买卖双方对运输途中的风险承担(　　)。

　　A. CIP　　B. DAP　　C. FCA　　D. CFR

14. FCA, CPT, CIP 三种术语涉及的国内费用与 FOB, CFR, CIF 相比较，它们的区别是前者不包括(　　)。

　　A. 装船费　　B. 邮电费　　C. 预计耗损　　D. 拼箱费

15. 某公司与国外一家公司以 EXW 条件成交了一笔买卖，在这种情况下，其交货地点是在(　　)。

　　A. 出口国港口　　B. 进口国港口　　C. 出口商工厂　　D. 进口商仓库

16. 外贸公司对外以 CFR 报价，如果该公司先将货物交到货站或使用滚装与集装箱运输时，应采用(　　)为宜。

　　A. FCA　　B. CIP　　C. CPT　　D. DDP

17. 按 DDP 成交，其合同性质属于(　　)。

　　A. 启运合同　　B. 装运合同　　C. 转运合同　　D. 到达合同

18. 某公司与美国一家公司以 CFR Ex Ship's Hold 的条件成交了一笔生意，按国际惯例，这批货物在目的港的卸货费用应由(　　)承担。

　　A. 买方　　B. 卖方　　C. 船方　　D. 港务部门

19. 我方出口大宗商品，按 CIF 新加坡术语成交，合同规定采用租船运输，如我方不想负担卸货费，我方应采用的贸易术语变形是(　　)。

　　A. CIF Liner Terms Singapore　　B. CIF Landed Singapore

　　C. CIF Ex Ship's Hold Singapore　　D. CIF Ex Tackle Singapore

20. 在 FOB 条件下，若采用程租船运输，如买方不愿承担装货费及理舱费，则应在合同中规定(　　)。

　　A. FOB Liner Terms　　B. FOB Under Tackle　　C. FOB Stowed　　D. FOB Trimmed

Ⅳ. 判断题

(　　) 1. 《1941 年美国对外贸易定义本》是美国法协会专门为解释 CIF 贸易条件而制定的。

(　　) 2. 在 CFR 条件下，如合同未规定"装船通知"条款，卖方将货物装船后可不发装船通知，此做法不算违法。

(　　) 3. FOB、CFR、CIF 三种常用贸易术语都是象征性交货。

(　　) 4. 按照 INCOTERMS 2010，CIF 术语属于装运合同，DAP 术语属于到达合同。

(　　) 5. 按照 CIF Landed 术语成交的一批货物，货物由船上卸至码头上的费用，包括舶船费、码头费应由买方承担。

(　　) 6. FOB 价格术语的变形是因装货费用的负担问题而产生的，而 CIF 价格术语的变形是因卸货费用的负担问题而产生的。

(　　) 7. 在出口贸易中，我们要尽量选择我方责任、费用和风险较少的贸易术语。

(　　) 8. 买卖双方以 CIF 条件成交，若双方在洽商合同时未规定具体的险别，则卖方投保时，只有投保最低限度的险别义务。

(　　) 9. 国际贸易惯例已得到各国的公认，因此，它对于买卖合同中的当事人都具有普遍的法律约束力。

(　　) 10. 当买方不愿负担装卸费时，在商定合同时可要求在 CIF 后加列 Liner Terms、Landed 或 Under Ship's Tackle 字样。

(　　) 11. 《国际贸易术语解释通则》是进行国际货物贸易关系最大，亦是最重要的一项国际公约。

(　　) 12. FOB 价格条件按各国惯例的解释都是由卖方负责申请领取出口许可证和支付出口税。

(　　) 13. 买方采用 FOB 条件进口散装小麦,货物用程租船运输,若买方不愿承担装船费用，可用 FOB Stowed 变形。

(　　) 14. 采用 FOB 贸易术语的各种变形是为了解决买卖双方在卸货费用上的负担问题。

(　　) 15. 按 FOB 旧金山从美国购进一批小麦，卖方理所当然应将货物装到旧金山港口的船上。

(　　) 16. CIF Landed Singapore 成交，货物在新加坡港的卸货费和进口报关费应由卖方负担。

(　　) 17. 贸易术语因其表示商品的价格构成，所以可以称为"价格术语"。

(　　) 18. EXW 术语是买方承担责任、费用和风险最小的术语。

(　　) 19. 所有的贸易术语下，出口报关的责任、费用均由卖方负担。

(　　) 20. 按一般惯例，凡是 FOB 后面未加"理舱"或"平舱"字样,则由买方负担理舱或平舱费用。

V. 案例分析

1. 我方某公司以 FOB 条件出口一批冻鸭。合同签订后接到买方来电,称租船较为困难,委托我方代为办理租船,有关费用由买方负担。为了方便合同履行,我方接受了对方的要求。但时至装运期我方在规定装运港无法租到合适的船,且买方又不同意改变装运港。因此,到装运期满时货仍未装船,买方因销售季节即将结束便来函以我方未按期履行交货义务为由撤销合同。试问:我方应如何处理?

2. 我方某公司按 CIF 条件向欧洲某国进口商出口一批草编制品,向中国人民保险公司投保了一切险,并规定了用信用证方式支付。我出口公司在规定的期限、指定的我国某港口装船完毕,船公司签发了提单,然后去中国银行议付款项。第二天,出口公司接到客户来电,称装货的海轮在海上失火,草编制品全部烧毁,客户要求我公司出面向中国人民保险公司提出索赔,否则要求我公司退回全部货款。问:对客户的要求我公司该如何处理?为什么?

3. 我方某公司按 CFR 术语与英国 A 客户签约成交,合同规定保险由买方自理。我方于 9 月 1 日凌晨 2 点装船完毕,受载货轮于当日下午起航。因 9 月 1、2 日是周末,我方未及时向买方发出装船通知。3 日上班收到买方急电称:货轮于 2 日下午 4 时遇难沉没,货物灭失,要求我方赔偿全部损失。试分析此案例。

4. 北京 A 公司拟向美国纽约 B 公司出口某商品 5 000 箱,B 公司提出按 FOB 天津新港成交,而 A 公司主张采用 FCA 北京的条件,试分析 A、B 公司各自提出上述条件的原因。

5. 我方某公司按每公吨 242 美元 FOB Vessel New York 进口 200 公吨钢材,我方如期开出 48 400 美元的信用证,但美商来电要求增加信用证金额至 50 000 美元,不然,有关出口关税及签证费用应由我方另行电汇。试分析美方此举是否合理?

CHAPTER 3

Terms of Price
价格条款

Focus

In this chapter, you will learn:

- ✧ Exporting pricing;
- ✧ Conversion of major trade terms;
- ✧ Exchange cost;
- ✧ Commission & discount;
- ✧ Price clauses in a contract.

3.1   Exporting Pricing 出口定价

Price is the value potential buyers put on a product when they make a purchasing decision. Most buyers have an upper price limit in mind. This is conditioned by prevailing prices in the market and by the buyers' perception of the product's attributes. Every business is confronted with a pricing problem. Businessmen are particularly interested in seeing the goods of their firm sold in sufficient volume and at profitable prices. Prices occupy a position of first-rank importance and present some of the key problems with which they are forced to contend.

价格是潜在的买家给他想购买的产品所设定的价值，大多买家在购买时都有一个价格上限，这主要由当前的市场价和买方对产品属性的认识而决定。每一宗交易都面临着定价问题。卖方都希望自己的商品能在有利的价格上卖得又多又好。价格在国际贸易中起着重要的作用，也是交易双方必须解决的关键问题。

3.1.1   Items Constituting an Export Quotation 出口价格的组成

In calculating an export price, the export has to take into account two things: cost and profit. Cost mainly involves cost of production, selling and delivering cost and customs duties.

★ Cost of Production

Cost of production is the sum of the costs of materials, labor and other processing employed in producing the merchandise. This price is also referred to as the factory price.

★ Selling and Delivering Cost

Selling and delivering cost can be divided into both fixed costs like salesmen's salaries and variable costs like packaging, transport, commissions, advertising and sales trip expenses, insurance premium.

★ Customs Duties

Customs duties are taxes imposed by a government on the import or export of goods or services, which should be taken into account by the exporter when he prices his products.

在定价时，出口商应考虑两个因素：成本和利润。成本包含生产成本、销售和运输成本以及关税三方面。

★ 生产成本

生产成本是指生产产品时所需要的原材料、人力和其他因素的成本。生产成本又称为出厂价。

★ 销售和运输成本

销售和运输成本由固定成本和可变成本两部分组成，固定成本主要指销售人员工资，可变成本则包含包装、运输、佣金、广告、差旅费、保险等费用。

★ 关税

关税是政府对进出口商品和服务所征收的税收，出口关税也是出口商在定价时必须考虑的。

3.1.2　Factor Considerations in Pricing
　　　　影响定价的因素

Pricing is a complex activity. The considerations listed below will help the exporter determine the best price for the export goods.

★ The international market level for similar products;

★ The market positioning the company conveys;

★ The objective the firm pursue, e.g. market penetrating or market-skimming pricing objectives;

★ The policies and regulations that apply to a particular market area;

★ Adequate profit margin;

★ The quality and quantity of the product contracted;

★ Terms of payment;

★ Possible fluctuations of foreign exchange rates.

出口定价是一项错综复杂的工作,出口商在确定出口商品的价格时,应考虑下列因素。

★ 同类商品的国际市场价;

★ 公司的市场定位;

★ 公司追求的目标,即渗透定价还是撇脂定价;

★ 对目标市场所适用的政策和法规;

★ 适当的利润;

★ 产品的品质和成交的数量;

★ 支付条款;

★ 汇率的波动。

3.2　Conversion of Major Trade Terms
主要贸易术语之间的换算

In this section, we discuss the conversion of some major trade terms, i.e. FOB, CFR and CIF, since they are most commonly used in international trade.

If FOB price is given, then we may get CFR and CIF price. Here is the formula:

CFR = FOB + overseas freight

$$CIF = \frac{FOB + overseas\ freight}{1-(1+insurance\ bonus\ rate) \times premium\ rate}$$

If CIF price is given, FOB and CFR can be figured out as per the following formula:

FOB = CIF×[1 – (1+ insurance bonus rate) × premium rate] – overseas freight

CFR = CIF×[1 – (1+insurance bonus rate) × premium rate]

If CFR price is given, FOB and CIF price can also be calculated as per the formula below:

这里,我们讨论常用贸易术语,即 FOB、CFR 和 CIF 之间的换算。

如已知 FOB 价,我们可以推算出 CFR 和 CIF 价,公式如下:

CFR = FOB+运费

CIF =(FOB+运费)/[1-(1+投保加成率)×保险费率]

如已知 CIF 价,则可根据以下公式算出 FOB 和 CFR 价:

FOB= CIF×[1-(1+投保加成率)×保险费率]-运费

CFR= CIF×[1-(1+投保加成率)×保险费率]

根据以下公式可将 CFR 换算成 FOB 和 CIF 价:

$$FOB = CFR - overseas\ freight$$

$$CIF = \frac{CFR}{1-（1+insurance\ bonus\ rate）\times premium\ rate}$$

FOB ＝ CFR-运费

CIF ＝ CFR/[1-(1+投保加成率)×保险费率]

Case Study

我某出口商品对外报价为每公吨 1 200 美元 FOB 宁波,对方来电要求改报 CIF 伦敦价,已知保险费率为 1.68%,运费合计为 9.68 美元,请问:我方应报的 CIF 价为多少?

3.3 Exchange Cost 换汇成本

Most countries in the world practice the foreign exchange control. China is of no exception. The State Administration of Foreign Exchange is the agency responsible for exchange administration. Therefore, we have to consider exchange cost, no matter whether we do exporting or importing. Exchange cost is the cost in terms of local currency for earning each unit of foreign currency. It is a special tool to evaluate whether the pricing is reasonable or profitable. Here is the formula:

$$Exchange\ cost = \frac{total\ export\ cost\ (local\ currency)}{net\ foreign\ revenues\ from\ export\ sale\ (foreign\ currency)}$$

Total export cost includes purchasing or production cost, domestic charges (storage, management, taxes, etc.). Net foreign revenue from export sale refers to the FOB net income in which freight and insurance premium are not included.

很多国家实行外汇管制,中国也不例外。国家外汇管理局是主要负责机构。因此,无论在进出口时,我们都需考虑换汇成本。换汇成本是指用多少本币可以换回一个单位的外币的比率,它是评价出口商品价格是否合理或盈利的一项重要指标,以下是计算公式:

出口商品换汇成本=出口总成本(人民币)/出口销售外汇净收入(外币)

出口总成本是指出口商的购货成本、国内费用(仓储费、管理费、税收等)。出口销售外汇净收入是出口商品的 FOB 净价,不包含国外运费和保险费。

Case Study

某外贸公司出口一批货物,国内进货价共 10 000 元人民币,加工费支出 1 500 元人民币,商品流通费是 1 000 元人民币,税金支出为 100 元人民币,该商品出口销售外汇净收入为 2 000 美元。请问:该商品的出口总成本为多少?出口销售换汇成本是多少?

3.4　Commission & Discount 佣金和折扣

Commission refers to the money paid to an agent for his intermediary service. Commission falls into two kinds: plain commission and hidden commission. The former means that the commission is included in the price. For example, "US$10.00 per piece CIFC2% New York". "C2%" means a commission of 2% is included in the price and will be given to the middleman. The later means that the commission is hidden. Contract price with commission is called commission-included price. We get commission by multiplying this price with the commission rate. The following is the formula:

Commission = commission-included price × commission rate

Net price = commission-included price–commission

So, commission-included price = $\dfrac{\text{net price}}{1-\text{commission rate}}$

Discount is a certain percent of price reduction granted by the seller to the buyer. There are different kinds of discount such as quantity discount, cash discount, and special discount for some special purposes. Discount is also specified in the price clause, as "US$10.00 per piece CIF New York including 3% discount". Discount is often used to promote sales.

Net price means that no commission or discount is included in the price.

佣金是代理人或经纪人为委托人进行交易而收取的报酬。佣金有两种：明佣和暗佣。前者的佣金包含在价格中，如"每件 10 美元 CIFC2% 纽约"，"C2%" 代表价格中包含给中间商的 2%的佣金。后者在价格中不体现出来，包含佣金的价格叫做含佣价。通过价格与佣金率的乘积算得佣金的计算方式如下：

佣金=含佣价×佣金率
净价=含佣价－佣金
所以，含佣价=净价/（1－佣金率）

折扣是卖方给予买方的价格减让，折扣分很多种，如数量折扣、现金折扣、特别折扣等等。折扣也在价格中表明，如"每件 10 美元 CIF 纽约，含 3%折扣"。折扣通常用于促销。

净价指价格中既不包含佣金也不包含折扣。

Case Study

If the seller makes an offer "US$100.00 per kg. CFRC2% New York", the agent requires to increase the commission to 5%, how should the seller modify the offer without reducing his profit?

3.5　Price Clauses in a Contract 合同中的价格条款

Price clause in a sales contract comprises four parts: the currency of sale, unit price figure, measurement unit and trade terms. Example: US$10.00 per piece FOB Shanghai	出口价格包含四个部分：计价货币、单位价格、计价单位和贸易术语。 如：每件 10 美元，FOB 上海

3.5.1　Choosing of Currency
计价货币

The currency used in a transaction can either be the currency of the importing country, or that of the exporting country, or the currency of a third country. As exchange risk is inevitable, fluctuation of exchange rates greatly increase the risks of commercial transactions. A depreciation of the currency used in export is likely to eliminate the exporter's profit in the transaction. In international trade, it is recommended to choose a hard currency in exporting. It's also recommended to choose a weak currency in importing.	计价货币可以选择出口国货币或进口国货币，也可以选择第三国货币。汇率的波动大大增加了国际贸易的风险，计价货币的贬值会降低出口商的利润。在国际贸易中，出口最好选择硬币，进口时要选择软币。

3.5.2　Measurement Unit
计量单位

Most countries have officially adopted metric system of units (e.g. kilogram, meter, liter, cubic meter). The imperial system of unit (e.g. pound, foot, gallon and cubic foot) and some local units are still in use in some countries. A unit of measurement like "ton" may refer to metric ton (2,204.6 lbs. or 1,000 kgs), short ton (2,000 lbs. or 970 kgs), or long ton (2,240 lbs. or 1,016 kgs). The metric ton is usually written "tonne" in American English. The exporter must be sure to indicate clearly proper units used in quotation and contract.	大多数国家采用公制度量衡（即千克、米、公升、立方米等）。有些地区仍在使用英制度量衡（即磅、英寸、加仑、立方英寸等）和地方度量衡。因此计量单位"吨"可以代表公吨（2 204.6 磅或者 1 000 千克），短吨（2 000 磅或 970 千克）或者长吨（2 240 磅或 1 016 千克）。在美国，公吨通常用"tonne"来表示，出口商在报价和合同中必须明确说明计量单位。

3.5.3　Selection of Trade Terms
贸易术语

The risks of international trade are not limited to the fluctuation of the price. Going through various formalities, shipping and taking delivery of the goods, arranging insurance, as well as subsequent claims are factors of potential risks. Trade terms are used to make clear the method of delivery, charges, responsibilities and risks of a transaction between the exporter and the importer.

For some reasons, CIF or CIP is preferred for exporting, and FOB or FCA for importing. In general, the selection of trade terms should follow the principle of being consistent with the means of transport and prevention of risks.

国际贸易中的风险不仅限于价格波动，办理各种官方手续、安排发货和提货、办理保险，以及后续的索赔等都存在风险，贸易术语可以明确交货方式以及买卖双方风险、责任和费用的划分点。

在我国，出口一般采用 CIF 或 CIP，进口则采用 FOB 或 FCA。总之，选择的贸易术语应与运输方式相符并注意防范风险。

Exercises

I. 术语翻译

佣金	货币贬值
折扣	硬币（硬通货）
换汇成本	关税
出口成本	汇率
出口外汇净收入	公吨

II. 单项选择题

1. 出口货物一批，国内进货成本为 100 000 人民币元，出口前一切费用为 9 000 人民币元，出口前一切税金为 25 470 人民币元，则该批货物的出口总成本为(　　　　)。
   A. 100 000 人民币元 　　　　　　　　　B. 109 000 人民币元
   C. 125 470 人民币元 　　　　　　　　　D. 134 470 人民币元
2. 以下出口商品的单价，只有(　　　　)的表达是正确的。
   A. 250 美元/桶 　　　　　　　　　　　B. 250 美元/桶 CIF 伦敦
   C. 250 美元/桶 CIF 广州 　　　　　　　D. 250 美元/桶 CFR 德国
3. 支付给中间商的酬金叫(　　　　)。
   A. 预付款　　　　B. 折扣　　　　　　C. 佣金　　　　　　D. 订金

4. 在货物的买卖中，收取佣金的通常是( )。
   A. 买方　　　　　B. 保险公司　　　　C. 船方　　　　D. 中间商

5. 凡货价中不含佣金和折扣的被称为( )。
   A. 折扣价　　　　B. 含佣价　　　　C. 净价　　　　D. 出厂价

6. 一笔业务中，若出口销售人民币净收入与出口总成本的差额为正数，说明该笔业务为
   ( )。
   A. 盈　　　　　B. 亏　　　　　C. 平　　　　D. 可能盈，可能亏

7. 在我国进出口业务中，选择计价货币应( )。
   A. 力争采用硬币收付
   B. 力争采用软币收付
   C. 进口时采用软币付款，出口时采用硬币收款
   D. 进口时采用硬币付款，出口时采用软币收款

8. 某公司对外发盘，200 台空调机，每台 150 美元 FOB 广州，外商要求改报 CIF 鹿特丹，
   经查，至鹿特丹总运费为 3 500 美元，保险费为 100 美元，则改报价应为( )。
   A. 168 美元　　　B. 3 750 美元　　　C. 184 美元　　　D. 150 美元

9. 某出口商品，对外报价为每公吨 FOB 上海 1000 美元，现外商要求改报 FOBC5%上海，我
   方的报价应为每公吨 FOBC5%上海( )。
   A. 1 050 美元　　B. 1 052.63 美元　　C. 950 美元　　D. 1 005 美元

10. 若我国外汇市场上美元和人民币的兑换价为：100 美元=686.72~686.86 人民币元，则将
    出口销售外汇净收入换算成出口销售人民币净收入所选择的价格应是( )人民
    币元。
    A. 686.72　　　B. 686.86　　　C. 686.79　　　D. 686

III. 判断题

( ) 1. 佣金和折扣都可分为明佣(扣)和暗佣(扣)两种。
( ) 2. 含佣价=净价/(1-佣金率)，其中的净价指 FOB 价。
( ) 3. 我出口合同中规定的价格应与出口总成本一致。
( ) 4. 出口销售外汇净收入是指出口商品的 FOB 价按当时的外汇牌价折合成人民币
       的数额。
( ) 5. 从一笔交易的出口销售换汇成本可以看出，在这笔交易中用多少人民币换回一美
       元，从而看出这笔交易是盈利还是亏损。
( ) 6. 硬通货是指在国际金融市场上汇价坚挺并能自由兑换、币值稳定、可以作为国际
       支付手段或流通手段的货币。
( ) 7. 折扣直接影响到商品的价格，对于卖方来说，同一商品的销售价格，给予买方 5%
       的折扣率比给予 3%的折扣率售价高。
( ) 8. 佣金是交易中买方给予卖方或卖方给予买方的报酬。

VI. 计算题

1. 我方某公司出口某商品 1000 箱，对外报价为每箱 22 美元 FOBC3%上海，外商要求改报为 CIFC5%汉堡。已知运费为每箱 1 美元，保险费为 FOB 价的 0.8%,请问：(1) 要维持出口销售净收入不变，CIFC5%应为多少? (2) 已知进货成本为每箱 160 人民币元，每箱的商品流通费为进货成本的 3%，出口退税为每箱 30 人民币元，该商品的换汇成本是多少?

2. 某公司出口单晶糖 200 公吨，每公吨 US$450CIFC2%利物浦，货物装船后，公司财务部门根据合同规定将 2%的佣金汇给中间商，请问：应付佣金为多少?

3. 我方出口某商品对外报价为 480 欧元/公吨 FOB 宁波,现外商要求将价格改报 CIF 旧金山,请问:我方的报价应为多少才能使 FOB 净值不变? (设运费为 FOB 价的 3%,保险费为 FOB 价的 0.8%)

4. 某商品的卖方报价为每打 60 美元 CIF 香港，若该商品的运费是 CIF 价的 2%，保险费是 CIF 价的 1%,现外商要求将价格改为 FOBC3%宁波，请问：(1) FOBC3%应报多少? (2) 若卖方国内进货价为每打 380 人民币，出口前的费用和税金合计为 15 元人民币/打，该商品的出口销售换汇成本?

CHAPTER 4

Terms of Commodity
商品条款

Focus

In this chapter, you will learn:

✧ Name of commodity;
✧ Quality of commodity;
✧ Quantity of commodity;
✧ Packing of commodity.

4.1   Name of Commodity 商品的品名

An international cargo trade involves any kind of commodities. The name of the commodity is an indispensable component of the contract. If the goods delivered are not in accordance with the name or description contracted, the buyer has right to lodge a claim against the seller for compensation, reject the goods or even cancel the contract.

国际货物买卖可以涉及任何商品，商品的品名是合同中的一个不可缺少的组成部分，如果卖方所交货物与合同中的品名不符，买方有权向卖方提出索赔、拒收货物甚至取消合同。

The Clause of "Name of Goods" in a Contract
合同中的"货物名称"条款

The clause of "Name of Goods" is also called the clause of the subject matter of sales contract. Usually, the parties to the contract just specify the name of the product under the subject "Name of Commodity". The clause of "Name of Goods" is subject to the kind and characteristics of the goods contracted. In some cases, the name of commodity and the quality description are merged into one.

There are points for attention in a sales contract:

★ The name of the commodity must be specific and concrete, not vague and general in stipulation.

★ The name of contracted goods must be that of the goods which the seller is able to supply and the buyer is in need of; any irrelevant or unfulfillable descriptions should be excluded.

★ World standardized names are advisable. If local names are used, both parties shall have a mutual understanding of the implication in advance. As to new commodities their naming and translation should be as precise and easy as possible and well up to world customs.

★ Proper choice of name can help to reduce customs tariff, and facilitates import and export and bring down freight.

合同中"货物名称"条款也称为合同的标的。交易双方通常在"货物名称"项下说明商品的名称，不同的商品，其"货物名称"的表达方式也不一样。有时，合同中商品的品名和品质条款合在一起。

在签订品名条款中，应注意以下四点：

★ 货物名称必须具体、明确，避免空乏、笼统的规定。

★ 交易的商品必须是卖方能够提供的，也是买方需要的，凡是做不到或不必要的描述性词句都不应列入。

★ 货物名称的使用应按照国际标准的要求。如果要采用本地名称，交易双方应事先达成共识。如果是新产品，其翻译应尽量准确简单，符合国际标准。

★ 选择合适的名称可以降低关税和运费，促进进出口。

Case Study

　　某出口公司与外商成交一批罐头，合同上的品名为"铁罐装洋梨罐头"，而信用证上的品名为"洋梨罐头"。问遇此情况应如何制作单据？

4.2　Quality of Commodity 商品的品质

Quality of goods refers to the intrinsic quality and outside form or shape of the goods, such as chemical composition, mechanical performance, biological features, modeling, structure, color and luster, and taste of a commodity. Terms of quality of goods are the main condition on which a contract is based and constructed. The goods the seller delivers must be up to the standard required in the contract. If the seller fails to deliver the goods as required by the contract, the buyer is entitled to claim damage, repair and substitutes, or reject goods, or sometimes even cancel the said contract.

商品的品质是指商品内在品质和外在形态，如化学成分、物理性能、生物特性、造型、结构、花色、味觉等。品质条款是合同的核心条款，卖方所交货物的品质必须与合同规定完全相符。如果卖方所交货物与合同不符，买方有权要求损害赔偿、修理或交付替代货物，甚至拒收货物或取消合同。

Case Study

回样未被认可，延期交货由谁负责

　　某出口公司凭买方样品成交金属拉手一批，合同规定3—4月份装船，但须卖方认可回样后方能装运。2月下旬买方开来信用证也有同样的字句。我方多次试制回样未得到买方认可，故我方不能如期装船。到了5月份，买方以延误船期而要求赔偿。问我方该如何处理？

4.2.1 Methods Describing Quality of Goods 描述商品品质的方法

Quality clause involves the methods of expressing the quality of goods. The qualities of different commodities can be expressed in different ways. The methods of stipulating quality of commodity depend on the quality, character and the customary usage in practice. The methods are often used as follows:

(1) Sale by Sample

A sample refers to the article which can be used to represent the quality of the whole lot. In merchandising, a sample is a small quantity of a product, often taken out from a whole lot or specially designed and processed that is given to encourage prospective customers to buy the product. Sale by sample means a sale made under the agreed condition that the quality of the bulk of the goods must be as good as the quality of the sample. It is suitable for commodities that are difficult to standardize and normalize, such as arts and crafts, garments, light industry products and agricultural native products.

According to the sample supplier, there are:

★ Sale by the Seller's Sample

Seller's samples are the samples which are usually sent by the seller to the buyer, which is also called original sample.

In this case, the seller shall supply a representative sample which will possess the moderate quality among a large quantity of the physical goods, and at the same time keep a duplicate sample, which shall be in strict conformity with the standard sample. The sample dispatched and the duplicate sample/file sample shall bear the same article number so as to make it convenient for delivery, verification when handling quality disputes or future transactions.

★ Sale by the Buyer's Sample

Sometimes the buyer may send a sample to the seller, who is asked to supply the goods in accordance with it. The transaction held is called Sale by the Buyer's Sample. In most

品质条款包含表示货物品质的方法。不同种类的商品，可以用不同的方法表示品质。确定商品品质的方法主要取决于商品的性质、特点及其在国际贸易中长期以来形成的习惯做法，表示品质的方法主要由以下几种：

（1）凭样品买卖

样品是指能够代表一整批货物质量的实物，通常是指从一批货物中抽取出来或由生产和使用部门设计加工出来能够代表出售货物品质的少量实物，用于向潜在的客户推广自己的产品。凭样品买卖是指买卖双方约定以样品作为交货品质依据的买卖方式。凭样品买卖的方法一般适用于难以标准化、规格化，难以用文字说明其品质的商品，如工艺品、服装、轻工产品及农副产品等。

按样品提供者的不同，交易方式可分为以下几种：

★ 凭卖方样品买卖

凭卖方样品是指卖方向买方提供货物的样品，即原样。

如果采用凭卖方样品的话，通常卖方要提供能够代表整批货物中等质量的实物，同时，卖方要自留与这些样品品质一致的复样。一般来说，发出的样品和复样具有相同的编号，以备交货时和处理品质纠纷时作核对之用。

★ 凭买方样品买卖

有时买方会向卖方提供样

cases, the seller may send to the buyer a sample of goods of the same quality for the buyer's confirmation. The sample that has been confirmed by the buyer is called return sample or counter sample. Furthermore, to avoid disputes upon the quality of goods, the method of Sealed Sample can be applied if necessary.

(2) Sale by Specification, Grade or Standard

If a trade is made in this way, the goods delivered should be of the same specifications, grade or standard as stipulated in the sales contract. Any discrepancy may lead to disputes and the buyer is in a position to make a claim for compensation or refuse to accept the goods.

★　Sale by Specifications

Specifications of a commodity are detailed descriptions of the goods to be sold. They include composition, content, purity, strength, size, etc. of the goods. For example, the specifications of China Sesame Seed are as follows:

Moisture 水分(Max 最高)	8%
Admixture 杂质(Max 最高)	2%
Oil Content 含油量 (Min.最少)	18%

★　Sale by Grade

The same kind of commodities with different specifications may be classified into different grades, such as large, medium or small; Grade A, Grade B, Grade C; Grade 1, Grade 2, Grade 3…For example, Chinese tungsten is of 3 grades according to its chemical contents for exporting, and each grade has its specifications.

品，要求卖方按此样品交货，这种交易叫做凭买方样品买卖。卖方大多会按买方样品打样并交由买方确认，这种经由买方确认的样品叫作回样或对等样品。另外，为了避免日后纠纷，必要时还可使用封样。

(2) 凭规格、等级或标准买卖

如果是凭规格、等级或标准成交的，卖方所交货物的规格、等级或标准必须和合同规定完全一致，如有任何不符都会产生纠纷，买方有权提出索赔或拒收货物。

★　凭规格买卖

规格是对所售商品的详细描述，如成分、含量、纯度、大小、长度、厚度等，以下是中国蓖麻籽的规格

★　凭等级买卖

同类商品但有不同的规格时，可以将其分等级，如大、中、小；A 级、B 级、C 级；一级、二级、三级等，以下是根据化学成分的含量对中国钨砂分的三个等级，每个等级有不同的规格：

Grade 等级 \ Contents 含量	Tungsten Trioxide (Min) 三氧化钨	Tin (Max.) 锡	Arsenic (Max.) 砷	Sulphur (Max.) 硫
Superior 特级	70%	0.2%	0.2%	0.8%
1 一级	65%	0.2%	0.2%	0.8%
2 二级	65%	0.1%	0.2%	0.8%

★　Sale by Standard

Standard means those specifications or grades that are laid down and proclaimed in a unified way by governmental departments or commercial organizations of a country. For example, Chinese raw silk is sold by standard and its standard consists of 12 grades: 6A, 5A, 4A, 3A, 2A, A, B, C, D, E, F and G. The quality of different lots of the goods that are of the same grade is the same.

It is worthy of note that the standard of a commodity is subject to change or amendment and a new standard often takes the place of the old one. So, in case of sale by standard, it is important and necessary to mention in the terms the name of the publication, in which the standard of the commodity appears, such as "tetracycline HCL Tablets (Sugar Coated) 250 mg. B.P. 1973" (B.P. stands for British Pharmacopoeia).

In trading agricultural products it is a regular practice to use FAQ (Fair Average Quality) or GMQ (Good Merchantable Quality) to indicate the quality of the goods. FAQ denotes the average quality level of the export commodity within a certain period of time while GMQ refers to the sound quality that is free from defects and is sufficiently good to satisfy the purpose for which the buyer intends to use the goods or for which the seller intends that they should be used. Both terms are rather too general and sweeping. When in use, therefore, they are usually supplemented by some concrete specifications.

(3) Sale by Brand and Trademark

A brand is a maker's name, trademark or sign, usually officially registered and protected, and is put on goods to make it easy for buyers to recognize the make or quality. A trademark is a special mark that is placed on a particular brand of article or commodity to distinguish it from similar goods sold by other producers. As to the goods whose quality is stable, reputation is sound and with which the customers are familiar, we may sell them by brand name or trademark. For example, "Haier Air Conditioner", "West Lake Longjing Tea". Since the goods with the same brand name or trademark possess the same quality and their

★　凭标准买卖

凭标准买卖标准是指政府机关或商业团体等统一制定或公布的规格或等级。如中国生丝就是按标准来表示品质的，它可以分为 6A、5A、4A、3A、2A、A、B、C、D、E、F 和 G 这 12 个等级，每个等级的品质是相同的。

值得注意的是，某种商品的标准或等级经常会进行变动和修改，新的标准常常会代替旧的标准。因此，如果按"标准"买卖的话，则必须注明是按照哪个版本的标准，并标明援用标准的版本年份。如：四环素片(糖衣)250毫克，1973 年英国药典标准

对于农副产品的贸易，通常采用"良好平均品质"和"上好可销品质"两种方式来表示其品质。"良好平均品质"即"大路货"，是国际农副产品市场上通用的标准，是指出口商品在某一特定的时期内所具有的中等平均水平，"上好可销品质"是指卖方保证其交付的货物品质良好，合乎销售，而在成交时无须以其他方式去证明商品的质量。这两种方式都太笼统，不易把握，在使用时要增加具体的规格。

(3) 凭牌号、商标买卖

牌号是制造商的名称、商标或标记，通常经由正式注册并受到保护，买方可以从牌号或商标中分辨出商品的制造商或品质。商标是一个特殊的标记，是生产者用以区分其他同类商品的一种标志。用牌号或商标表示品质，一般都是在国际市场上享有良好信誉、品质稳定的商品，被广大

quality remain unified and unchanged, their brand names or trademarks are often used to indicate the quality of these goods.

(4) Sale by Description, Drawing or Diagram

Machines, apparatus, and complete sets of equipment are apt to sell by description, drawing or diagram. It is difficult to indicate completely their quality in detail by merely using specifications, brand or trademark because their structure and function are complicated and their installation, application and maintenance are subject to specified rules. Consequently, relevant technical manuals, booklets of directions, drawings or diagrams will serve the purpose.

客户所喜爱，因而可以凭牌号或商标买卖。例如，"海尔空调"、"西湖龙井茶叶"等，由于这些同一牌名或商标的商品具有相同的品质，且品质统一、稳定，因此，这些牌名或商标通常用来表示商品的品质。

(4) 凭说明书、图样或图表买卖

机器、仪器和成套设备等一般用说明书或图样来表示品质。因结构和功能复杂，其安装、使用和维护都需遵循特定的规定，所以很难用规格、牌名或商标来详细描述其品质，因此，技术手册、说明书、图表等用来表示商品的品质。

Case Study

我方出口纺织原料一批，合同规定水分最高 15%，杂质不得超过 3%，但在成交前曾向买方寄过样品，订约后，我方又电告对方成交货物与样品相似。货到后，买方提出货物的质量比样品低 7%的检验证明，据此要求赔偿损失。问我方是否该赔？

4.2.2　Quality Clauses in a Contract
　　　合同中的品质条款

Quality clauses in a sales contract are subject to the method used in describing the subject matter of the contract. In the case of "sale by sample", in addition to the description of commodity, "sample number", "sending date" or an elastic clause like "Quality to be about equal to the sample", "Quality to be similar to the sample", "Quality to be nearly the same as the sample", or "for reference only", should be added. In international trade, to avoid violation of the contract as a result of the deviation from a given standard of size, quality or some other measurable characteristic allowed in the specifications for a product, quality tolerance and flexible ranges are commonly used.

合同中的品质条款由表示合同标的品质的方法来决定。如果用样品表示品质，除了商品描述外，还需写明样品号、寄样日期或者"品质与样品大致一致"、"品质与样品相似"、"品质与样品几乎相同"或者"仅供参考"等机动条款。在国际贸易中，为了避免因交货品质与合同中规定的尺寸、质量或其他衡量的品质标准不符而造成违约，可以在合同的品质条款中做出某些变通规定，如品质公差和品质机动幅度条款。

(1)   Quality Tolerance

The quality tolerance refers to the quality deviation internationally recognized. Quality tolerance means the permissible range within which the quality supplied by the seller ma be either superior or inferior to the quality stipulated in the contract. For deviation within the internationally recognized range, the seller is deemed to have fulfilled his obligation even without such mention in the contract. For example, "Oil Content (Min.) 18%", "Should the oil content of the goods actually shipped be 1% higher or lower, the price will be accordingly increased or decreased by 1%."

(2)   Quality Flexible Ranges

It allows for quality differences within some flexible ranges, which may be stipulated as:

★   a given range—meaning certain quality index can change within the given range

For example:

Yarn-dyed Gingham   Width 41/42″

★   a limit—setting a limit to the specifications, such as maximum and minimum

For example:

Belgian Flavor Animal Chocolate

cocoa solids	min. 26%
black chocolate	min. 25%
white chocolate	min. 20%
milk solids	min. 14%
milk chocolate	min. 11%

★   a more or less clause—stipulating a more or less allowance for a certain quality index

For example:

Gray Duck Feather   The Content of Duck's down 18% (allowing 1% more orless)

(1)   品质公差

品质公差是指国际同行业所公认的产品品质的差异，品质公差允许卖方交付商品的品质可以高于或者低于合同所规定的幅度。即使在合同中未明确规定，如果卖方所交货物品质在品质公差范围之内，卖方也属已履行合同，例如："含油量（最少）18%，含油量增减 1%，则合同价增减 1%。"

(2)   品质机动幅度

品质机动幅度是指对特定品质指标在一定幅度内有灵活性。具体有以下三种规定方法：

★   规定一定的范围，即对品质指标的规定允许有一定的差异范围

例如：色织条格布　宽度 41/42″

★   规定一定的极限，指对所交货物的品质规格，规定上下极限，如最大最小等

例如：

比利时风味动物巧克力

可可粉	最少 26%
黑巧克力	最少 25%
白巧克力	最少 20%
乳固体	最少 14%
牛奶巧克力	最少 11%

★   规定上下差异，即规定一定的机动幅度，

如：灰鸭毛，含绒量 18%(上下 1%)

Case Study

我方先后向某国出口纯毛纺织品数批，货到国外后买方一一收货，从未提出异议。但数月后，买方寄来制成的服装一套，声称用我毛料制成的服装色差严重，难以投入市场销售，因而要求赔偿。问对此我方应如何解决？

4.3 Quantity of Commodity 商品的数量

It is evident that a business deal cannot be completed without caring for the quantity of the goods sold or bought. Calculation of quantity is often made by weight, by capacity, by number, by length, by area and by volume. Quantity of goods is an indispensable part of a business contract.

任何交易都会涉及数量，计量方法有按重量、容积、数量、长度、面积、体积等。数量条款是合同中不可缺少的因素。

4.3.1 Unit of Measurement
计量单位

The following are the units of measurement widely used in international trade:

★ Weight: gram or gm.; kilogram or kg.; ton or t.; metric ton or m/t.; pound or lb.; ounce or oz.; long ton or l/t.; and short ton or s/t. These are for natural products and some industrial products, such as wool, cotton, corns, minerals, oil .

★ Capacity: liter or l.; gallon or gal.; bushelor bu. They are for products such as grain, gas, gasoline and beer.

★ Numbers: piece or pc.; package or pkg.; pair; set; dozen or doz.; gross or gr.; roll or rl.; coil; head; case; bag, etc. They are for daily industrial and general products such as stationery, paper, toys, ready-made clothes, vehicles and live animals.

★ Length: yard or yd; meter or m.; foot or ft.; centimeter or cm., etc. They are for textiles, ropes and wires, and so on.

★ Area: square yard or yd^2; square meter or m^2; square foot or ft^2 and square inch, etc. They are for glass，floor and leather.

★ Volume: cubic meter, cubic yard, cubic foot, cubic nch, etc. They are for chemical gas, wood and so on.

以下是国际贸易中最常用的计量单位：

★ 重量：克、千克、吨、公吨、磅、盎司、长吨、短吨。用于农副产品及工业制成品如羊毛、棉花、玉米、矿产、油等。

★ 容积：公升、加仑、蒲式耳等。常用于谷类、石油、啤酒等升。

★ 数量：件、包、双、套、打、箩、卷、圈、头、箱、袋等，用于一般杂货和工业制品，如文具、纸、玩具、成衣、车辆、活牲畜等。

★ 长度：码、米、英尺、厘米等。用于纺织品、绳索、电缆线等。

★ 面积：平方码、平方米、平方英尺、平方英寸等。常用于玻璃、皮革、地板等。

★ 体积：立方米、立方码、立方英尺、立方英寸等。用于化学气体、木材等。

In international trade, different countries adopt different metrology apart from their different means of calculation and unit of measurement. At present, there are four metrologies commonly used in international trade：The Metric System，The UK System，The US System and The International System of Units. What units of measurement should be chosen in the contract should go in accordance with the nature of goods.

在国际贸易中，不同的国家采用不同的度量衡制度，使用的计量方法和计量单位也不一样。目前主要有四种度量衡制度，公制、英制、美制和国际单位制，合同中选择何种度量衡单位应根据商品的性质而定。

4.3.2　Calculation of Weight
重量的计算

In international trade, goods are most often measured in the units of weight. The method to measure the weight of goods are stated as follows:

★ By Gross Weight: the total weight of a package, including its contents and the packing.

★ By Net Weight: the weight of the contents only, i.e. after deducting the weight of packing, which is often called the tare. (gross weight – are = net weight).Tare can be calculated by actual tare, by average tare, by customary tare or by computed tare.

★ By Conditioned Weight: the weight equals to dry weight plus standard moisture content, used in calculating products of high economic value and with unsteady moisture content such as wool, cotton and raw silk.

★ By theoretical weight: the weight is calculated by multiplying the total number and the weight of each unit. This method is applicable to commodities with regular specifications and regular size, such as galvanized iron and steel plate.

★ By legal weight: the weight equals to the net weight plus direct packing (inner packing), used mainly for tax calculation.

国际贸易中，大多数商品的买卖按重量计算，计算重量的方法有以下几种：

★ 按毛重：商品的总重量，包含本身的重量和包装的重量。

★ 按净重：货物自身的重量，不包含包装，即皮重。（毛重－皮重=净重）。衡量皮重有四种方法：实际皮重、平均皮重、习惯皮重和约定皮重。

★ 按公量：采用科学方法抽出商品中的水分后，再加上标准含水量所得出的重量即为公量。用于价值较高而水分含量不稳定的商品，如羊毛、棉花和生丝等。

★ 按理论重量：由数量乘以每件的重量得出。这种方法适用于有固定规格形状和尺寸的商品，如马口铁和钢铁。

★ 按法定重量：实际净重加上直接接触商品的包装物料的重量，海关征收从量税时一般按照法定重量计算。

4.3.3 Quantity Clauses in a Contract
合同中的数量条款

The quantity clause in a contract should cover the quantity of the goods, the measurement unit and the method to calculate the weight. In international trade, some commodities are difficult to weigh accurately such as agricultural and mineral products because of their own nature, their supply condition, packing, or shipment condition. Quite often the actual shipment is over-delivered or under-delivered in quantity. To meet this, flexible range of quantity of commodities should be reasonably stipulated.

(1) About or Approximately

In international sales contract, such expression as "about 5,000 metric tons" is used in quantity clause. But here the word "about" may be given several interpretations: some refer to 2.5% more or less, some 5%, and some 10%. This kind of indefinite wording will surely give rise to dispute and should, therefore, be avoided.

(2) More or Less Clause

A "more or less clause" means over-load and under-load by the seller are permitted but should not surpass a certain percentage of the stipulated quantity. That's to say both the seller and the buyer agree to allow some more or less of the goods delivered, but not exceeds the fixed quantity agreed upon. For example, "20,000 metric tons, 5% more or less at seller's option". "Plus or minus" or the sign "±" may also be used. Under the "more or less" clause, the payment for the over-load or under-load will be made according to the contract price or at the market price at the time of shipment.

合同中的数量条款包括商品的数量、计量单位及计算重量的方法。在粮食、矿砂等大宗商品的交易中，由于受商品特性、货源变化、包装、装运条件等因素的影响，难以准确称重，实际交付的货物通常会比合同的规定的要多或少。因此，需要在合同中规定合理的数量机动幅度。

(1) 大约或近似于

在国际贸易中，有时会在数量前加"约"，如"约5000公吨"。但各国对"约"的解释不同，有的解释为2.5%的增减幅度，有的解释为5%，而有的则理解为10%，这样可能引起日后的纠纷，应避免。

(2) 溢短装条款

溢短装条款的意思是允许卖方多装或少装，但以不超过合同规定数量的百分之几为限。即规定交货数量可在一定幅度内增减。例如："20000公吨，允许5%的溢短装，由卖方选择"，也可采用"增加或减少"，或用"±"符号表示。在此条款下，溢短装部分可按合同价计价，或按装船时的市场价计算。

Case Study

溢短装条款运用

我公司订购钢板400公吨，计6英尺、8英尺、10英尺、12英尺四种规格各100公吨，并用每种数量可增减5%的溢短装条款，由卖方决定。今卖方交货为：6英尺，70公吨；8英尺，80公吨；10英尺，60公吨；12英尺，210公吨，总量未超过420公吨的溢短装上限的规定。对于出口商按实际装运数量出具的跟单汇票，进口商是否有权拒收拒付？

4.4 Packing of Commodity 商品的包装

4.4.1 Types of Packing
包装的种类

Whatever mode of transport is used, the goods require packing. Packing is a part of export business. Ocean voyages may be most damaging to the goods that are not properly packed. So proper packing could prevent or minimize the damage to the shipment.

Many goods have little or no form of packing and carried loose. They are nude cargo or bulk cargo. The former included iron and steel plates, steel rails, heavy vehicles, etc., and the latter oil, ores, grain, coal, etc. But most goods need proper packing in international trade. Packing is generally divided into two types.

★ Transport packing, is also called large/outer packing. Its main function is to protect the quality and quantity of the commodity, to facilitate loading, unloading and stowage, and even to prevent pilferage.

★ Selling packing, i.e. inner packing or small packing, is the immediate packing that can go into market. It is designed not only to protect goods, but also to aid marketing.

无论以何种方式运输，产品都需要包装，包装是出口贸易的一部分。包装不当可能使货物在运输途中受损，尤其是海运。因此，适当的包装可以预防或者将货物在运输途中的损失降到最低。

很多货物无包装，我们称之为裸装货物和散装货物。像钢板、铁板、钢轨、重型车辆等属于裸装货，油、矿石、谷物、煤等则属于散装货。但国际贸易中大多货物需要包装，包装有以下两种：

★ 运输包装，也叫做大包装或外包装，其主要作用是保护运输途中的商品、便于装卸甚至防止盗窃。

★ 销售包装，也叫内包装或小包装，是直接接触商品并随商品进入市场销售的包装，这类包装不仅必须具有保护商品的功能外，还应具有促销的功能。

4.4.2 Marking of Goods
商品的标志

When talking about transport packing, the packing mark (or the marking of packing) has to be referred to. Packing mark refers to different diagrams, words and figures which are written, printed, or brushed on the outside of the shipping packing in order that it is easy and convenient for goods' loading, unloading,

运输包装涉及到包装标志问题。包装标志是指在商品的包装上书写、压印、刷制各种有关的标志，如图形、文字、数字等，以便识别货物，有利于装卸、运输、仓储、

store, inspection and discharge. Marks are generally categorized into the shipping mark, indicative mark, warning mark, weight/volume mark and mark of origin, etc.

(1) Shipping Mark

A shipping mark is composed of a geometric figure, a simple code or initials. Usually four types of information are included in shipping marks:

★ The initial letters or abbreviation of the consignee or the buyer;

★ The reference number, such as the number of the contract, order, invoice, Bill of Lading or Letter of Credit;

★ The destination, i.e. the name of the port or place of destination;

★ The package number, i.e. the consecutive number of each package or the total number of the shipment.

For example:

ABCCO	←Name of Consignee
LONDON	←Port of Destination
S/C 9756	←Contract No.
No.4-20	←Serial No.

(2) Indicative Mark

Simple, noticeable design, remarkable diagrams and words on the packages are often used to remind the relative workers of the items for attention when they load, unload, carry and store the goods, such as "HANDLE WITH CARE" THIS SIDE UP", etc.

(3) Warning Marks

Warning marks, also called dangerous cargo marks, are to warn dockers and crew against dangerous cargoes such as explosive, corrosive, inflammable and radioactive products.

检验和交接工作的顺利进行。包装标志可分运输标志、指示性标志、警告性标志、重量/尺码标志和原产地标志等。

（1）运输标志或唛头

运输标志由简单的几何图形、代码或字母组成，一般包含四类信息：

★ 收货人缩写；

★ 参考号码，如合同号、订单号、提单号、信用证号等；

★ 目的地，即目的港或目的地名称；

★ 件号，即每件货物的号码或整批货物的件数。

例如：

ABC CO	←收货人名称
LONDON	←目的港
S/C 9756	←合同号
No.4-20	←件号

（2）指示性标志

人们通常会在包装上使用简单、醒目的图形和文字标出货物在运输、装卸、搬运、保管过程中应注意的事项，如"小心轻放"、"此端向上"等。

（3）警告性标志

警告性标志又称危险货物包装标志，是指凡在包装内有易爆物品、腐蚀物品、易燃及放射性物品等危险货物时，都必须在运输包装上显示。

4.4.3　Packing Clauses in a Contract
合同中的包装条款

Clause of packing is one of the important terms in a sales contract. It must be clearly stipulated in a contract. Clause of packing usually includes packing material, means, speci-fications, marks and charges, etc. For example: In sturdy wooden case of 200 kgs net weight each.

The following points are to be taken good care of:

★　For packing means, the amount of containing of the packing should be clearly stated.

★　The packing material is usually provided by the seller. If the buyer is responsible for the packing and packing material, its time of arrival and means of packing should be clearly stated as well as the responsibility for failure in timely delivery resulting from late arrival of the packing or packing material.

★　Specifying the bearer of packing charges.

★　Usually the seller decides the shipping mark, but sometimes the buyer would designate the shipping mark. If doing so, the time of providing shipping mark should be clearly stated in the contract as well as the responsibility for failure in timely delivery resulting from late arrival of the shipping mark.

包装条款是合同中的主要条款，必须明确。包装条款通常包括包装材料、包装方式、包装规格、包装标志和包装费用的负担等内容。如：用结实的木箱包装，每箱净重 200 公斤。

在商定包装条款时，要注意下列事项：

★　每件包含的数量应在包装方式中明确规定。

★　包装材料通常由卖方提供，如由买方负责提供包装或包装物料，则应明确规定买方提供包装或包装物料的时间，以及由于包装或包装物料未能及时提供而影响发运时买卖双方所负的责任。

★　明确包装费用由谁承担。

★　通常由卖方制定唛头，但有时买方也可以提供唛头，如买方提供唛头，则应在合同中明确规定由于买方未及时提供唛头而影响发运时买卖双方所负的责任。

Case Study

包装规格不符，买方有无权力拒收

英国穆尔公司以 CIF 伦敦的条件，从兰陀公司购买 300 箱澳大利亚水果罐头。合同的包装条款规定："箱装，每箱 30 听。"卖方所交货物中有 150 箱为每箱 30 听装，其余 150 箱为每箱 24 听，买方拒收。卖方争辩说，"每箱 30 听"字样并非合同的重要部分，不论是 24 听还是 30 听，其品质均与合同相符，因此，买方应接受。请问，买方有权拒收吗？

Exercises

I. 名词解释

1. 公量
2. 对等样品
3. FAQ
4. ISO9000 系列标准
5. 中性包装

II. 单项选择

1. 在国际货物贸易中，对交易双方无约束力的样品是（　　　　）。
   A. 卖方样品　　　　B. 买方样品　　　　C. 参考样品　　　　D. 对等样品
2. 按《联合国国际货物销售合同公约》规定，如卖方交货数量大于约定的数量，买方
   （　　　）。
   A. 可以拒收约定的和多交的全部货物
   B. 只能拒收多交中的一部分货物，而不能拒收多交中的全部货物
   C. 只能拒收多交的全部货物，而不能只拒收多交中的部分货物
   D. 可以接受多交中的一部分或全部货物，也可以拒收多交中的一部分或全部
3. 联合国欧洲经济委员会简化国际贸易程序工作组指定的标准运输标志中不包括（　　　　）。
   A. 件数代号　　　　B. 参考号　　　　C. 收货人代号　　　　D. 几何图形

III. 多项选择

1. 按照买方提供的样品，卖方复制后寄买方确认，确认后的样品被称为（　　　　）。
   A. 复样　　　　B. 回样　　　　C. 对等样　　　　D. 参考样
2. 根据《联合国国际货物销售合同公约》规定，还盘时，变更（　　　）均视为在实质上
   变更发盘的条件。
   A. 品质　　　　B. 数量　　　　C. 价格　　　　D. 货运保险

IV. 判断题

（　　　）1. 商品质量是构成商品说明的组成部分，如卖方交货不符合约定的品质，买方有
权提出索赔，甚至拒收货物。

（　　　）2. 若卖方交货违反约定的包装条件，买方可提出损害赔偿要求，但不得拒收货物。

（　　　）3. 《联合国国际货物销售合同公约》成员国之间进行交易，若卖方交货数量少于约
定的数量，只要卖方在规定的交货期届满前补交了少交的货物，则在任何情况
下，买方都无权提出损害赔偿的要求。

（　　）4. 鉴于凭样品成交，卖方必须严格按样品交货，其承担的责任太大，且容易引起
争议，故我国出口贸易中，最好都不采用凭样交易。

（　　）5. 为了从不同角度说明商品的品质，在约定成交商品的品质时，最好采用既凭规
格，又凭样品买卖。

V. 简答题

1. 何谓品质机动幅度和品质公差？在买卖合同中约定品质机动幅度和品质公差的意义何在？

2. 何谓溢短装条款？溢短装的选择权由谁掌握合适？

3. 何谓条形码？为什么在我国出口果品包装上应标明条形码？

VI. 计算题

1. 买卖双方按每箱单价 150 美元出售某商品 1 000 箱，并约定"交货数量允许有 5% 的伸缩性，由卖方决定"。试问：卖方最多可装多少箱？最少可装多少箱？如实际装运 1 040 箱，则其应收货款多少？

VII. 案例分析

1. 凭我方样品成交，对美国出口高档瓷器一批，合同中规定有"货到目的港 60 天内复检，索赔有效"条款。货到经对方复检后，并未提出异议。事过一年，对方来电称："这批瓷器全部釉裂，必须按原价降低 60%，否则全部退回。"接电后，检验我方留存复样，也发现釉下裂纹。问我方应如何处理？

2. 我国某公司对印度某商号出口烧碱一批，在合同中对产品的规格规定得十分复杂，并且把一些次要的规格一并罗列进去。如规定产品的颜色为：白色结晶状并带微蓝色阴影。而作为工业用烧碱，其颜色一般只要求白色即可，是否带有"微蓝色阴影"对该商品的品质和用途不起重要作用。最后，我方在执行合同时发生困难，造成交货品质不符合合同规定的被动局面。问：我方应该从此案例中吸取什么教训？

3. 某出口公司与国外成交红枣一批，合同与来证上均写的是三级品，但到发货时发现三级红枣库存告罄，于是改以二级品交货，并在发票上加注"二级品红枣仍按三级计价"。 问这种以好顶次原价不变的做法妥当吗？

4. 我某公司向科威特出口冻羊肉 20 吨，每吨 FOB 价 400 美元，合同规定数量可增减 10%。国外按时开来信用证，证中规定金额为 8 000 美元，数量约 20 吨。结果我方按 22 吨发货装运，但持单到银行议付时遭拒绝。问原因何在？

5. 我某商品出口，在与外商签订合同时规定由我方出唛头，因此，我方在备货时就将唛头刷好，但到装船前不久，国外开来的信用证上又制定了唛头。问这种情况应如何处理？

CHAPTER 5

International Cargo Transportation Insurance
国际货物运输保险

Focus

In this chapter, you will learn:

✧ Basic concepts in insurance;

✧ The scope of ocean marine cargo insurance;

✧ Terms and coverages of ocean marine cargo insurance of China;

✧ Overland, air transportation & parcel post insurance;

✧ Marine cargo insurance of the Institute of London Underwriters;

✧ Cargo insurance practice in import & export business;

✧ Insurance clauses in a contract.

5.1　Basic Concepts in Insurance 保险中的基本概念

In international trade, goods traveling long distances to another country, out of the direct physical control of both the buyer and the seller, may face all kinds of risks and losses and therefore must be insured against loss and damage at each stage of their journey. In this way, whatever mode of transport is being used, neither the exporter nor the customer suffers any loss. So, insurance exists to protect the importer or exporter against the financial loss which he would otherwise suffer in case damage or loss was inflicted upon him. It is an indispensable adjunct of international trade. Without adequate insurance and protection of the interest of those with goods in transit, international trade can not be guaranteed.

Usually, insurance can be classified into four types as property insurance, liability insurance, credit insurance and personal insurance. Cargo insurance falls under the type of property insurance.

在国际贸易中，货物必须经由一个国家运到另一个国家，路途遥远，途中可能遇到各种买卖双方都无法控制的风险，因此必须投保。无论采用何种运输方式，只要将货物投保，买卖双方都不会遭受任何损失。所以，保险可以将运输途中的风险转嫁给保险公司，保护买卖双方免受经济损失。保险是国际贸易中一个重要的环节，它可以保障货物运输途中各方的利益，使国际贸易得以顺利进行。

保险可分财产险、责任险、信用险和人寿险，运输货物保险属于财产险。

5.1.1　Parties to Insurance
###　　　　保险中的当事人

The parties to be involved in insurance are as simple as only two. One is the insurer, the other is the insured. In some cases, there may be an insurance broker in betwe en. Once damage occurred, the party who suffers will lodge a claim against the insurance policy. The party is called the claimant.

The insurer is the party to the insurance contract who promises to indemnify losses or service, which usually indicates the insurance company or the individuals who run an insurance firm. In China, the People's Insurance Company of China has made great contributions to the prevention of Chinese exports/imports from perils and dangers.

The insured refers to the one who buys insurance from the insurer or the insurance company. The insured may be the buyer under FOB contract, or the seller under CIF contract.

保险中涉及的当事人有两个，保险人和被保险人，有时也会涉及保险经纪人。当发生货损时，遭受损失的一方凭借保险单提出索赔，此时他被称为索赔人。

保险人通常为保险公司或者经营保险业务的人，他们在保险合同中承诺对损失做出赔偿或服务。在中国，中国人民保险公司在进出口货物保险中起了重要的作用。

被保险人是指向保险公司或者保险人购买保险的人。他可以是FOB业务中的买方，也可以是CIF业务中的卖方。

The insurance broker, in fact, is the middleman in insurance business. The broker has the advantage of being familiar not only with the technicalities of marine insurance but also has an unbiased view over the coverage and premium rates offered by all insurance companies. He is in a good position to obtain for his client the coverage that best fits his needs at the lowest possible cost.

Whenever an actual loss occurs, the insured can get fair, efficient and rapid adjustment of his claim. While insurance may be arranged by the exporter, the importer is the rightful owner. Consequently, claims are usually made by the importer, after discovering a loss.

保险经纪人是保险业务中的中间人，经纪人不仅通晓熟悉保险业务，而且对各家保险公司的保险险别和费率了如指掌，他可以为他的客户以最优惠的费率投保最合适的险别。

无论何时发生货损，被保险人都可获得公正、有效和快速的赔偿。虽然保险可由出口商安排，但进口商才是合法的索赔人，因此，当发生货损时，索赔手续通常由进口商办理。

5.1.2　The Fundamental Principles of Insurance
保险的基本原则

Both the applicant (insured) and the insurer under any kind of insurance coverage are required to enter into an insurance contract and to observe the fundamental principles. The fundamental principles are mainly as follows:

★　Principle of insurable interest

It refers to the legal right to enter into insurance contract. A person is said to have an insurable interest if the event insured against could cause a financial loss.

★　Principle of utmost good faith

It means that both the applicant and the insurer should keep their utmost good faith without any misrepresentation or concealment while entering into the insurance contract and also in the validity of the policy.

★　Principle of indemnity

It means that the insurer should be responsible for the loss of or damage to the subject matter insured according to the terms of the insurance contract if such loss or damage falls within the scope of insurance coverage.

无论投保什么险，保险人和被保险人都必须签订保险合同并遵循下列原则：

★　可保利益原则

指拥有签订保险合同的合法权利，当发生货损时，只有拥有可保利益的人才能获得赔偿。

★　最大诚信原则

指投保人和保险人在签订保险合同及保险单的有效期内要保持最大诚信，不能欺骗或隐瞒。

★　补偿原则

指保险人必须对保险标的在保险责任范围内产生的损失进行赔偿。

5.2　The Scope of Ocean Marine Cargo Insurance
海上货物运输保险承保的范围

Obviously, cargo insurance is a contract whereby the insurer (insurance company), on the basis of a premium paid, under-takes to indemnify the insured against loss from certain risks or perils to which the cargo insured may be exposed. Cargo insurance may be classified into Ocean Marine Cargo Insurance, Overland Transportation Cargo Insurance, Air Transportation Cargo Insurance and Parcel Post Insurance according to the different modes of transportation, among which Ocean Marine Cargo Insurance is the oldest. The insurance company covers different risks under different types of cargo insurance because of the different mode of transportation, but there is minor difference in the scope of the coverage.

国际货物运输保险是指保险人与被保险人订立保险合同，被保险人向保险人缴纳相应的保险费，保险人对货物运输过程中发生的承保责任范围内的损失给予被保险人赔偿。根据运输方式不同，国际货物运输保险分为海洋货物运输保险、陆上运输货物保险、航空运输货物保险和邮政包裹保险四种，其中海洋货物运输保险是最早的一个险种。不同运输方式的货物保险，保险人承担的责任有所不同，但所保障的范围都是相似的。

5.2.1　Types of Marine Risks
海上风险的种类

There are two types of risks covered under Ocean Marine Cargo Insurance. One is the perils from the sea, which refer to the risk that occurs when the vessel or the cargo is in the course of sea transportation. It includes both natural calamities and unexpected accidents. Natural calamities include heavy weather, lighting, tsunami, earthquake, volcanic eruption and so on. Accidents refer to fire, explosion, vessel being stranded, grounded, sunk or capsized, collision or contact of vessel with any external object other than water, etc.

海洋货物运输风险有两类，一是海上风险，主要指船舶和货物在海上运输途中可能遭遇的风险，包括自然灾害和意外事故。自然灾害是指恶劣气候、雷电、海啸、地震、火山爆发等，意外事故是指火灾、爆炸、船舶触礁、搁浅、沉没、碰撞或互撞等。

The other type of risks is external (extraneous) risks, which refer to the risk that is caused by external factors when the vessel or the cargo is in the course of sea transportation, including general external risks and special external risks. General external risks include theft and pilferage, contamination, leakage, breakage, sweating and/or

另一类风险是外来风险，是指海上风险以外的其他外来原因造成的风险，包括一般外来风险和特殊外来风险。一般外来风险包含偷窃、玷污、渗漏、破碎、受潮受热、串味、生锈、钩损、

heating, taint of odor, rusting, hook damage, fresh and/or rain water damage, short-delivery and non-delivery, shortage in weight and so on. Special risks include war, strike, failure to deliver, etc.

淡水雨淋、短交和提货不着、短重等。特殊外来风险包含战争、罢工、交货不到等。

5.2.2 Types of Losses
损失的种类

Two types of losses are covered by marine insurance. One is total loss and the other is partial loss. Total loss is divided into actual total loss and constructive total loss.

Actual total loss refers to the events that the whole consignment insured is totally lost in the course of transit or is so damaged to the extent that it is without its original shape and validity or it can no longer be in the possession of the insured. It means the complete loss of the insured cargo in value.

A constructive total loss refers to the loss where an actual loss appears to be unavoidable though the cargo is not actually lost; or the cost to be incurred in recovering or reconditioning the goods together with the forwarding cost to the named destination would exceed their value on arrival. Then the loss is treated as totally lost.

Partial loss means a partial damage to or the total loss of part of the insured cargo. It can be divided into general average and particular average.

General average refers to sacrifices voluntarily made and extraordinary expenses incurred to rescue a ship and its cargo from impeding danger or for the common safety under fortuitous circumstance while it is at sea or at anchor in a port. It is based upon a relationship between the ship owner and all shippers who have cargo aboard the same vessel on a particular voyage. All these parties are bound together in the "adventure". Sometimes, when the whole ship was threatened by a peril of the sea or some other hazard, in order to save the ship and some of the cargo, part of cargo or vessel has to be sacrificed, then an act of general average would be declared. According to maritime law, those interests whose property was

海损有两种，全部损失和部分损失，全部损失又分为实际全损和推定全损。

实际全损是指被保险货物在运输途中完全灭失，或者受到严重损坏完全失去原有的形体、效用，或者不能再归被保险人所拥有。这意味着被保险货物价值的完全损失。

推定全损是指被保险货物在运输途中受损后，虽未达到完全灭失的状态，但实际全损已不可避免，或为了避免全损需要支付的抢救、修理费用加上继续将货物运抵目的地的费用之和将超过货物到达目的地时的价值。在这种情况下，被保险人可以推定货物发生了全部损失。

部分损失是指货物的损失只是部分的，分为共同海损和单独海损。

共同海损是指载货的船舶在海运途中或港口遭到自然灾害或意外事故，船长为了解除船货的共同风险或为了使航行能够继续，有意地、合理地、人为地做出牺牲，或采取其他救难措施所带来的损失和额外费用。共同海损是基于船方和所有货运

saved must contribute proportionally to cover the losses of the one whose property was voluntarily sacrificed.

Particular average refers to a partial loss suffered by a part of the cargo caused by an insured peril such as a storm or fire, other than a general average loss, i.e. the loss which should be borne by the party who suffers.

方具有共同面临风险的关系这一特点。有时，当整船受到海上风险或其他灾害的威胁时，为了保护船只和部分货物，部分货物或船只需要牺牲，在这种情况下，共同海损即产生。通常，共同海损的牺牲和费用应由受益方，即船方、货运、运费方三方最后按获救价值的比例进行分摊，称为共同海损分摊。

单独海损是指除共同海损外的部分损失，即被保险货物在海上遭遇风险损失后如风暴和火灾，其损失未达到全损的程度，仅涉及船舶或货物所有人单方面的利益，该损失应由受损方单独来承担。

Case Study

某货轮从天津港驶往新加坡，在航行途中船舶货舱起火，大火蔓延到机舱，船长为了船货的共同安全，决定采取紧急措施，往船中灌水灭火。火虽被扑灭，但由于主机受损，无法继续航行，于是船长决定雇用拖轮将货船拖回新港修理，检修后重新驶往新加坡。事后调查，这次事件造成的损失有：①1 000 箱货物被烧毁；②600 箱由于灌水灭火而受损失；③主机和部分甲板被烧坏；④拖轮费用；⑤额外增加的燃料和船长、员工的工资。从上述各项损失的性质看，哪些属于单独海损？哪些属共同海损？

5.2.3   Expenses
费用

Ocean cargo insurance also covers the expenses incurred to avoid or reduce damage to or loss of the subject matter insured. There are mainly two types of expenses. One is sue and labor expenses and the other is salvage charges or salvage.

Sue and labor expenses are any reasonable expense incurred by the insured or his agent or his employees in

海洋货物保险还包括为了减少被保险货物的损失而产生的费用，主要有施救费用和救助费用。

施救费用是指保险标的物遭受承保范围内事故时，被保险人或其代理人、雇用人员为防止或

preventing or minimizing a loss when the subject matter insured is endangered.

Salvage charges is an award payable to a third party for service rendered to preserve maritime property from peril at sea and is payable only when the property has been saved.

减少货损所采取的抢救措施而支出的合理费用。

救助费用是指保险标的物遭受承保范围内的事故时，由保险人和被保险人以外的第三者采取措施并获得成功而向其支付的报酬。

5.3 Terms and Coverages of Ocean Marine Cargo Insurance of China 我国海洋货物运输保险条款和险别

The most commonly used terms in cargo insurance in China is China Insurance Clause (CIC). The terms of Ocean Marine Cargo Insurance of China mainly includes four aspects as follows.

在我国，海洋货物运输保险主要适用中国保险条款，主要有以下四方面内容。

5.3.1 The Insurance Coverages 保险险别

The scope of the subject matter insured depends on different insurance coverages. There are two types of insurance coverage under Ocean Cargo Insurance, basic coverage and additional coverage. Basic coverage can be applied for independently, but additional coverage is the amendment to the basic coverage.

(1) Basic Coverage

Basic coverage mainly includes FPA, WPA and All Risks.

FPA (Free from Particular Average) is a limited form of cargo insurance cover under which no partial loss or damage is recoverable. It only provides coverage for total losses and general average emerging from the actual "marine perils" like vessel stranded, grounded or sunk.

WPA or WA (With Particular Average) is a wider cover than FPA. Apart from the risks covered under FPA, it also covers partial losses of the insured goods caused by natural calamities like heavy weather.

All Risks is the most comprehensive of the three basic coverages. Aside from the risks covered under FPA and

被保货物的责任范围取决于其所投保的险别。中国保险条款有两大险别：基本险和附加险。基本险可单独投保，而附加险则是对基本险的补充。

（1）基本险

基本险有平安险、水渍险和一切险三种。

平安险是一种有限制的货物保险形式，承保人不对部分损失进行赔偿，仅对全部损失或者船舶搁浅或沉没等引起的共同海损进行赔偿。

水渍险的责任范围比平安险广，除了平安险外，水渍险还负责被保险货物在运输途中由于恶劣天气等自然灾害所造成的部分损失。

在三种基本险中，一切险承保的范围最广，除了平安险和水渍险

WPA, it also covers all total loss or partial loss of, or damage to the goods insured either arising from sea or perils or general external causes. However, it does not cover loss, damage or expense caused by delay, inherent vice or nature of the goods insured, or special external risks of war, strike, etc.

(2)   Additional Coverages

Additional coverage includes general additional coverage and special additional coverage.

General additional risks include:

★   TPND (Theft, Pilferage and Non-Delivery);

★   Fresh Water Rain Damage;

★   Risk of Shortage;

★   Risk of Intermixture and Contamination;

★   Risk of Leakage;

★   Risk of Clash and Breakage;

★   Risk of Odor;

★   Damage caused by Heating and Sweating,

★   Hook Damage;

★   Risk of Rust.

These additional risks can not be covered independently and should go with FPA, WPA and are included in All Risks coverage.

Special additional risks include:

★   War Risk;

★   Strikes Risk;

★   Failure to Delivery Risk;

★   Import Duty Risk;

★   On Deck Risk;

★   Rejection Risk.

These additional coverages are usually taken out together with FPA, WPA and All risks.

To choose an insurance coverage that is effective and economical, the exporter or the importer should be aware of the possible losses to be expected of a particular consignment. Different items have different natures and may apply to different insurance types. For example, cargo like iron ore faces little risk of partial loss, so FAP will be sufficient. Most

的各项责任外，该保险还负责被保险货物在运输途中由于外来原因所致的全部或部分损失。要注意的是，一切险不包括由于延误、货物固有的缺陷和特性以及战争、罢工等引起的损失。

（2）附加险

附加险包含一般附加险和特殊附加险。

一般附加险包含以下几种：

★   偷窃提货不着险；

★   淡水雨淋险；

★   短量险；

★   混杂玷污险；

★   渗漏险；

★   碰损破碎险；

★   串味险；

★   受潮受热险；

★   钩损险；

★   锈损险。

这些附加险不能单独投保，可在平安险和水渍险的基础上加保，但已包含在一切险中。

特殊附加险包含：

★   战争险；

★   罢工险；

★   交货不到险；

★   进口关税险；

★   舱面险；

★   拒收险。

特殊附加险也不能单独投保，必须和平安险、水渍险或一切险一起投保。

进出口商必须了解货物可能产生的损失才能选择经济有效的险别，不同的商品有不同的特性，所以投保的险别也应不同。例如，铁矿砂产生部分损失的可能性很

manufactured goods are covered against All Risks as they are prone to damage caused by sea perils or external risks.

小，只要投保平安险就足够了，但大多工业制成品很容易因海上风险和外来风险受损，所以应该投保一切险。

Case Study

由于罢工而造成的大豆损失赔偿案

我方按 CIF 条件出口大豆 1000 吨，计 10000 包，合同规定投保一切险加战争、罢工险。货卸目的港码头后，当地码头工人便开始罢工。在工人与政府的武装力量对抗中，该批大豆有的被撒在地上，有的被当成掩体，有的丢失，总计共损失近半。问这种损失保险公司是否负责赔偿？

5.3.2 Exclusions of Ocean Marine Cargo Insurance
海洋货物运输保险除外责任

Exclusions refer to the loss or expenses that the insurer is not responsible for compensation on the condition that the subject matter insured is covered under basic coverages.

海洋货物运输的除外责任是指保险标的在投保了基本险的情况下，保险人不负责赔偿的损失和费用。

Case Study

货物变质索赔案

我方向海湾某国出口花生糖一批，投保的是一切险。由于货轮陈旧，速度慢，加上该轮船沿途到处揽载，结果航行 3 个月才到达目的港，卸货后，花生糖因受热时间过长已全部潮解软化，无法销售。问这种情况保险公司可否拒赔？

5.3.3 Commencement and Termination of Ocean Marine Cargo Insurance
海洋货物运输保险责任起讫

Commencement and Termination of Ocean Marine Cargo Insurance refers to time limits of insurance. It is stipulated in the terms of commence ment and termination of Ocean Marine Cargo Insurance Clauses that a Warehouse to Warehouse

海洋货物运输保险责任起讫是指保险人承担保险责任的期限，按照国际保险业的习惯，采用的是"仓至仓"条款。"仓

Clause is adopted. The insurance attaches from the time the goods hereby insured leave the warehouse or place of storage named in the policy for the commencement of the transit until the insured goods are delivered to the consignee's final warehouse or place of storage at the destination named in the policy or to any other place used by the insured for allocation or distribution of the goods or for storage. This insurance shall be limited to sixty days after completion of discharge of the insured goods from the seagoing vessel at the final port of discharge before they reach the above mentioned warehouse or place of storage.

至仓"条款是指保险责任自被保险货物远离保险单所载明的起讫地仓库或储存所开始,到该货物抵达保险单所载明目的地收货人的最后仓库或储存所或被保险人用作分配、分发的其他储存所为止。如未抵达上述仓库或储存处,则以被保险货物在最后卸载港全部卸离海轮后满 60 天为止。

5.3.4   The Time of Validity of a Claim
保险索赔期限

The time of validity of a claim under basic coverages shall not exceed a period of two years counting from the time of completion of discharge of the insured goods from the seagoing vessel at the final port of discharge.

保险索赔期限从货物在最后卸载港全部卸离海轮后满两年为止。

5.4   Overland, Air Transportation & Parcel Post Insurance
陆运、空运和邮包运输险

Insurance coverage for land transportation can be divided into two categories:
★   Land Transportation Risk, almost equivalent to WPA;
★   All Risks for land transportation, almost equivalent to Marine All Risks.

There are also two types of air coverage:
★   Air transportation risk;
★   Air transportation All Risks.

Air transportation risk is similar to WPA, while air transportation All Risks is similar to Marine All Risks.

陆上运输险有两种:
★   陆运险,与海运的水渍险相似;
★   陆运一切险,与海运的一切险相似。

航空运输险也有两种:
★   航空运输险;
★   航空运输一切险。

航空运输险与水渍险相似,而航空运输一切险与一切险相似。

Parcel post insurance covers the losses of or damage to the parcel caused by natural calamities, fortuitous accidents or external risks. It includes :

★ Parcel post risk;

★ Parcel post All Risks.

On the basis of these two basic coverages, some additional risks may also be added if circumstances required.

邮包运输险承保邮包在寄送过程中因自然灾害、意外事故或外来原因而遭受的损失，包含：

★ 邮包险；

★ 邮包一切险。

除了这两种基本险，必要时还可加保附加险。

5.5 Marine Cargo Insurance of the Institute of London Underwriters
伦敦保险协会海运货物保险条款

London Institute Cargo Clauses was first drafted by the Institute of London Underwriters in 1912. The newly revised one in 1982 include six coverages:

★ Institute Cargo Clauses A (ICC (A));

★ Institute Cargo Clauses B (ICC (B));

★ Institute Cargo Clauses C (ICC (C));

★ Institute War Clauses (Cargo);

★ Institute Strikes Clauses (Cargo);

★ Malicious Damage Clauses.

(1) Institute Cargo Clauses A (ICC (A))

Institute Cargo Clauses A gives the most extensive coverage.

This covers all risks of loss of or damage to the subject matter insured except general exclusions, unseaworthiness and unfitness exclusion, war exclusion, and strike exclusion.

(2) Institute Cargo Clauses B (ICC (B))

Clause B lists all risks covered so that the insured may choose the proper insurance cover. The terms of Institute Cargo Clauses B are identical to those of WPA.

(3) Institute Cargo Clauses C (ICC (C))

This insurance covers only big accidents. It is similar to FPA.

《协会货物条款》最早由伦敦保险协会在 1912 年制定，现在适用的是 1982 年 1 月 1 日的版本，主要条款由 6 种：

★ 协会货物条款(A)；

★ 协会货物条款(B)；

★ 协会货物条款(C)；

★ 协会战争险条款（货物）；

★ 协会罢工险条款（货物）；

★ 恶意损害险条款。

(1) 协会货物条款(A)

(A)条款包括的范围最广，采用的是"一切风险减除外责任"的办法，除外责任包括：一般除外责任、不适航、不适货除外责任、战争和罢工除外责任。

(2) 协会货物条款(B)

(B)条款采用"列明风险"的办法，即把保险人所承保的风险一一列出，以便投保人选择合适的险别。B 条款和水渍险相似。

(3) 协会货物条款(C)

协会货物条款(C)只承保重大意外事故，相当于平安险。

5.6   Cargo Insurance Practice in Import & Export Business
进出口业务货物保险实务

When dealing with cargo insurance on import & export goods, the insured should often ascertain insurance amount, make an application, pay the insurance premium, obtain an insurance document and lodge a claim at the time of loss, etc.

(1)   Insurance Amount

Insurance amount is the highest amount of indemnity or benefit of an insurance contract and also the basis on which the insurer calculates the insurance premium.

(2)   Application

According to the insurance stipulation of our country, insurance is arranged by the seller when the export contract is concluded on the term of CIF or CIP. When export enterprises are applying for insurance from local insurance companies, he is required to fill in the application form. Then he pays the premium.

(3)   Insurance Premium

It is the precondition that the applicant pays premium so that the insurance contract becomes valid. The insurer is entitled not to issue any insurance policy before the applicant or insurant pays the insurance premium.

An insurance document is the evident of the insurance contract entered into by the insurer and the applicant or insurant. It serves as a document defining obligations and titles both of the insurer and the insured. It is a document according to which the insured lodges a claim and the insurer settles a claim when the loss occurs which is answerable under the terms of the coverage. There are mainly four kinds of insurance documents:

★   Insurance policy

Insurance policy, issued by the insurer, is a legal document setting out the exact terms and conditions of an insurance transaction—name of the insured, name of the commodity insured, the amount insured, the name of the carrying vessel, the precise risks covered, the period of cover and any exception

办理进出口货物运输保险包括以下几个程序：确定保险金额、办理投保手续、交保险费、领取保险单证，发生货损时进行索赔等。

（1）保险金额

保险金额是指保险人承担赔偿或者付给保险金责任的最高限额，也是保险人计算保险费的基础。

（2）投保

根据我国保险条款，以 CIF 或 CIP 条件成交的合同，出口商负责办理保险手续；出口商在向保险公司办理投保时应填写投保单，并付保险费。

（3）保险费

只有在投保人交了保险费后，保险人才签署保险单，保险合同生效。

保险单据是保险人和被保险人之间订立保险合同的证明文件。既反映了保险人和被保险人之间的权利和义务关系，又是保险人的承保证明。当发生保险责任范围内的损失时，还是保险索赔和理赔的依据。保险单据共有四类：

★   保险单

保险单是保险人签发的一种更具有法律效力的单据，它严格规定了一笔保险业务的条款和条件——被保险人姓名、保险货物名称、保险数量、载货船只名称、承保险别、保险期限和可能发生的免

there may be. It also serves as a written contract of insurance between the insurer and the insured.

★　Insurance certificate

Insurance certificate is the simplified version of the insurance policy serving the same function in the transaction. It only contains the key items and does not list all the contents of a formal insurance contract.

★　Open policy

Open policy is recommended for exporters and importers who do a large volume of business. It is a convenient method for insuring the goods where a number of consignments are intended to be covered. An open policy covers these shipments, as soon as they are made, under previous arrangement between the insured and the insurance company.

★　Endorsement

Any amendment and addition to an existing document such as policy, certificate or cover note is made by endorsement. The endorsement giving effect to the amendment or addition is affixed to the document.

(4)　Claim

The insured shall lodge a claim against the insurer according to the regulations stipulated in the insurance policy when any loss answerable under insurance conditions occurs to the import and/or export goods during the validity of the insurance policy.

责事项。它也是保险人和被保险人之间订立的书面契约。

★　**保险凭证**

保险凭证是简化了的保险单，与保险单具有同样的法律效力。它仅包含了主要项目，并没有列出保险合同的所有条款。

★　**预约保单**

如果进出口商的贸易量大的话，可以选择预约保单。这种预约保单非常方便。根据投保人和保险公司签订的合同，货物一经起运，保险人即自动承保。

★　**批单**

在保险办完后，如果投保人想要更改保险条款，他可向保险公司提出申请。保险公司会发出修改，这就是保险更改批单。

（4）索赔

根据保险单上的规定，如果进口或出口的货物发生保险责任范围内的损失，被保险人可以在保险单的有效期内向保险人提出索赔。

5.7　Insurance Clauses in a Contract 合同中的保险条款

Insurance terms are one of the most important components in sales contracts and they should be made in a clear and definite way. The contents of insurance terms may vary under different trade terms.

As to contract concluded on FOB, CFR, FCA, or CPT, insurance terms could be "Insurance: To be covered by the buyer". In the event the seller is entrusted to arrange insurance for the buyer, it must be specified as to insurance amount,

保险条款是合同的主要条款，必须明确规定。贸易术语不同，保险条款的内容也不同。

以 FOB、CFR、FCA 或 CPT 几个贸易术语成交的合同中，保险条款可以这样表示："保险：由买方办理"。如果买方委托卖方办理保险，则可以在合同中写明保险金额、险

insurance coverage required, which insurance clause would be adopted, and insurance premium shall be paid by the buyer. Time and way of premium payment should also be stipulated herein.

As to contract entered into on CIF or CIP, it must be definitely stipulated which party is to arrange for insurance, coverage needed, method to ascertain insurance amount, which insurance clause should be applied to and date on which term is to attach.

For example,

Insurance: To be covered by the seller for 110% of total invoice value against WPA as per (and subject to the relevant) Ocean Marine Cargo Clause of the People's Insurance Company of China, dated January 1st, 1981.

别、适用的保险条款，以及保险费由买方承担等内容，买方付保险费的时间和方式也需在合同中写明。

在以 CIF 和 CIP 贸易术语成交的合同中，必须明确规定投保人、应保的险别、计算保险金额的方法、适用的保险条款及该条款生效时间等内容。

例如：

由卖方按发票金额 110%投保水渍险，按 1981 年 1 月 1 日中国人民保险公司海运货物保险条款承保。

Exercises

I. 名词解释

1. 共同海损
2. "仓至仓"条款
3. 施救费用
4. 战争险
5. 保险单

II. 单项选择题

1. 根据"仓至仓"条款规定，当被保险货物从目的港卸离海轮时起算满(   )天，不论货物是否进入收货仓库，保险责任均告终止。
   A. 60   B. 45   C. 30   D. 15

2. 中国人民保险公司的海洋货物运输保险的索赔实效为(   )。
   A. 在货到目的港开始起最多不超过两年
   B. 在货到目的港开始起卸货时不超过两年
   C. 在货到目的港后将全部货物卸离海轮时起最多不超过两年
   D. 在货到最终目的仓库起最多不超过两年

3. 平安险的责任范围不包括(   )。
   A. 由于恶劣气候、雷电、海啸、地震洪水等自然灾害造成整批货物的全部损失
   B. 被保险人对承包范围内的货物采取抢救措施以减少损失而支出的合理费用
   C. 由于恶劣气候、雷电、海啸、地震洪水等自然灾害造成整批货物的部分损失
   D. 在装卸货转运时由于一件或数件整件货物落海造成的全部或部分损失

4. 一般附加险种不包括(　　　　)。

    A. 碰损破碎险   B. 淡水雨淋险   C. 黄曲霉素险   D. 受潮受热险

5. 按英国伦敦保险协会的《海运货物条款》的规定,(　　　　)不能作为独立的险别进行投保。

    A. ICC (A)险   B. ICC (B)险   C. 协会战争险   D. 恶意损害险

6. 构成保险上"推定全损"有各种不同的情况,(　　　　)不能算作推定全损的范畴。

    A. 被保险货物受损后,修理费用超过货物修复后的价值

    B. 被保险货物受损后,修理和续运至目的地的费用超过货物到达目的地的价值

    C. 必须是属于非常性质的损失

    D. 为避免实际全损需要花费的施救费用,超过施救后的标的价值

III. 多项选择题

1. 单独海损和共同海损的主要区别在于(　　　　)。

    A. 单独海损是承担风险直接导致的损失,而共同海损则为解除共同危险有意做出的合理牺牲

    B. 单独海损由受损方单独承担,共同海损由受益方共同分摊

    C. 单独海损仅指某项货物的损失,共同海损包括所有货物的损失

    D. 单独海损只限货物一方受到损失,共同海损即指船、货各方均受到损失

2. 共同海损分摊涉及的受益方包括(　　　　)。

    A. 船方   B. 货方   C. 运费方   D. 救助方

3. 英国伦敦保险协会的《协会货物条款》规定的险别与中国人民保险公司的《海运货物保险条款》规定的险别,在承包范围上大体相当的是(　　　　)。

    A. ICC (A)与一切险   B. ICC (B)与水渍险

    C. ICC (C)与一切险   D. ICC (A)与平安险

4. 向中国人民保险公司投保平安险的情况下,如被保险货物发生(　　　　),保险公司不负赔偿责任。

    A. 自然损耗   B. 发货人责任引起的损失

    C. 共同海损的牺牲、分摊和施救费用   D. 由于战争引起的损失

IV. 判断题

(　　) 1. 构成共同海损的条件之一是,在海难中船舶和货物都必须遭受到一定的损失。

(　　) 2. 按 CIF 条件,出口玻璃制品时,因其途中容易破损,故因在投保一切险的基础上加保破损险。

(　　) 3. 平安险与水渍险的重要区别在于:前者保险公司不承担自然灾害造成的部分损失,而后者则承担此项损失。

（　　）4.航空运输货物保险期限适用"仓至仓"条款，如被保险货物未运抵保险单所载明的仓库或储存所，则货到最终卸货地卸离飞机满30天为止。

（　　）5.战争险的保险期限仅限水上危险或运输工具上的危险，如货物未卸离运输工具，则保险责任延长至货到目的港当日午夜起算满15天为限。

（　　）6.凡被保险人或其代理人为防止被保险标的损失扩大而采取抢救行为所支出的一切费用，不论其数量大小，保险人均应一律给予补偿。

V. 简答题

1. 在海运货物保险中，保险公司承包哪些风险、损失与费用？
2. 共同海损与单独海损有哪些主要区别？
3. 何谓救助费用？此项费用属什么性质？
4. 试述陆运、航空货物运输保险的险别及其责任范围。
5. 试简述 ICC(A)、ICC(B)、ICC(C)三种险的责任范围及其与我国海运货物保险条款中三种基本险的比较。

VI. 计算题

1. 浙江某出口公司出售200套服装，保险金额为10000美元，因途中货物不幸遭水渍，故只能按八折降价出售，约定目的地的完好价每套为50美元，试问保险公司应赔付多少？

2. 广东某出口公司按 CIF 条件出售一批食品，根据交易双方约定成交额为10000美元，保险费率为0.4%，按 CIF 价加成10%投保平安险，试计算出保险金额和保险费各多少？

VII. 案例分析

1. 有一货轮在航行中与流冰相撞，船身一侧裂口，海水涌进，舱内部分货物遭浸泡。船长不得不将船驶向浅滩，进行排水，修补裂口，而后为了起浮，又将部分笨重货物抛入海中。问这一连串的损失都是单独海损吗？

2. 某货轮在航行途中因偏离航道而搁浅，为了摆脱困境，船长下令抛弃部分货物，以减轻船舶的负重，但仍无效。船长只好下令发出求救信号，请救助船将货轮退至深水处，使其能继续航行至目的港。由此造成下列损失和费用：①在救助过程中使货轮船底划破受损；②给救助船一笔救助费用；③抛弃船上部分货物的损失；④额外增加的燃料费、船员工资、给养开支。试问：上述各项损失应作何种性质的损失处理？

3. 我方向澳大利亚出口坯布 100 包，按合同规定加一成投保水渍险。货在运输途中因舱内食用水管漏水，致使该坯布中的 30 包浸有水渍。问对此损失应该向保险公司索赔还是向船公司索赔？

4. 卖方以 CIF 条件出口 100 箱茶叶，投保一切险。由于承运人的工作疏忽，将茶叶与樟脑装载于相邻的货位上。收货人提货后，发现茶叶已严重串味，不具有饮用价值，提出退货。问：收货人的要求合理吗？

5. 我方按 CIF 条件向中东某国出口一批货物，根据合同投保了水渍险，附加提货不着险，但在海运途中，因两伊战争轮船被扣押，之后进口商因提货不着向保险公司进行索赔，问其结果如何？

CHAPTER 6

International Cargo Transportation
国际货物运输

Focus

In this chapter, you will learn:

- ✧ Modes of transport;
- ✧ Major shipping documents;
- ✧ Shipment clauses in a contract.

Transportation is a very important step in international trade. It is one of the basic obligations for the exporter to deliver the goods, according to the stipulated time, place, and mode of transport in the contract, to the buyer or carrier or agreed conveyance after signing the contract.

International cargo transportation is work of strong timeliness, wide involved aspects, long distance and complicated techs. Therefore, the two parties shall decide the right mode of transport which will be the best for goods to be transported so as to ensure the contract be fulfilled without any trouble.

运输是国际贸易中非常重要的一个环节。它是出口方的基本义务之一。签约后，出口方根据合同规定的时间、地点和运输方式向买方或承运人或商定的运输工具交付货物。

国际货物运输具有时间性强、涉及面广、距离远、技术复杂的特性。因此，买卖双方应选定适合货物的正确的运输方式，以确保合同的顺利履行。

6.1　Modes of Transport 运输方式

In international transportation, there are many modes of transport which may be suitable to different goods and contracts, such as ocean transport, rail transport, air transport, road transport, inland water transport, postal transport, pipelines transport, land bridge transport, container transport, international multimodal transport / international combined transport. The buyer and the seller can decide which mode will be the best for goods to be transported according to goods characteristics, quantity, transit journey, value, time, the natural conditions, and so on.

国际运输中，有很多适用于不同商品和合同的运输方式，如海洋运输、铁路运输、航空运输、公路运输、内河运输、邮政运输、管道运输、大陆桥运输、集装箱运输、国际多式联运/国际联合运输。买方和卖方可以根据货物的特点、数量、过境情况、价值、时间、自然条件等决定最佳的运输方式。

6.1.1　Ocean Transport
海洋运输

Ocean transport is the most widely used form of transportations in international trade as well as the most efficient form in terms of energy. At present, about 80% of international transportation is in the ocean transport. It has strong ability to travel around the whole world without the limits from roads or railways, strong deadweight capacity and of low freight.

海洋运输是国际贸易中使用最广、能源利用最有效的运输方式。目前，大约 80%的国际运输是海洋运输。它具有不受道路或轨道限制、运量大、运费低廉的优点。

◆   **Liner Transport 班轮运输**

A liner is a vessel with regular sailing and arrival on a stated schedule between a group of specific ports. In international ocean transport practice, goods transport is mostly done by liners except the charter transport for bulk cargo. The main features of liners are as follows:

★   The liner has a regular line, port, timetable and comparatively fixed freight, which is the basic features of liners.

★   The carrier is responsible for loading and unloading operations, i.e. Gross Terms.

★   The B/L drawn by the shipping company is the evidence of the shipping contract between the carrier and the consignor. The rights and obligations of the carrier and the consignor are based on the B/L drawn by the shipping company.

Liner freight is the remuneration payable to the carrier for the carriage of goods. It has two parts: basic freight and surcharge.

The basic freight includes the loading and discharge expenses at the ports of shipment and destination, and the freight between the port of shipment and port of destination. The basic standards for calculating freight are stipulated as follows:

★   According to gross weight in terms of Weight Ton (WT), which is indicated by "W" in the tariff. 1 MT is to be considered as 1 weight ton or one long ton (1,016 kg) or one short ton (907.18 kg).

★   According to volume, i.e. Measurement Ton, which is indicated by "M" in the tariff. 1 measurement ton equals one cubic meter or 40 cubic feet.

★   According to the value of the cargo which is indicated by "AV" (Ad Valoren) in the liner freight tariff.

★   According to gross weight or volume, i.e. choosing the higher rate between the two, which is indicated by "W/M" in the tariff.

★   According to the number of the cargo.

班轮是在固定航线上、固定港口停靠、定期开航的船舶运输。在国际海洋运输实践中，除了租船运输用于散装货物外，货物运输大多数是由班轮运输的。班轮的主要特点如下：

★   按固定航线、固定停靠港口、固定的航行时间表航行，按相对固定的运费率计收运费。

★   承运人负责配载装卸，即班轮条件。

★   船公司出具的提单作为承运人和托运人双方的运输合同的证明。承运人和收货人之间的权利和义务在船公司出具的提单上予以体现。

班轮运费是支付给承运人运送货物的报酬。它包括基本运费和附加费两部分。

基本运费包括货物在装运港和目的港的装运费和卸货费，以及货物从装运港运送到目的港应收取的运费。它的计收标准规定如下：

★   按货物毛重，又称重量吨计收运费，运价表中用"W"表示。1重量吨为1长吨（1016 kg）或1短吨（907.18 kg）。

★   按货物的体积，即尺码吨计收运费，运价表中用"M"表示。1尺码吨为1立方米或40立方英尺。

★   按商品价格计收，运价表中用"AV"（Ad Valoren)表示。

★   按货物的毛重或体积计收，即选择其中收费较高的作为计费吨，运价表中用"W/M"表示。

★   按每件货物的数量计收。

★ According to the temporary / interim or special agreement entered into between the ship owner and the consignor.

The main surcharges are shown as follows:

★ Bunker Adjustment Factor—BAF;

★ Heavy lift additional;

★ Over length additional;

★ Tank cleaning charge;

★ Direct additional;

★ Optional additional;

★ Port additional;

★ Port congestion surcharge;

★ Transshipment surcharge.

★ 由船方和货主临时议定运价。

主要的附加费有以下几种：

★ 燃油附加费；

★ 超重附加费；

★ 超长附加费；

★ 洗舱费；

★ 直航附加费；

★ 选港附加费；

★ 港口附加费；

★ 港口拥挤附加费；

★ 转船附加费。

◆ **Charter Transport 租船运输**

Charter transport is also called tramp. It has no regular route or fixed schedule of sailing, just a bit like a marine taxi-cab. It is suitable for the carriage of goods, primarily in bulk, such as coal, grain, timber, ores, etc. There are three kinds of mode for charter: voyage charter, time charter and demise charter.

★ Voyage charter

It includes single voyage charter, return voyage charter and successive voyage charter. The ship owner is responsible for managing the ship and bearing all expenses.

The payment by the charterer is usually based on an agreed rate per ton for a full and complete cargo. Should the charterer fail to provide sufficient cargo to fill the ship he is liable for what is termed dead freight, a prorate payment for the space not used. A voyage charge also stipulates the number of days known as lay days, for loading and unloading. Should these be exceeded, the charterer is liable for a demurrage charge for each day in excess, and conversely is entitled to dispatch money for each day not taken up. The liability of the shipowner is to provide a ship that is seaworthy and to avoid unjustifiable deviation en route.

租船运输又称不定期船运输。它没有固定的航线或固定的船期表，有点像海洋出租船。它主要适合运送散装货物，如煤炭、木材、矿产等。租船运输有三种方式：定程租船、定期租船和光船租船。

★ 定程租船

包括单程租船、来回航次租船和连续航次租船。船方负责船舶的经营管理并负担所有的费用。

租船人支付的费用通常基于议定的运费率以载满货物时计算的。如果租船人不能使船只载满，空舱费由租船人按载重吨支付。定程租船还规定了装卸货物的天数，即装卸货物日期，如果超过了规定的装卸期限，租船人应对超期向船方支付滞期费，相反，如果租船人提前完成装卸作业，船方要对节省的时间支付速谴费。船方的责任是保证船舶的适航性，并避免航途中不必要的绕航。

★　Time charter

The charterer charters the ship for a period of time during which the ship is managed, deployed and used by the charterer, but control remains with the shipowner. The fuel expenses, port expenses, etc., should be borne by the charterer while the shipowner should bear the wages and board expenses of the crew, and be responsible for sea-worthiness during the period of chartering and the so-caused expenses and the vessel insurance premium.

★　Demise charter

It is also called Bare-Boat Charter (BBC), the charterer takes a lease of the entire ship for an agreed time. So demise charter belongs to time charter, but there are some differences: as to time charter, during the period of chartering, the shipowner provides the charterer with a crew, while as to bare-boat charter, the shipowner only provides the charterer with a bare-boat, the charterer shall employ the crew and pay the crew's wages and provisions, ship's maintenance and stores, etc. by himself.

★　定期租船

船舶所有人将船舶出租给承租人，供其使用一段时间，在此期间，船舶由承租人自由使用、经营和调度，船舶经营中产生的燃料费、港口费等也由承租人负责，船方则承担船员薪金、伙食等费用，保证租赁期间船舶具有适航价值并承担相关费用和船舶的保险费。

★　光船租船

光船租船方式下，租船人向船东承租一定期限，所以光船租船也是期租的一种，但他们有不同点：在定期租船方式下，船主不仅提供货船，还提供船员，而在光船租船方式下，船主只提供船只，租方自行配备船员、负责船舶的经营管理和航行各项事宜（如船舶的维护、修理及机器的正常运转等）。

◆　**Differences between Liners and Tramps 班轮与不定期货船的区别**

The differences between liners and tramps are as follows: 班轮与不定期货船的区别如下：

Liners 班轮	Tramps 租船
General cargo and passengers 一般货物和乘客	Mostly bulk cargo 大多为散装货物
Regular sailing schedules 固定航行时间表	No schedule(react to demand) 没有时间表（根据需求）
Regular routes 固定航线	No fixed routes 不定航线
Firm freight rates 固定运费率	Rates subject to negotiation 议定运费率
Bill of lading 提单	Charter party 租船契约

6.1.2　Rail Transport
铁路运输

Rail transport is the secondly most popular transport mode in daily trade. It is capable of attaining relatively highly speeds with large quantities and safe, at low cost, punctual, rather economical and less influenced by weather.

Rail transport falls into three kinds:

★　Railway transport at home;

★　Railway transport to HK and Macao;

★　International railway cargo through transport.

According to the stipulation of the International Railway Cargo Through Agreement, the goods belonging to the export country may be transported directly to the place of destination as long as the carrier issues a railway bill of lading at the place of dispatch.

One way of international railway cargo through transport is to use the land bridge. There are two famous land bridges to be used in our country: one is Siberian Land Bridge and the other is New European-Asia Land Bridge. The transport by using land bridge is called Land Bridge Transport which connects the ocean transport on the two sides of the land by the railway and land which runs across the continent, i.e. ship-train-ship. Land Bridge Transport uses the container as a medium, so it has all advantages of container transport.

铁路运输是日常贸易中排名第二的最受欢迎的运输方式。它具有运量大、安全可靠、速度费用低廉、运输准时，并且受天气影响较小。

铁路运输有三种类型：

★　国内铁路运输；

★　对香港和澳门的铁路运输；

★　国际铁路货物联运。

根据国际铁路货物联运协定的规定，只要承运人在起运地签发铁路运输提单，出口货物就可以直接运往目的地。

大陆桥运输是铁路运输的一种方式，我国目前主要使用两个大陆桥：西伯利亚大陆桥和欧亚大陆桥。使用大陆桥来运输的方式叫大陆桥运输。它使用连贯大陆上的铁路或公路运输系统作为中间桥梁，把大陆两端的海洋运输连接起来，构成海—陆—海的连贯运输。它以集装箱为媒介，具有集装箱运输的优点。

6.1.3　Air Transport
航空运输

Air transport is one of the modern modes of transport. Its features are as follows:

★　Fast speed;

★　High quality of transport to diminish the damages during the transport process into the lowest level;

★　Free from the limits on the ground.

航空运输是现代化的运输方式之一，它具有以下特点：

★　航行速度快；

★　运输质量高，可以将运输途中货物破损率降到最低；

★　不受地面条件的限制。

The chief disadvantage is the limited capacity of air freight and overall dimensions of acceptable cargo together with weight restrictions. It is also subject to the influence of weather. Therefore, it is suitable for those goods that are of time pressing, small quantity but urgent need, light but precious. The air transport can be divided into the following kinds:

★ Scheduled airliner;

★ Charted carrier;

★ Consolidation;

★ Air express.

Airline rates are normally based on actual weight for heavy cargo or measurement weight for large volume cargo, subject to the higher rate.

航空运输的缺点是运量小、运价高，易受恶劣气候的影响。因此，它适用于一些时间性强、量少而急需、体轻而贵重的货物运输，航空运输可分为以下四种：

★ 班机运输；

★ 包机运输；

★ 集中托运；

★ 急件速送。

航空运价是按货物的实际重量和体积重量两者之中较高者为准。

6.1.4 Postal Transport
邮包运输

Postal transport is one of the easiest modes of transport. Its features are easy procedure, low payment and "Door to Door" transport. It is a kind of international transport. However, the restriction of the size and weight on the parcels limits the practicality of this mode; it is only suitable for exactitude instruments, machinery components, and other small size and precious goods.

邮包运输是最简便的运输方式，其特点为手续简便、费用不太高，具有"门到门"的运输性质。然而，邮包运输只适用于量轻体小的商品，如精密仪器、机器零件以及小而贵重物品等。

6.1.5 International Multimodal Transport
国际多式联运

International multimodal transport means the carriage of cargo by at least two modes of transport on the basis of a multimodal transport contract from the place of dispatch to destination. Under this method, the container is used as an intermedium to make up of an international multimodal and join transport mode by sea, air and land. The use of containers in multimodal transport means high efficiency, better quality of transport, lower cost and less time being required for cargo movement between the point of origin and the place of delivery.

国际多式联运是指利用两种或两种以上运输方式来完成货物运输。它以集装箱为媒介，把海、陆、空多种传统的单一运输方式有机地结合起来，组成一种国际连贯运输。多式联运中集装箱的使用使得货物运输更快捷、高效，降低了运输成本，缩短了货物从原产地到目的地的运输时间。

Although different modes of transport are combined, only one Multimodal Transport Operator (MTO) is responsible for taking the cargo from the consignor and delivering them to the consignee. This adds the simplicity to the transport.

在国际多式联运方式下,货物运程无论多远或由几种运输方式共同完成运输任务,从发货人处提货到送达收货人,所有事项都由多式运输经营人负责,这使得运输变得更加简便。

6.1.5 Container Transport
集装箱运输

With the expansion of international trade, the container service has become more and more popular. Nowadays, container transport has become a very convenient and modern transport method in international practice.

The most widely used type are twenty-foot equivalent unit (TEU) and forty-foot equivalent unit (FEU). But recently, containers are becoming larger and larger. For instance, American President Lines adopt 53-foot container. The generally adopted sizes in China are: 8'×8'×20' and 8'×8'×40'.

Container transport falls into two kinds (methods of consignment): Full Container Load (FCL) and Less than Container Load (LCL). As for the consignment that reaches the demand of FCL, the vanning FCL is done either by the consignor himself or the carrier at the production side or the warehouse, then it is sent to the Container Yard (CY) for consolidation by the carrier. As for the consignment that does not reach the demand of a full container, we call it less than container, the vanning LCL is done by the consignor himself and then send the consignment to the Container Freight Station (CFS) or inland container depot for consolidation by the carrier, who will piece together the goods according to the nature, destination, weight and so on in the container and then send it to the container yard.

随着国际贸易的发展,集装箱服务越来越流行,集装箱运输已成为国际上普遍采用的一种便捷的现代运输方式。

目前国际航运上使用的集装箱多为 20 英尺和 40 英尺集装箱。但近年来,集装箱的发展向大型化方向发展,如美国总统轮船公司采用 53 英尺型集装箱。我国采用的规格为:20 英尺集装箱和 40 英尺集装箱。

集装箱运输可分两类:整箱货(FCL)和拼箱货(LCL)。对于托运数量达到整箱要求的整箱货,可以由发货人在自己的工厂或仓库自行装箱,也可以由承运人代为装箱,装箱后直接运往设在港口码头的集装箱堆场(简称 CY)。对于数量不足装满整箱的货物,称之为拼箱货,托运人自己将货物送到集装箱堆场或内陆集装箱货运站(简称 CFS),由承运人根据货物的性质、目的地、重量等对其进行分类、整理、集中和装箱后,送至集装箱堆场。

6.2　Major Shipping Documents 主要运输单据

6.2.1　Ocean Bill of Lading
　　　海运提单

A Bill Of Lading is a document issued by a carrier to a shipper, signed by the captain, agent, or owner of a vessel, representing both a receipt for the goods shipped and a contract for shipment between the shipping company and the shipper. It is also a document of title to the goods, giving the holder or the assignee the right to possession of the goods (see Table 6.1). There are a number of different types of bills of lading. Main types are as follows:

★　Shipped (On board) B/L and received for shipment B/L

According to whether the goods are loaded or not, the bills of lading can be classified into on board (shipped) B/L and received for shipment B/L.

Shipped B/L is issued by the shipping company after the goods are actually shipped on board the designated vessel. The importer will normally require the exporter to produce shipped B/L. According to general foreign trade practices, only the shipped on board B/L is accepted by banks for payment under the L/C.

Received for shipment B/L arises where the word "shipped" does not appear on the bill of lading. It merely confirms that the goods have been handed over to, and are in the custody of the shipowner.

★　Clean B/L and unclean B/L

According to whether there are notes on the B/L, it falls into two kinds: clean B/L and unclean B/L.

A clean B/L is the one where the carrier has noted that the goods have been received in apparent good order and condition (no apparent damage, loss, etc.) and there is no modification of the shipowner.

Unclean B/L, or Foul B/L is the one that contains unfavorable notation about the external condition of the cargo. E.g. "packages in damaged condition", "iron strap loose or missing". An unclean B/L is not acceptable to banks.

海运提单是船长或船公司或其代理人签发的，证明已收到特定货物，允诺将货物送至指定的目的港，并交付给收货人的凭证。提单也是物权证明，持有提单的人即拥有货物（见表6.1）。提单有不同的种类，以下为常见的提单：

★　已装船提单和收妥待运提单

根据货物是否装船可分为已装船提单和收妥待运提单。

已装船提单是承运人已将货物装上指定的船舶后所签发的提单，进口商一般要求出口商提供已装船提单。根据国际贸易惯例，信用证支付方式下，银行只接受已装船提单。

收妥待运提单上没有"已装船"字样，它仅仅证明船方已收到货物，但没有实际装上船。

★　清洁提单和不清洁提单

根据提单上有无不良批注可分为清洁提单和不清洁提单。

清洁提单是指货物在装船时表面状况良好，船公司在提单上未加任何有关货物受损或包装不良等批注。

不清洁提单是指船公司在提单上对货物表面状况或包装加有不良或存在缺陷等批注的提单。例如，提单上批注"包装损坏"、"铁条松散"等，银行不接受不清洁提单。

★ Straight B/L, blank B/L and order B/L

According to whether the B/L is transferable, it is divided into three kinds: straight B/L, blank B/L and order B/L.

A straight B/L is made out so that only the named consignee at the destination is entitled to take delivery of the goods under the B/L. The consignee is designated by the shipper. The carrier has to hand over the cargo to the named consignee. The shipper cannot pass the bill to a third party by endorsement. This kind of B/L is not transferable.

Blank B/L also called open B/L or bearer B/L, means that there is no definite consignee of the goods. Words like "To bearer" usually appear in the box of consignee. Anyone who holds the bill is entitled to the goods the bill represents. No endorsement is needed for the transfer of the blank bill. Due to the exceedingly high risk involved, this bill is rarely used.

Order B/L, or a shipper's order B/L, is widely used in international trade. It is a title document to the goods, issued "to the order of" a party, usually the shipper, whose endorsement is required to effect its negotiation. Because it is negotiable, a shipper's order B/L can be bought, sold, or traded while goods are in transit and is commonly used for L/C transaction. In international trade practice, the bill made out "to order" and endorsed in blank is mostly used which is called "made out to order and blank endorsed".

★ Direct B/L, transshipment B/L and through B/L

According to the modes of transport, it can be divided into three kinds:

Direct B/L means that the goods are shipped from the port of loading directly to the port of destination without involving transshipment.

Transshipment B/L means that the goods need to be transshipped at an intermediate port as there is no direct service between the shipment port and the destination port. This kind of bill usually bears such a clause "Transshipment to be made".

★ 记名提单、不记名提单和指示提单

根据提单的抬头可分为记名提单、不记名提单和指示提单。

记名提单的收货人栏内（抬头人）直接写明收货人的名字，这就表明该提单项下的货物只能由该特定收货人提取，不能用背书的方式转让给第三者，此类提单不能流通转让。

不记名提单意味着货物没有特定的收货人，在收货人一栏往往写着如"来人"之类。提单的持有人即收货人，不需要通过背书手续就可以任意转让，所以这种提单不安全，风险较高，很少使用。

指示提单在国际贸易中广泛使用，它是物权凭证，收货栏内填写"凭某人指定"，常常是凭发货人指定。发货人经背书可转让。因其可转让性，货物在运输途中即可买卖提单，所以在信用证业务中被大量使用。在实际业务中，使用最多的是"凭指定"并经空白背书的提单，习惯上称为"空白抬头、空白背书"提单。

★ 直达提单、转船提单和联运提单

根据运输方式可分三种提单：

轮船从装运港装货后，中途不经过换船而直接驶往目的港卸货的称为直达，这种情况下签发的提单为直达提单。

转船意味着从装运港装货的轮船，不直接驶往目的港，需要在中途港换装另一艘船驶往目的港，这种情况下签发的提单为转船提单。

Through B/L means that the goods need to be carried by more than one mode of transport, and the ocean shipment forms only part of the complete journey and, subsequent thereto, the goods have to be carried by other land or sea carrier. The first carrier issues the bill and collects the freight for the entire voyage, and arranges transshipment and forwarding of the goods at the intermediate port.

联运是指需经两种或两种以上的运输方式，但其中一种必须是海运，由第一承运人所签发提单并收取全程运费，安排货物中途转换运输工具和交接工作。

Table 6.1 BILL OF LADING FOR PORT TO PORT SHIPMENT OR
COMBINED TRANSPORT SHIPMENT

SHIPPER:	B/L NO.:
CONSIGNEE (NOT NEGOTIABLE UNLESS CONSIGNED TO ORDER):	**DELMAS**
NOTIFY PARTY (CARRIER NOT TO BE RESPONSIBLE FOR FAILURE TO NOTIFY):	

Pre-carriage by:	Place of receipt (*):	SERVICE:
Vessel: Voy.:	Port of loading:	CONTAINERS STATUS:
Port of discharge:	Place of delivery:	

CARRIER'S RECEIPT:	PARTICULARS FURNISHED BY SHIPPER—CARRIER NOT RESPONSIBLE

Marks and Nos.	Number of Containers/Packages —Kind of Packages, Description of Goods	Gross Weight	Measurement

FREIGHT & CHARGES(indicate whether PREPAID OR COLLECT)	Received by the Carrier from the shipper in apparent good order and condition, unless otherwise noted herein, for transportation on board the ocean vessel mentioned herein or any substituted vessel or on board the feeder vessel of other means or transportation.
Payable at:	It is further agreed that the Carrier is at liberty to stow any goods on deck without notice to the shipper. There goods will be considered as goods under-deck in regard to responsibility and limits of liability as well as general average.
Declared Value Charges For Declared Value of	

LAW AND JURISDICTION: Any claim or dispute against the Carrier arising under this Bill of Lading, including third party proceedings or those involving several defendants, shall be governed, for the maritime part of the carriage, either by the International Convention for the unification of certain rules relating to Bills of Lading dated Brussels, the 25th August 1924 as enacted in the country where the Bill of Lading is issued or, when the Convention is not compulsorily applicable, by the said Convention non amended and, for the non maritime part of the carriage, either by the provisions contained in any International Convention or National Law compulsorily applicable, or by the French Law applicable to the means of transport utilized and shall be determined in France by the "Tribunal de Commerce du Havre."

In accepting this bill of lading the Merchant expressly accepts and agrees to be bound by all its stipulations, terms, conditions and exceptions—INCLUDING THE TERMS ON THE REVERSE HEREOF AND THE TERMS OF THE CARRIER'S APPLICABLE TARIFF—stated herein whether printed, stamped or written, or otherwise incorporated, of which the merchant is fully aware not withstanding the non-signing of the bill of lading by the Merchant.

Number of Original B(s)/L:	IN WITNESS of the contract herein contained the number of original stated opposite have been issued, each one being the same contents and date, one of which being accomplished the other(s) to be void.
Place of issue:	
Date of issue:	

FOR THE SHIPPER AND/OR THE CONSIGNEE	FOR THE CARRIER

（*）Applicable when this document is used as a Combined Transport Bill of Lading

Case Study

One export company exported 350 cartons of garments on the basis of CFR, payment by irrevocable L/C, containerized, CY/CY. After shipment, the exporter got the clean on board B/L indicating "Shippers Load and Count." Then the exporter made presentation for negotiation within the validity of the L/C. 20 days later, the importer sent to the seller a mail informing that after the joint inspection of the vessel party, the customs, the insurance company and the public surveyor, 20 cartons of packages were found seriously damaged and the garments were found missing in each package, totaling up to 512 pieces while the container is in good condition in appearance. Therefore, the buyer asked the seller to compensate for the loss of shortage of goods, and to undertake all inspection fee of US$2,500.

Question: Is the buyer's requirement reasonable? Why?

6.2.2　Air Waybill
航空运单

The Air Waybill (AWB), also called air consignment note, is a document used for the carriage of goods by air supplied by the carrier to the consignor. It is not a document of title. However it is a formal proof evidencing the consignor has made shipment of the goods, with which the consignor could make settlement with the consignee.

航空运单是航空公司出具的承运货物的收据，它不能作为物权凭证进行转让，但它是证明发货人业已交运货物的正式凭证，发货人可凭其向收货人结算货物。

6.2.3　Multimodal Transport Document
多式联运单据

Multimodal Transport Document (MTD) evidences the contract of carriage of goods by at least two modes of transport, issued by a Multimodal Transport Operator (MTO) under a multimodal transport contract. It is quite similar to "through B/L" but is of difference in some respect. Through B/L and combined transport B/L are always connected with sea, used for any transport combined with sea, while MTD is broader than them, it can be applied to any kind of combined transport.

多式联运单据是证明多式联运合同以及证明多式运输经营人接管货物并负责按合同条款交付货物的单据，它和联运提单相似，但又有不同，联运提单和联合运输提单仅限于由海运与其他运输方式所组成的联合运输时使用，而多式联运单据使用的范围更广，适用于任何运输方式。

6.3　Shipment Clauses in a Contract 合同中的装运条款

When negotiating a transaction, the buyer and the seller should reach an agreement on time of shipment, port of shipment and port of destination, partial shipment and transshipment, shipping advice, etc., and specify them in the contract of sale. Clear stipulation of shipment clause is an important condition for the smooth execution of the contract.

在交易磋商中，买卖双方必须就装运时间、装运港、目的港、分批装运、转运、装运通知等事项达成协议并在合同中明确规定，以保证合同的顺利履行。

6.3.1　Time of Delivery
　　　　装运时间

The time of delivery refers to the time limit during which the seller shall deliver the goods to the buyer at the agreed place by the agreed mode of transport. There are several ways to stipulate it in the contract.

★　Stipulate a period of fixed time. The seller can arrange shipment during whichever date, for example:
Shipment during March, 2012;
Shipment during Feb./Mar./Apr. 2012.

★　Stipulate a definite time of delivery, for example:
Shipment at or before the end of May, 2012;
Shipment not later than the end of May, 2012.

★　Stipulate shipment within…days after receipt of the letter of credit. In order to prevent the buyer from opening L/C late, it is necessarily accompanied by another clause "The relevant L/C must reach the seller not later than…" In this way a somewhat indefinite clause is made more or less definite.

For example:
Shipment within 45 days after receipt of L/C. The buyer must open the relative L/C to reach the seller before June 5th, 2012.

装运时间又称装运期，是指卖方按照合同规定的时间和期限内，按约定的方式和地点将货物交给买方。合同中装运时间的规定有几种方法。

★　规定某一段时间，卖方可以选择其中任何一天装运，如：
2012 年 3 月装运；
2012 年 2/3/4 月装运。

★　明确规定具体时间按，如：
2012 年 5 月底前装运；
装运期不迟于 2012 年 5 月底。

★　规定在收到信用证后 XX 天后装运。为了防止买方延迟开立信用证，还必须加上"信用证不得迟于……到达卖方"的字句。在某种意义上说，也是对装运时间的限制。例如：
在收到信用证后 45 天内装运；买方必须在 2012 年 6 月 15 日前将信用证送达卖方。

★ Stipulate the goods shall be shipped in the near future, for example:

Immediate shipment.

Shipment as soon as possible.

Prompt shipment.

But there are not unanimous explanations about these terms in the international trade, and thus, it is quite easy to result in disputes, so we should try to avoid using them.

★ 规定即将安排装运。例如：

立刻装运；

尽速装运；

即刻装运。

但这类术语在国际上并无统一的解释，极易引起争议和纠纷，因此应尽量避免使用。

6.3.2   Port/Place of Shipment and Port/Place of Destination
装运港/地和目的港/地

◆ **Port/Place of Shipment 装运港/地**

In international trade practice, port/place of shipment is usually proposed by the seller and determined by both parties. When we choose the port/place of shipment, we should pay attention to the following points:

★ The port of shipment shall be close to the origin of the goods;

★ Specific transportation conditions and the standards of freight and various charges should be taken into consideration;

★ Normally, one specific port/place of shipment are stipulated, but sometimes when large amount of goods are involved and, in particular, the goods are stored at different places, two or more ports of shipment are also specified, such as "Port of shipment: Shanghai and Guangzhou", "Port of shipment: Dalian/Qingdao/ Shanghai". Sometimes, as the port of shipment is not yet determined at the time the transaction is being concluded, a general clause like "China ports" may be used.

在国际贸易中，装运港/地通常由卖方提出，经买方同意后确认，在商定装运港/地时，应注意以下问题：

★ 选择靠近产地的装运港；

★ 要考虑装运港口的装卸条件、具体的运输条件和收费标准等。

★ 在出口贸易中，习惯做法是只规定一个装运港，但如果该批货物过多，特别是分放在几个地方，则可规定两个或以上装运港，如"装运港：上海和广州"，"装运港：大连、青岛、上海"。有时在签订合同时装运港还没定下来，也可以规定为"中国港口"。

◆ **Port/Place of Destination 目的港/地**

The port of destination is usually proposed and determined by the buyer. When we choose the port/place of destination, we should pay attention to the following points:

目的港一般由买方提出，在商定目的港/地时，应注意以下问题：

★ The stipulations on the port of destination shall be as clear as possible, and not to use ambiguous terms, such as "main ports in Europe".

★ Port regulations, facilities, charges and possible sanctions should be taken into consideration.

★ In order to make it convenient for the buyer to resell the goods afloat, the "optional port" may be accepted upon the request of the foreign party, the buyer is allowed to choose one from the several ports of destination provided.

★ Pay attention to the names of foreign ports. Many ports have the same names. For example, there are 12 "Victoria" ports. We'd better indicate the name of the country after the name of the destination.

★ 目的港的规定必须明确具体，不要用模棱两可的措辞，如"欧洲主要港口"；

★ 要考虑港口的规则、设备、费用及相关的处罚条款等；

★ 为方便买方转售货物，可根据国外客户的要求，接受买方的"选择港口"条件，买方可以在合同中规定的那几个港口中选择一个；

★ 注意国外港口的重名问题，世界上重名的港口很多，如"维多利亚"就有12个，最好在目的港后面注明国名。

6.3.3 Partial Shipment and Transshipment
分批装运和转运

◆ **Partial Shipment 分批装运**

Partial shipment means shipping the commodity under one contract in more than one lot. It should be defined in the clause of shipment whether "Partial shipment is (or is not) allowed". Meanwhile, the time and quantity of each shipment should be specified. For example:

★ Shipment during Jan./Feb. 2012 in two equal lots;

★ Shipment during Jan./Apr. 2012 in four equal monthly lots.

所谓分批装运，是指一笔成交的货物分若干批于不同航次装运。在合同中必须表明是否允许分批装运，同时，每一批的装运时间和数量也必须一并明确，例如：

★ 2012年1月和2月分两批平均装运；

★ 2012年1月到4月分四批等量装运，每月各装一批。

◆ **Transshipment 转运**

Transshipment means when there is no direct ship between the port of shipment and the port of destination, or no suitable ships available at that particular period, the goods have to be transferred from one ship to another at an intermediate port. It should also be defined in the clause of shipment whether "Transshipment is (or is not) allowed". For example:

转运意味着装运港到目的港之间没有直达船，或在那特定的时期内没有合适的船只，货物需要在中途港换装另一艘船驶往目的港。在合同的运输条款中必须明确是否允许转船，例如：

★ During Mar./Apr. 2012, in two shipments, transshipment is prohibited.

★ During Mar./Apr. 2012, in two equal monthly shipments, to be transshipped at Hong Kong, China.

★ 2012 年 3 月和 4 月分两批装运，不允许转运；

★ 2012 年 3 月和 4 月分两批等量装运，在中国香港转运。

◆ **Stipulations in the UCP600《跟单信用证统一惯例 600》中的有关规定**

According to the relevant stipulations of the UCP600 (Uniform Customs and Practice for Documentary Credits),

(1) Transport documents which appear on their face to indicate that shipment has been made on the same means of conveyance and for the same journey, provided that they indicate the same destination, will not be regarded as covering partial shipments, even if the transport documents indicate different dates of issuance and/or different ports of shipment, place of taking in charge, or dispatch.

(2) If any installment is not shipped within the period allowed for that installment, the credit ceases to be available for that and any subsequent installments, unless otherwise stipulated in the credit.

(3) Unless the credit stipulations otherwise stipulated, partial shipment and transshipment are allowed. But contractual laws in some countries stipulate that: Partial shipment and transshipment, if not stipulated in the contract, shall not be deemed to be allowed.

根据《跟单信用证统一惯例》第 600 号出版物的相关规定：

（1）如果运输单据表面注明货物是使用同一运输工具并经过同一路线运输的，而且运输单据注明的目的地相同，那么即使每套运输单据注明的装运日期不同及/或装运港、接受监管地、发运地不同，也不视作分批装运。

（2）除非信用证中另有规定，否则其中任何一批未按规定装运，则本批以及以后各批均告失效。

（3）除非信用证有相反的规定，可允许分批装运和转运，但按有些国外的合同法，如果没有在合同中规定允许分批装运和转运，将视作禁止。

Case Study

The ABC Co. exported 2,000 M/Ts of soy beans. The buyer opened the L/C as scheduled which said partial shipments not allowed. Then the exporter made shipment of 1,000 M/Ts in Dalian Port and on the same vessel and for the same journey made another 1,000 M/Ts in Qingdao Port respectively. The B/L indicated different dates of issuance and different ports of shipment.

Question: Did the ABC Co. violate the contract? Can the company present the documents to the bank for negotiation?

6.3.4 Shipping Advice
装运通知

When the goods are shipped on board the vessel, the seller needs to, within three working days according to international trade practice, give the buyer prompt notice of the port of shipment, the Estimated Time of Departure (ETD), the name of the carrying vessel, the Estimated Time of Arrival (ETA) of the vessel, etc., to enable the buyer to effect the insurance, and also send the buyer the copies of the necessary documents for the buyer to get ready to take delivery of the goods. In the event of the seller's failure to send shipping advice to the buyer within the prescribe time period, the seller would bear the consequential cost incurred (as follow).

根据相关国际贸易惯例，当货物装上船后，卖方应该在三个工作日内发出装运通知，内容包括：装运港、预计离港时间、船名、预计到达时间等，以便买方及时办理保险手续，卖方还需寄交买方相关单据的副本以使其做好提货准备。如果卖方未在规定时间内发出装运通知，则需承担由此引起的一切后果（装运通知如下）。

KUNSHAN HUACHENG WEAVING AND DYEING CO., LTD
HUANGLONG RD., LIUJIA ZHEN, SUZHOU，JIANGSU, CHINA
TEL: 86-520-76713862
SHIPPING ADVICE

TO: YOU DA TRADE CO., LTD   DATE: APR. 11th, 2012

RE: L/C NO. HK1112234   INV. NO. 04HK-99WS061

WE HEREBY INFORM YOU THAT THE GOODS UNDER THE ABOVE MENTIONED CREDIT HAVE BEEN SHIPPED. THE DETAILS OF SHIPMENT ARE STATED BELOW:

COMMODITY: 100 PCT NYLON FABRICS, DETAILS AS PER S/C NO. 99WS061

QUANTITY: 100,000 YARDS (1,000 ROLLS)

INVOICE VALUE: US$33,680.00

OCEAN VESSEL/SHIPPED PER S.S.: DANUBHUM/S009

DATE OF SHIPMENT: APR. 10th, 2012

PORT OF LOADING: SHANGHAI, CHINA

PORT OF DESTINATION: HONG KONG, CHINA

SHIPPING MARKS: YOU DA

                HONG KONG

                C/NO.: 1-1000

WE HEREBY CERTIFY THAT THE ABOVE CONTENT IS TRUE AND CORRECT.

Signature

KUNSHAN HUACHENG WEAVING AND DYEING CO., LTD

XXX

Exercises

I. 术语翻译

班轮	国际多式联运
指示提单	航空运单
凭指定	空白抬头、空白背书
滞期费	速遣费
发货人	收货人
整箱货	拼箱货
集装箱货运站	集装箱堆场

II. 填空

1. 在国际货物运输中，运用最广泛的是(　　　　)运输方式，其运量在国际货物运输总量中所占的比重为(　　　　)以上。

2. 海洋运输按照船舶经营方式不同，可以被分为(　　　　)和(　　　　)运输。其中后者又可被分为(　　　)、(　　　)和(　　　)三种形式。

3. 新欧亚大陆桥运输于(　　　)年正式开通，它进一步促进了我国对外贸易的发展。

4. 根据惯例，一般情况下，滞期费相当于速遣费的(　　　)倍。

5. 在采用租船运输大宗进出口货物的情况下，货物被装上船后，卖方应在约定的时间内，通常是在(　　　)小时内向买方发出装运通知，通知其货物装船的有关信息。

6. 在外贸运输中，如果船公司已经收到被托运的货物，在等待装运期间给发货人签发的提单被称为(　　　)，又称(　　　)提单。

7. 班轮运费的计算包括两部分，即(　　　)和(　　　)。

8. 租船运输通常适用于(　　　)货物的运输。

9. 提单按收货人的抬头可分为(　　　)提单、(　　　)提单和指示提单。其中指示提单又可分为(　　　)指示提单和(　　　)指示提单，要转让必须经(　　　)形式。

10. 海运提单的性质和作用为：提单是货物的(　　　)；是货物所有权的(　　　)和运输协议的证明。

III. 单项选择题

1. 经过背书才能转让的提单是(　　　)。
   A. 指示提单　　　B. 不记名提单　　C. 记名提单　　　D. 清洁提单
2. 目前，在实际业务中使用最多的提单是(　　　)。
   A. 记名提单　　　　　　　　　　　B. 不记名提单
   C. 空白抬头、空白背书提单　　　　D. 空白抬头、记名背书提单

3. 轮船公司在提单上未作任何不良批注的提单是( )。

    A. 不清洁提单　　　　B. 清洁提单　　　　C. 不记名提单　　　　D. 已装船提单

4. 运价表中注是"W/M"表明( )。

    A. 运费按实际重量计收　　　　　　　　B. 运费按体积或容积计数

    C. 运费按重量或体积计收　　　　　　　　D. 运费按商品价格计数

5. 按 UCP600 解释，若信用证条款中未明确规定是否"允许分批装运"、"允许转运"，则应视为( )。

    A. 可允许分批装运，但不允许转运　　　　B. 可允许分批装运和转运

    C. 可允许转运，但不允许分批装运　　　　D. 不允许分批装运和转运

6. 海运提单日期应理解为( )。

    A. 货物开始装船的日期　　　　　　　　B. 货物装船过程中任何一天

    C. 货物装船完毕的日期　　　　　　　　D. 签订运输合同的日期

7. 班轮运费应该( )。

    A. 包括装卸费，但不计滞期费、速遣费　　B. 包括装卸费，但应计滞期费、速遣费

    C. 包括装卸费和滞期费，但不计速遣费　　D. 包括装卸费和速遣费，但不计滞期费

8. 信用证的到期日为 12 月 31 日，最迟装运期为 12 月 16 日，最迟交单日期为运输单据出单后 15 天，出口人备妥货物安排出运，并于 12 月 10 日装货完毕取得提单，则出口人最迟应于( )向银行交单议付。

    A. 12 月 16 日　　B. 12 月 25 日　　C. 12 月 28 日　　D. 12 月 31 日

9. 我国对北美出口货物通常所使用的运输单据是( )。

    A. 铁路运单正本　　B. 承运货物收据　　C. 海运提单　　　　D. 航空运单

10. 下列关于航空运单的说法错误的是( )。

    A. 它是一种运输契约　　　　　　　　B. 它是一种货物收据

    C. 它是代表货物所有权的凭证　　　　D. 它不是代表货物所有权的凭证

11. 在进出口业务中，能够作为物权凭证的运输单据有( )。

    A. 铁路运单　　　　D. 海运提单　　　　C. 航空运单　　　　D. 邮包收据

12. 在海洋运输中，规定了装卸期限和装卸率，并凭以计算滞期费和速遣费的合同是( )。

    A. 班轮运输合同　　B. 定程租船合同　　C. 定期租船合同　　D. 光船租船合同

13. 滞期费是( )。

    A. 买方向卖方收取的因卖方延期交货而造成损失的补偿费

    B. 卖方向买方收取的因买方延期交货而造成损失的补偿费

    C. 租船人未按约定日期完成装卸定额，延误了船期而付给船方的罚款

    D. 船方装卸太慢而向货方支付的赔偿费

14. 下列单据中，只有( )才可用来结汇。

    A. 大副收据　　　　B. 铁路运单副本　　C. 场站收据副联　　D. 铁路运单正本

15. 关于程租船装卸费用划分问题，使用较多的是(　　　　)。
    A. FO
    B. FIO 或 FIOST
    C. FOB LINER TERMS
    D. FI

16. 信用证规定"于或约于 2012 年 5 月 31 日装船"，我方应在(　　　)期限内装船。
    A. 2012 年 5 月 26 日—6 月 5 日
    B. 2012 年 6 月 5 日以前
    C. 2012 年 6 月 5 日以后
    D. 2012 年 6 月 5 日左右

17. 如果卖方未按期装运货物，则买方的权利是(　　　　)。
    A. 只能要求卖方赔偿损失
    B. 只能撤销合同
    C. 只能要求卖方马上装运
    D. 撤销合同并要求卖方赔偿其损失

18. 国内铁路运输中使用的运输单据是(　　　)。
    A. 记名提单
    B. 清洁提单
    C. 国际货协运单
    D. 承运货物收据

19. 签发多式联运的承运人的责任的是(　　　)。
    A. 只对第一种运输负责
    B. 必须对全程运输负责
    C. 对运输不负责
    D. 只对最后一种运输负责

20. 国际多式联合运输是以至少两种不同的运输方式将货物从一国境内接受货物的地点运至另一国境内指定交付货物的地点的运输，它由(　　　)。
    A. 一个联运经营人负责货物的全程运输，运费按全程费率一次计收
    B. 一个联运经营人负责货物的全程运输，运费按不同运输方式分别计收
    C. 全程运输方式的经营人负责货物的全程运输，运费按全程费率一次计收
    D. 多种运输方式，分别经营，分别计费

Ⅳ. 判断题

(　　　) 1. 所有运输单据都是承运人签发给托运人的货物收据，故都是物权凭证，都可凭此向目的地承运人提货。

(　　　) 2. 海运提单如有三份正本，则凭其中任何一份即可在卸货港向船公司或船代理提货。

(　　　) 3. 海运提单是货物所有权的凭证，铁路运单是否是货物所有权的凭证，须视具体情况而定。

(　　　) 4. 海运提单的签发日期 就是货物开始装船的日期。

(　　　) 5. 提单日期是说明装船开始的日期。

(　　　) 6. 信用证规定的装运期是 6 月 30 日，有效期是 7 月 15 日，交单期是提单日期后 21 天。若实际装船日是 6 月 25 日，受益人可以于 7 月 16 日交单。

(　　　) 7. 清洁提单是指提单的表面整洁、没有污点。

(　　　) 8. 不清洁提单是指船公司或其代理在签发提单时，在提单上对货物的品质加注不良批注的提单。

(　　　) 9. 记名提单和指示提单同样可以背书转让。

(　　　) 10. 记名提单比不记名提单风险大，故很少使用。

( ) 11. 中国内地通过铁路运往港澳地区的出口货物所使用的货运单据为承运货物收据。

( ) 12. 在航空运输中，收货人提货是凭航空公司的提货通知单。

( ) 13. 航空运单可以做成指示性抬头。

( ) 14. 我国对外贸易海洋运输是使用班轮运输。

( ) 15. 我方出口大宗商品。如以 CIF 班轮条件成交，我方就必须用班轮来装运货物。

( ) 16. 根据《跟单信用证统一惯例》的规定，如果信用证中没有明确规定是否允许分批装运及转船，应理解为允许。

( ) 17. 国外来证规定分两批装运，我们就必须将货物装在不同航次的两条船上。

( ) 18. 如合同中规定装运条款为"2012 年 7/8 月份装运"，那么我出口公司必须将货物于 7 月、8 月两个月内，每月各装一批。

( ) 19. 凡装在同一航次、同一条船上的货物，即使装运时间和装运地点不同，也不作分批装运。

( ) 20. 按惯例，速遣费通常为滞期费的一半。

V. 案例分析

1. 我国出口 4000 公吨大米至新加坡，国外开来信用证规定：不允许分批装运，装运时间为 2012 年 1 月/2 月。结果我方分别于 2 月 20 日在烟台、于 2 月 28 日在上海装运 2000 公吨大米于同一航次的同一船上，提单也注明了不同的装运地和不同的装船日期。请问这是否违约？银行能否议付？

2. 某公司向坦桑尼亚出口一批货物，目的港为坦塥。国外来证未明确可否转船，而实际上从新港到坦塥无直达船。问：这种情况下是否需要国外改证加上"允许转船"字样？

3. 我公司与外商签订销售合同，出售中国大米 10000 公吨，合同规定："自 2 月份开始，每月装船 1000 公吨，分十批交货。"卖方从 2 月份开始交货，但交至第五批大米时，大米品质霉变，不适合人类食用，因而买方以此为由，主张以后各批均应撤销。在上述情况下买方能否主张这种权利？为什么？

4. 我某外贸公司以 FOB 中国口岸与日本 M 公司成交矿砂一批，日商即转手以 CFR 悉尼价售给澳大利亚的 G 公司，日商来证价格为 FOB 中国口岸，目的港为悉尼，并提出在提单上表明"运费已付"。请问：日商为何这样做？我们应如何处理才使我方的利益不受损害？

CHAPTER 7

International Payment & Settlement (I)
国际支付和结算（一）

Focus

In this chapter, you will learn:

✧ Credit instruments;

✧ Modes of international payment.

7.1   Credit Instruments 信用工具

In international trade, the main issues concerning the settlement of payment are means of payment, time and place of payment and mode of payment. Issues in this regard should be clearly specified in the contract by the parties concerned.

A credit instrument is a term used in the banking and finance world to describe any item agreed upon that can be used as currency.

In international trade, the most frequently used means of payment include currencies and bills. The former are used for account, settlement and payment; the latter for settlement and payment. In practice, sellers of goods, in general, almost never insist on their rights to demand cash for payment, but readily take certain bills, such as bill of exchange (draft), promissory note and cheque (check) for substitutes among which draft is widely used.

在国际贸易中，货款的结算主要涉及支付工具、付款时间和地点、支付方式等问题，交易双方应在合同中做出明确规定。

信用工具是银行业的一个术语，表示可以代替货币用于结算的单据。

在国际贸易中，最常用的支付工具是货币和票据。前者用于计价、结算和支付，后者用于结算和支付。实际上卖方几乎从不坚持用现金支付，而乐意用一些票据，如汇票、本票、支票等来代替现金支付，其中以使用汇票为主。

7.1.1   Bill of Exchange
汇票

◆ **Definition of Bill of Exchange (Draft)**

A bill of exchange, also called draft, is defined as "an unconditional order in writing, addressed by one person to another, requiring the person to whom it is addressed to pay on demand, or at a fixed or determinable future time, a sum certain in money, to, or to the order of a specified person, or to the bearer". The operation process of draft includes: drawing, presentation, acceptance, endorsement, payment, dishonor and recourse.

◆ **Content of Bill of Exchange (Draft)**

A bill of exchange contains the following items:

★ The term "bill of exchange";

★ An unconditional order to pay a determinate sum of money;

★ The name of the person who is to pay (drawee);

◆ **汇票的含义**

汇票是一种无条件书面支付命令，是由出票人签发的，命令付款人在见票时或者在指定日期无条件支付确定的金额给收款人或者持票人的票据。汇票使用过程中票据行为主要有出票、提示、承兑背书、付款、拒付和追索。

◆ **汇票的内容**

汇票包含以下内容：

★ 标明"汇票"字样；

★ 无条件支付一定金额的命令；

★ 受票人名称；

★ A statement of the time of payment;

★ A statement of the place where payment is to be made;

★ The name of the person to whom or to whose order payment is to be made;

★ A statement of the date and of the place where the bill is issued;

★ The signature of the person who issues the bill (drawer).

◆ **The Parties to a Bill of Exchange**

A bill of exchange involves three parties:

★ Drawer: the person who writes the order and gives directions to the person to make a specific payment of money. He is usually the exporter or his banker in import & export trade; usually, he is also a creditor of the drawee.

★ Drawee (or the payer): the person to whom the order is addressed and who is to pay the money. He is usually the importer or the appointed bank under a Letter of Credit in import & export trade. In addition, when a time bill has been accepted by the drawee, he becomes an acceptor who is the same person as the drawee. The drawer and the acceptor must be different persons.

★ Payee: the person (individual, firm, corporation, or bank) to whom the payment is ordered to be made. The drawer and the payee may often be the same person. In this case, the bill maybe worded "Pay to our order…" The payee is usually the exporter himself or his appointed bank in import & export trade. The payee may also be the bearer of the bill. The payee may be the original payee in the bill, or may be some party to whom the original payee has transferred the instrument. If a bill bears such instruction "Pay… Co. or order" or "Pay to the order of… Co.", it means to pay to the payee or to anyone to whom he in turn directs payment to be made. In this way, the bill should be endorsed by the payee, now the endorser, and can be passed on to a new payee, the endorsee, thus making it negotiable. A bill may have many numbers of endorsers.

★ 支付的时间；

★ 支付的地点；

★ 收款人名称；

★ 出票地点和时间；

★ 出票人签名。

◆ **汇票的当事人**

汇票主要涉及三个当事人：

★ 出票人：签发命令要求另一人支付一定金额的人。在进出口贸易中，他通常是出口商或出口地银行，他也经常是受票人的债权人。

★ 受票人（付款人）：接受命令并将付款的人。在进出口业务中，他通常是进口商或信用证项下的指定银行。当受票人承兑一张远期汇票时，他就成为承兑人。出票人和承兑人必须是不同的人。

★ 受款人：接受付款的人（个人、商号、公司或银行）。出票人和受款人通常是同一个人，在这种情况下，汇票上可能有这样的字句"付款给我们……"。在进出口业务中，受款人通常是出口商本人或他指定的银行。受款人也可能是持票人。受款人可以是汇票中的原有受款人，也可以是原有受款人所转让汇票的人。如果一张汇票有这样的指示："付xxx公司或其指定人"，则意味着汇票可以经受款人（现在是背书人）转让给新的受款人（被背书人），使之成为可以转让的票据。一张汇票可以有多个背书人。

◆ **Classification of Bills of Exchange**

On the basis of different criteria, bills of exchange may be classified into several types:

★ **Commercial Bill and Banker's Bill**

According to different drawers, the bills of exchange can be classified into commercial bill and banker's bill. If the drawer is a commercial concern, the bill is called a commercial bill. It is often used in foreign trade finance. If the drawer is a bank, the bill is called a banker's bill. It is mainly used in remittance.

★ **Clean Bill and Documentary Bill**

Clean bill is a draft to which no shipping documents are attached. It is usually adopted to collect commission, interest, sample fee and cash in advance. On the contrary, if a draft with some shipping documents, such as bill of lading, insurance policy, invoice, etc., attached to it, the draft is called documentary bill. It is usually used to collect the payment of import and export goods.

★ **Sight (or Demand) Bill and Time (or Usance) Bill**

According to the time when the bill falls due, bills of exchange may be divided into sight (or demand) bill or a time (or usance) bill. A sight bill requires the drawee to pay the bill on demand or at sight. As for a time bill, the drawee is required to accept it first and pay it at a fixed or determinable future time, in other words, it requires acceptance before payment. The fixed or determinable future time may be a certain number of days after acceptance;

(1) At…days after sight, such as "30 days sight" or "60 days after sight";

(2) At…days after date of draft, such as "90 days after date of this draft";

(3) At fixed date in the future, such as "On Dec. 18, 2012".

★ **Commercial Acceptance Bill and Banker's Acceptance Bill**

In time or usance commercial bills, when the drawer is a commercial firm and the drawee is another commercial firm, the bill after acceptance by the commercial firm is called a commercial acceptance bill. If the drawee is a bank, the bill after acceptance by the bank or the drawee is called a banker's acceptance bill.

◆ **汇票的类型**

根据不同的标准，汇票可以分为以下几种：

★ 商业汇票和银行汇票

按出票人不同，汇票可分为商业汇票和银行汇票。商业汇票由工商企业开出，它经常用于对外贸易的资金融通，银行汇票的出票人是银行，它主要用于汇付。

★ 光票和跟单汇票

光票不随附货运单据，主要用于收付佣金、利息、样品费及预付款。随附货运单据（如提单、保险单、发票等）的汇票则为跟单汇票，在国际贸易货款的结算中，大多数使用跟单汇票。

★ 即期汇票和远期汇票

根据付款期限的不同，可分为即期汇票和远期汇票。汇票上规定受票人见票后立即付款的成为即期汇票。汇票上规定受票人先承兑，然后在指定的或将来的一个确定的日期付款的，换句话说，要求先承兑后付款的为远期汇票。指定的或将来的一个可确定的日期是承兑后的若干天：

（1）见票后若干天付款，如见票后 30 天或 60 天付款；

（2）出票后若干天付款，如出票后 90 天付款；

（3）定日付款，如 2012 年 12 月 18 日付款。

★ 商业承兑汇票和银行承兑汇票

在远期汇票中，由工商企业出票而以另一工商企业为付款人时，经付款人承兑后，该汇票即成为商业承兑汇票。如果受票人是银行，经银行承兑的汇票就是银行承兑汇票。

◆   **Use of Bill of Exchange in Foreign Trade**

A bill of exchange (draft) is an order to pay. It is made out by an exporter and presented to an importer, usually through a bank. It may be payable immediately on presentation (a sight or demand draft), or so many days after presentation (a time draft). In the later case, the drawee writes "Accepted" across it and signs his name. The exporter can get immediate payment by discounting the draft and supplying a letter of hypothecation. If a time draft is not honored at maturity, it will be noted and protested by a Notary Public, and represented to the drawee. Such a draft, and the corresponding payment terms, "Documents against Acceptance", obviously involve risks to the exporter or his bank.

◆   **汇票的使用**

汇票是支付的命令。由出口商开出，通过银行向进口商提示，可以见票即付（即期汇票），也可以是提示后若干天后付（远期汇票）。在后一种情况下，受票人在汇票上写上"承兑"字样并签上自己的名字。出口商可以将汇票贴现，凭借押汇质押书后立即取款。如果远期汇票的付款人到期不付款，持票人需通知公证人，由其出具拒付证书并再次向受票人提示。这种汇票以及相应的"承兑交单"支付方式,显然对出口商或其银行有一定的风险。

7.1.2   Cheque (Check)
支票

A cheque is an unconditional order in writing drawn on a banker signed by the drawer, requiring the banker to pay on demand a sum certain in money to or to the order of a specified person or to the bearer.

The payer of a check is also the drawer of the check. In foreign trade, a cheque drawn on a bank overseas cannot be readily negotiated by the exporter. If the exporter's bank were prepared to negotiate it for him, he would receive payment immediately but at the cost of the discount. If his bank is not willing to negotiate it, the exporter would have to ask his bank to collect the cheque for him, which would be time consuming as well as relative expensive.

支票是出票人签发的，委托支票存款业务的银行或者其他金融机构在见票时无条件支付确定的金额给收款人或者持票人的票据。

支票的出票人就是付款人。出口商不能把以海外银行为付款人的支票立即议付货款，如果出口商的银行愿意议付，出口商就可以立即得到付款，但他需要支付贴现的费用。如果出口商的银行不愿议付，则出口商只能委托其银行收款，这既费时又费钱。

7.1.3　Promissory Note
本票

A promissory note is an unconditional promise in writing made by one person to another signed by the maker, engaging to pay, on demand or at a fixed or determinable future time, a sum certain in money, to or to the order of, a specified person or to the bearer. The main difference between a promissory note and a draft lies in that there are three parties, namely drawer, drawee and payee involved in a draft but only two, drawer and payee in a promissory note. The payer of promissory note is the drawer himself.

本票是一人向另一人签发的，保证在见票时或在指定的或可以确定的将来的某一天，支付一定的金额给特定的人或其指定的人或持票人的无条件的书面承诺。本票和汇票最大的区别在于，汇票有三个当事人，即出票人、受票人和受款人，而本票只有两个当事人——出票人和受款人，本票的付款人是出票人本身。

7.2　Modes of International Payment 国际支付方式

Trading with other countries is not the same as trading within one's own country. Both exporters and importers face risks in export or import transactions because they will inevitably experience the possibility that the other party may not fulfill the contract.

For exporters, they are likely to take the risk of buyer's default; the customers might not pay in full for the goods. There are several reasons for this: the importers might go bankrupt; a war might break out or the importers' government might ban trade with the exporting country; or they might ban imports of certain commodities. Moreover, the importers might run into difficulties getting the foreign exchange to pay for the goods, or they are even not reliable and simply refuse to pay the agreed amount of money.

For importers, they may face the risk that the goods will be delayed and they might only receive them a long time after paying for them. This may result form port congestion or strikes. Delays in fulfillment of orders by exporters and difficult customs clearance in the importing country can cause

国际贸易与国内贸易不同，出口商和进口商在交易时都可能遇到风险，因为可能有一方不能履行合同。

对出口商来说，可能遇到买方违约或不支付全部货款的风险，这主要由以下几个原因引起：进口商破产、战争爆发、进口商所在国家政府禁止与出口商所在国的贸易往来、或者他们可能禁止进口某些商品。另外一种可能的原因是进口商无法获取外汇以支付货款，也可能是进口商不可靠或根本不想支付合同款项。

对进口商来说，他们要面临延期交货或付款很长时间后才收到货物的风险。这可能是港口拥挤或码头工人罢工引起的。出口商延期发货以及进口国复杂的清

loss of business. There is also a risk that the wrong goods might be sent.

It is to prevent such risks that different methods of payment have been developed. The modes of payment in international trade can be generally divided into three categories: remittance, collection and Letters of Credit.

Remittance and collection belong to commercial credit, Letter of Credit, banker's credit. If the payment is made by remittance, it is called favorable exchange, by which the buyer makes the payment by bank of his own accord; if by collection or L/C it is adverse exchange, by which the exporter takes the initiative to gather payment from the buyer. In foreign trade, "credit" stipulates who takes the responsibility of paying money and surrendering the shipping documents that represent the title to the goods. In remittance or collection, the buyer is responsible for making payment, the seller handing over documents. While in Letter of Credit transaction, the banker is responsible for paying money and tendering documents on behalf of both parties.

关手续都可能给进口商带来损失。另外，进口商也面临出口商发错货的风险。

为了预防这些风险，人们采取了不同的支付方式。国际贸易中的支付方式主要有三种：汇付、托收和信用证。

汇付和托收属于商业信用，信用证则属于银行信用。汇付属于顺汇，买方通过银行主动将款项汇给卖方，托收属于逆汇，卖方委托银行向买方收款。在国际贸易中，"信用"在货物的交接和货款的支付上规定由谁承担付款和提供所有权单据的责任问题。在汇付和托收项下，买方负责付款，卖方负责提交装船单据。在信用证项下，银行代替买卖双方负责付款和提交单据。

7.2.1 Remittance
汇付

Under remittance, the payer instructs his bank or other institutions to have a payment made to the payee. Four parties are involved in the remittance business: the remitter, the payee, the remitting bank and the paying bank. In foreign trade, remittance is often adopted in those sales: under the terms of cash in advance, cash with order, cash on delivery or open account. Remittance can be made by mail, telegraph and draft.

汇付是指付款人通过银行或其他途径将款项汇给受款人。在汇付业务中，通常有四个当事人：汇款人、收款人、汇出行和汇入行。在对外贸易中，汇付通常在预付货款、随订单付现、交货付现和记账贸易下使用。汇付方式包括信汇、电汇和票汇三种。

◆ Types of Remittance 汇付种类

★ Mail Transfer (M/T)

Mail Transfer is the process under which the remitter gives money to the remitting bank (his local bank) which, then, issues an order for payment and sends it to the paying bank (his branch or correspondent bank) at the seller's place

★ 信汇

信汇是汇出行应汇款人的申请，将信汇委托书寄给汇入行（其分行或代理行），授权解付一定金额给收款人的一种付款方式。信

by mail instructing him to pay the specific amount to the seller. This method costs less, but slower.

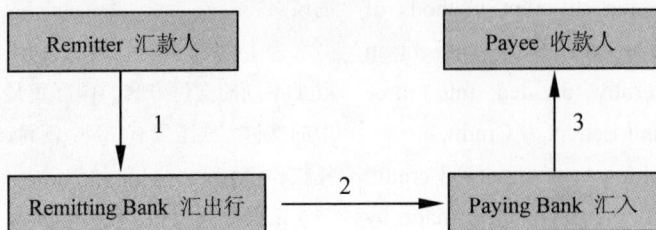

汇成本低，但速度较慢。

Remitter 汇款人		Payee 收款人

Fig. 7.1   Remittance Workflow of M/T信汇的流程

Notes:

1. Remitter applies for remittance;

2. Remitting Bank debits the remitter's account (amount to be remitted, bank commission, airmail expense), issues and sends a payment order by airmail;

3. Paying Bank verifies the authentication of the payment order, notifies and pays the payee, claiming reimbursement.

★ Telegraphic Transfer (T/T)

The procedure under T/T is similar to that of M/T except that the instructions from the buyer's bank to its branch or correspondent bank at the seller's end are made by cable instead of by mail. This means that the payment can be effected more quickly and the seller can receive the money promptly. But the buyer has to be charged more for it.

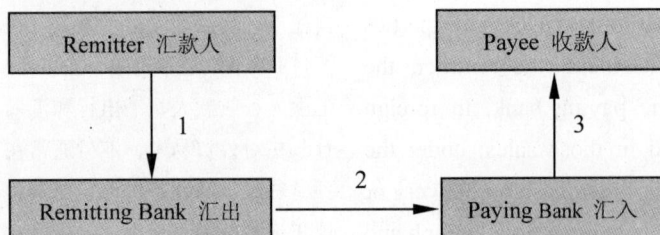

Fig. 7.2   Remittance Workflow of T/T电汇的流程

Notes:

1. Remitter applies for remittance;

2. Remitting Bank debits the remitter's account, issues and sends a payment order by telegraph, or by telex or through SWIFT;

3. Paying verifies the authentication of the payment order, notifies and pays the payee, claiming reimbursement.

【注】

1. 汇款人提出申请；

2. 汇出行从汇款人账户中扣款（汇出的款项、银行佣金、航空邮寄费），用航空邮递的方式发出汇款委托书；

3. 汇入行核对签字无误后，解付并索偿。

★ 电汇

电汇与信汇相似，其不同之处在于汇出行给汇入行的汇款委托书是用电报的方式发出的。电汇方式下受款人可以迅速收到货款，但费用较高。

【注】

1. 汇款人提出申请；

2. 汇出行从汇款人账户中扣款，用电报、电传或 SWIFT 的方式发出汇款委托书；

3. 汇入行核对密押无误后，解付并索偿。

★ Demand Draft (D/D)

Under demand draft, the remitting bank, at the request of the buyer, draws a demand draft on its branch or correspondent bank instructing it to make a certain amount of payment to the seller on behalf of the buyer.

★ 票汇

票汇是指汇出行应汇款人的申请，代汇款人开立以其分行或代理行为付款人的银行即期汇票，命令其支付一定金额给受款人的一种汇款方式。

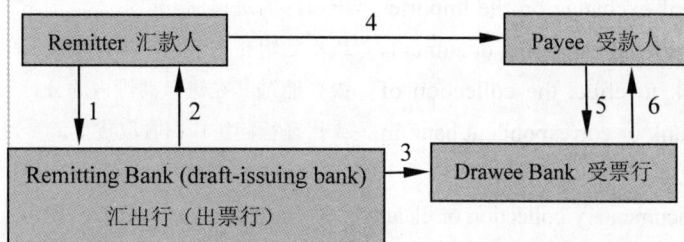

Fig. 7.3 Remittance Workflow of D/D票汇的流程

Notes:

1. Remitter requests to issue a banker's draft;

2. Remitting Bank debits the remitter's account (amount of the draft, bank commission), issues a draft and hands to remitter;

3. Remitting Bank sends an advice or non-negotiable copy of the draft;

4. Remitter sends the draft;

5. Payee presents the draft for payment;

6. Drawee bank verifies and pays the draft, and claims reimbursement.

【注】

1. 汇款人委托汇出行出票；

2. 汇出行从汇款人账户中扣款（汇票金额、银行佣金），出票并将汇票交给汇款人；

3. 汇出行寄送汇票通知书；

4. 汇款人寄送汇票；

5. 受款人提示汇票；

6. 付款行付款并索偿。

◆ **Advantages and Disadvantages of Remittance 汇付的利与弊**

In international trade, most of transactions are paid through M/T and T/T if remittance is used. T/T is beneficial to the seller because it enables him to obtain money promptly, accelerate the turnover of funds, increase the income of interests and avoid the risk of fluctuation in exchange rate. But it is disadvantageous to the buyer in that he has to bear more cable expenses and bank charges. When the amount of payment is comparatively large, or the money market fluctuates greatly, or the currency of settlement being used is likely to devaluate, it is wise for the buyer to use T/T. In a word, the choice of T/T or M/T should be clearly stipulated in the contract according to specific situation. As far as D/D is concerned, it is transferable, which is different from M/T and T/T.

在国际贸易中，如果使用汇付时，大多是通过信汇和电汇来完成的，电汇对卖方有利，他可以较快地收到货款，加速资金周转，增加利息收入和避免汇率变动的风险，但买方却要多付电报费用和银行费用。有时，当款项较大或因货币市场动荡，使用的结算货币有贬值的可能时，通过电汇付款是买方明智的选择。总之，无论是用电汇还是信汇，都要根据实际情况在合同中明确规定。就票汇而言，它是可以转让的，这一点和信汇与电汇不同。

7.2.2 Collection
托收

Under collection, the exporter takes the initiative to collect the payment from the buyer. Upon delivery of the goods, the exporter draws a bill of exchange on the importer for the sum due, with or without relevant shipping documents attached, and authorizes his bank to effect the collection of the payment through its branch bank or correspondent bank in the country of the importer.

Collection can be of either documentary collection or clean collection. Documentary collection has the relevant shipping documents attached to the draft, while in clean collection only draft is used.

Documentary collection is most often used in the payment of goods in international trade while clean collection is occasionally used in the payment of balance, extra charges, etc.

In the course of collection, banks only provide the service of collecting and remitting and are not liable for non-payment of the importer. The procedure of collecting payment is illustrated as follows (See Fig. 7.4):

托收情况下，出口商主动向进口商收取货款。装运货物后，出口商向进口商开出汇票，随附或不随附相关装运单据，委托其银行通过其在进口商国内的分行或代理行向进口商收取货款。

托收可以是跟单托收，也可以是光票托收。跟单托收随附相关的装运单据，而光票托收则无任何单据。

国际贸易中大多使用跟单托收，光票托收仅在货款余额的支付、附加费的收付等中偶尔使用。

在托收过程中，银行只提供托收和汇付服务，对进口商的不付款不承担责任。托收的流程如下（如图7.4）：

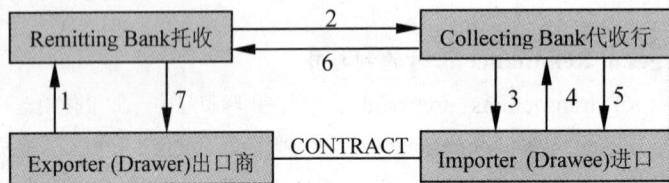

Fig. 7.4 Workflow of Collection托收流程

Notes：

1. The exporter dispatches the goods and draws a draft, then sends the draft together with shipping documents to the remitting bank to make an application for collecting money on his behalf;

2. The remitting bank sends the draft and shipping documents to a correspondent bank overseas—the collecting bank;

3. The collecting bank presents the draft and documents to the importer for Documents against Acceptance (D/A) or Documents against Payment (D/P);

4. The importer makes Documents against Payment (D/P) or endorses the bill for acceptance;

【注】

1. 出口商发货并开立汇票，填写托收委托书，将汇票和装运单据交予托收行委托其代收货款；

2. 托收行将全套单据寄交其代理行——代收行，委托其代收货款；

3. 代收行将汇票和单据向进口商提示承兑或付款；

4. 进口商付款或承兑；

5. The collecting bank hands over the documents to the importer;

6. The collecting bank notifies the remitting bank of crediting the money to their account;

7. The remitting bank makes payment to the exporter.

5. 代收行将单据交给进口商;

6. 代收行通知托收行款已收妥,并办理转账;

7. 托收行将货款付给出口商。

◆   **Document Against Payment (D/P) 付款交单**

Under this payment term, the exporter is to ship the goods ordered and deliver the relevant shipping documents to the buyer abroad through the remitting bank and the collecting bank with instructions not to release the documents to the buyer until the full payment is effected. According to the different time of payment, document against payment can be further divided into D/P at sight and D/P after sight.

★   D/P at Sight

Under this term, the seller draws a sight draft, and sends it with the shipping documents to the collecting bank. Then, the collecting bank presents the sight draft and shipping documents to the buyer. When the buyer sees them he must pay the money at once, then he can obtain the shipping documents. This method is also called "Cash against Documents", the procedure of which can be seen in the Fig. 7.5:

付款交单是指出口商的交单以进口商的付款为条件,即出口商发货并取得装运单据后,委托出口地银行办理托收,并在托收委托书中指示银行,只有在进口商付清货款后才能向进口商交付货运单据。按照付款时间的不同,可以分为即期付款交单和远期付款交单。

★   即期付款交单

在这种方式下,卖方开具即期汇票并通过银行向买方提示,买方见票后必须立即付款,只有付清货款后买方才能取得装运单据。这种方式也叫做"凭单据付款",其流程如图7.5:

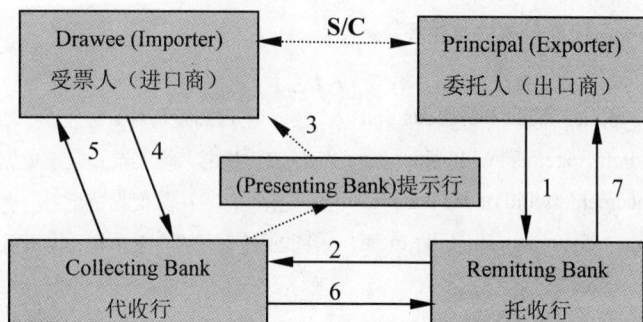

Fig. 7.5   Workflow of D/P at Sight 即期付款交单流

Notes:

1. According to the contract, the exporter loads the goods and draws a sight draft, then sends the draft together with shipping documents to his bank for collecting a documentary bill on his behalf;

2. The remitting bank sends the documentary bill to a correspondent bank overseas—the collecting bank for collecting money;

【注】

1. 根据合同,出口商发货并开立即期汇票,填写托收委托书,将汇票和装运单据交予托收行委托其代收货款;

2. 托收行将全套单据寄交其代理行——代收行,委托其代收货款;

3. The collecting bank presents the bill and documents to the importer for payment;

4. The importer makes payment;

5. The collecting bank hands over the documents to the importer;

6. The collecting bank notifies the remitting bank of crediting the money to their account;

7. The remitting bank makes payment to the exporter.

★ D/P after Sight

Under this term, the seller draws a time (or usance) draft. The collecting bank presents the time draft for acceptance and then present again for payment and shipping document at maturity of the draft. When receiving the money from the buyer, the collecting bank hands over the shipping documents to him. The procedure of D/P after sight is shown as follows (see Fig. 7.6):

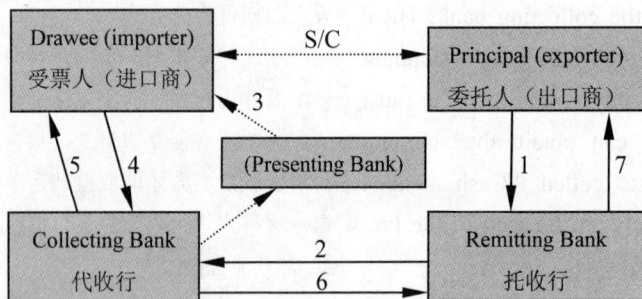

Fig. 7.6 Workflow of D/P after Sight远期付款交单流程

Notes：

1. According to the contract, the exporter loads the goods and draws a time draft, then sends the draft together with shipping documents to his bank for collecting a documentary bill on his behalf;

2. The remitting bank sends the documentary bill to a correspondent bank overseas—the collecting bank;

3. The collecting bank presents the bill and documents to the importer for acceptance. After the importer accepts the draft, the collecting bank takes back the draft and documents;

4. The importer makes payment when time falls due;

5. The collecting bank hands over the documents to the importer;

6. The collecting bank notifies the remitting bank of crediting the money to their account;

7. The remitting bank makes payment to the exporter.

3. 代收行将汇票和单据向进口商提示付款；

4. 进口商付款；

5. 代收行将单据交给进口商；

6. 代收行通知托收行款已收妥，并办理转账；

7. 托收行将货款付给出口商。

★ 远期付款交单

远期付款交单方式下，卖方开立远期汇票。代收行将此汇票向买方提示，买方见票后承兑汇票，等汇票到期后支付货款，代收行收到货款后即向他交付单据，其流程如图7.6：

【注】

1. 出口商发货并开立汇票，填写托收委托书，将汇票和装运单据交予托收行委托其代收货款；

2. 托收行将全套单据寄交其代理行——代收行，委托其代收货款；

3. 代收行将汇票和单据向进口商提示承兑，进口商承兑后，代收行收回汇票和单据；

4. 进口商在汇票到期日付款；

5. 代收行将单据交给进口商；

6. 代收行通知托收行款已收妥，并办理转账；

7. 托收行将货款付给出口商。

◆　**Documents Against Acceptance 承兑交单**

Documents against Acceptance is applicable only to a time bill that is used in documentary collection, in which the collecting bank will release the shipping documents to the buyer without any payment but merely against the acceptance of the bill by the buyer to

shonor the draft at a certain future date agreed upon between the seller and the buyer.(see Fig. 7.7）

这种付款方式仅适用于跟单托收中的远期汇票。在此方式下，代收行向买方交付单据不以后者付款为条件，仅以后者承兑为条件，即买方做出的在买卖双方同意的将来某个时间支付款项的书面承诺。(如图7.7)

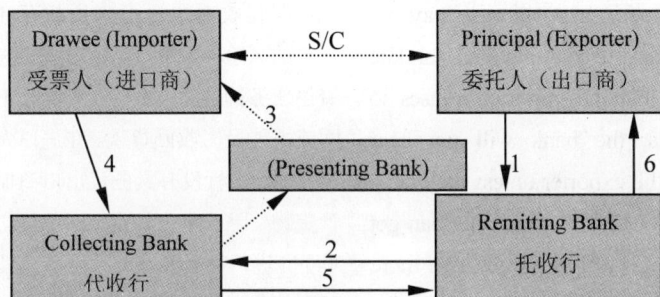

Fig.7.7　Workflow of D/A 承兑交单流程

Notes：

1. According to the contract, the exporter loads the goods and draws a time draft, then sends the draft together with shipping documents to his bank for collecting a documentary bill on his behalf;

2. The remitting bank sends the documentary bill to a correspondent bank overseas—the collecting bank;

3. The collecting bank presents the bill and documents to the importer for acceptance. And after that, the collecting bank takes back the draft and gives the shipping documents to the importer;

4. The importer makes payment when time falls due;

5. The collecting bank notifies the remitting bank of crediting the money to their account;

6. The remitting bank makes payment to the exporter.

【注】

1. 根据合同，出口商发货并开立汇票，填写托收委托书，将汇票和装运单据交予托收行委托其代收货款；

2. 托收行将全套单据寄交其代理行——代收行，委托其代收货款；

3. 代收行将汇票和单据向进口商提示承兑，进口商承兑后，代收行收回汇票并将全套运输单据交给进口商；

4. 进口商在汇票到期日付款；

5. 代收行通知托收行款已收妥，并办理转账；

6. 托收行将货款付给出口商。

◆ Advantages and Disadvantages of Collection 托收的利与弊

Collection has the following advantages for the importer: ★ It facilitates the importer to get financing. ★ The expenses are low. At the time of market with intense competition, collection is often used by the exporter to get customers and promote sales. But collection has some disadvantages for the exporter: if the importer goes bankrupt or is not in a position to pay the debts, the exporter will bear the risk of non-payment or late payment by the importer. In case that the importer refuses to make payment for the documents, the bank will not bear obligations to handle the goods for the exporter unless they have reached agreement in advance. Under D/A, the importer can get the shipping documents and take delivery of the goods after mere acceptance is made on the draft. Whether the exporter gets the payment or not will depend on the credit standing of the importer. Should the importer fail to make payment when the draft falls due, the exporter will suffer great loss.	托收对于进口商来说具有以下优点： ★ 有利于资金融通； ★ 费用低。 在市场竞争激烈的情况下，托收常被出口商用来作为一种争夺客户、扩大销售的竞争手段。 但托收对出口商来说却存在一定的风险：如进口商破产或丧失清偿债务的能力，出口商可能收不回或不能及时收回货款。在进口人拒付后，银行没有义务代出口商保管货物，除非事先约定。在承兑交单下，进口商只要在汇票上承兑就可取得货运单据并提走货物。进口商是否支付货款取决于进出口商的信用。一旦进口商到期不付款，出口商就会遭受极大的损失。

Case Study

I. Have a try.

The following are common payment clauses in contracts. Please figure out the types of each payment.

Payment by remittance, Payment by collection, Payment by L/C

1. The Buyers shall pay the total value to the Sellers in advance by T/T (M/T or D/D) not later than XXX.

_____

2. The Buyers shall pay the Sellers XX% of the contract price (USD XXX) in advance by T/T within thirty days after signing this contract.

_____

3. Payment by T/T: Payment to be effected by the Buyers shall not be later than XX days after the receipt of the documents listed in the contract.

_____

D/P at sight, D/P after sight, D/A

1. Upon first presentation the Buyers shall pay against documentary draft drawn by the Sellers at sight. The shipping documents are to be delivered against payment only.

   _____

2. The Buyers shall duly accept the documentary draft drawn by the Sellers at XX days sight upon first presentation and make payment on its maturity. The shipping documents are to be delivered against payment only.

   _____

3. The Buyers shall duly accept the documentary draft by the Sellers at XX days sight upon first presentation and make payment on its maturity. The shipping documents are to be delivered against acceptance.

II. How will you do?

Under D/P, if the Buyer refuses to make payment, what will you do if you are the Seller?

Exercises

I. 术语互译

1. 承兑交单 _____
2. 现金预付 _____
3. 托收 _____
4. 汇票 _____

5. Document Against Payment _____
6. Remittance _____
7. Check _____
8. Credit Instruments _____

II. 填空

1. 根据表格所给内容，在标号的位置填入相对应的内容。

	Draft	Promissory Note	Check
无条件支付	1.	承诺	2.
基本当事人	出票人、付款人、收款人	3.	出票人、付款人、收款人
期限	4.	远期	即期(见票即付)
出票份数	5.	6.	7.
付款人	8.	9.	10.

2. 为左列各项找到所对应的内容。

(   ) M/T   (1) 汇票的出票人是工商企业

(   ) Trader's Acceptance Bill   (2) 汇票的承兑人是银行

(   ) Bank Draft   (3) 票汇

(   ) Commercial Draft   (4) 信汇

(   ) T/T   (5) 电汇

(   ) D/D   (6) 汇票的出票人是银行

(   ) Banker's Acceptance Bill   (7) 汇票的承兑人是工商企业

III. 单项选择题

1. 承兑是(   )对远期汇票表示承担到期付款责任的行为。

     A. 付款人   B. 收款人   C. 出口人   D. 议付银行

2. 托收方式下的 D/P 和 D/A 的主要区别是(   )。

     A. D/P 是属于跟单托收；D/A 是属于光票托收

     B. D/P 是付款后交单；D/A 是承兑后交单

     C. D/P 是即期付款；D/A 是远期付款

     D. D/P 是远期付款；D/A 是即期付款

3. 汇付方式主要包括信汇、电汇和票汇三种(   )。

     A. 汇付方式属商业信用，银行只是提供服务

     B. 信汇、电汇属商业信用，票汇因为使用银行汇票，所以属银行信用

     C. 信汇属商业信用，电汇和票汇属银行信用

     D. 电汇属银行信用，信汇和票汇属商业信用

4. 无须提示承兑的汇票是(   )。

     A. 定日付款的汇票   B. 出票后定期付款的汇票

     C. 见票后定期付款的汇票   D. 见票即付的汇票

5. A documentary collection is an operation which a bank collects payment on behalf of the seller by delivering (   ) to the buyer.

     A. goods   B. documents

     C. goods and documents   D. bills of lading

6. Remitting bank is the bank to which the (   ) entrusts the collection items.

     A. drawer   B. payer   C. drawee   D. importer

7. The presenting bank is the collecting bank which presents the documents to the (   ).

     A. drawer   B. bank   C. drawee   D. exporter

8. (   ) are payable when presented to the payer by the payee.

     A. After draft   B. On time draft

     C. Sight draft   D. Time draft

9. The documentary collection provides the seller with a greater degree of protection than shipping
   on (   ).

    A. open account   B. bank's letter of guarantee

    C. banker's draft   D. documentary credit

Ⅳ. 判断题

(   ) 1. To the seller, payment by D/P is much safer than by D/A.

(   ) 2. In letter of credit transaction, the banker is responsible for paying money and tendering
documents on behalf of both beneficiary and applicant.

(   ) 3. The documentary bill is a bill accompanied by the contract between the drawer and the
drawee.

(   ) 4. If the payment is to be made "30 days' sight", it means that the payment will have to be
made 30 days after the issuing of the draft.

(   ) 5. In the course of collection, banks only provide the service of collecting and remitting and
are not liable for non-payment of the importer.

(   ) 6. Unlike the bill of exchange, the promissory note has two parties: the maker and the
payee.

(   ) 7. In the context of international trade, the drawer and payer is usually the seller and the
drawee and payee is usually the buyer.

(   ) 8. Bills of Exchange can be transferred over and over again by means of endorsement.

Ⅴ. 案例分析

1. 我国某企业与国外 A 商达成一份合同，支付条件为托收付款交单见票后 45 天付款。当跟单汇
   票通过托收行寄抵进口地代收行后，A 商及时承兑了汇票，货抵目的港后，A 商提货心切，
   出具信托收据向代收行借单提货并转售。汇票到期后，A 商因经营不善，不能偿付货款，代
   收行以汇票付款人拒付为由，通知托收行，并建议我方直接向 A 商索取货款。对此，你认为
   我方应如何处理？理由何在？

2. 天津 M 出口公司出售一批货物给香港，价格条件为 CIF 香港，付款条件为 D/P 见票后 30 天
   付款，M 出口公司同意 G 商指定香港汇丰银行为代收行。M 出口公司在合同规定的装船期内
   将货物装船，取得清洁提单，随即出具汇票，连同提单和商业发票等委托中行通过香港汇丰
   银行向 G 商收取货款。五天后，所装货物安全运抵香港，因当时该商品的行市看好，G 商凭
   信托收据向汇丰银行借取提单，提取货物，并将部分货物出售。不料，因到货过于集中，货
   物价格即下跌，G 商以缺少保险单为由，在汇票到期时拒绝付款，你认为 M 公司如何处理此
   事？并说明理由？

CHAPTER 8

International Payment & Settlement (II)

国际支付和结算（二）

Focus

In this chapter, you will learn:

✧　A brief introduction to the Letter of Credit;

✧　Merits and circulation of the Letter of Credit;

✧　Types of documentary credit.

8.1   A Brief Introduction to the Letter of Credit 信用证概述

A documentary credit is the written promise of a bank, at the request of the buyer, undertaking to pay the seller the amount specified in the credit provided the seller complies with the terms and conditions set forth in the credit. The terms and conditions of a documentary Letter of Credit revolve around two issues: (1) the presentation of documents that evidence title to the goods shipped by the seller, and (2) the payment.

Documentary credits provide a high level of protection and security to both the buyers and the sellers engaged in international trade. The seller is assured that payment will be made by the issuing bank the buyer so long as the terms and conditions of the credit are met. The buyer is assured that payment will be released to the seller only after the bank has received the title documents called for in the credit.

跟单信用证是银行根据买方的要求向卖方做出的书面承诺，只要卖方遵循信用证规定的条款，银行保证付款。信用证条款涉及两方面内容：（1）提交代表卖方所交货物的单据；（2）支付。

信用证为买卖双方提供了高度保障。对卖方来说，只要他按信用证规定的要求去做，开证行保证付款；对买方来说，开证行将在卖方提交了符合信用证要求的代表货物所有权的单据后才付款。

8.1.1   Definition of Documentary Credit
跟单信用证的定义

A Letter of Credit is the payment undertaking given by a bank to the seller and is issued on behalf of the applicant, i.e. the buyer. The buyer is the applicant and the seller is the beneficiary. The bank that issues the L/C is referred to as the Issuing Bank which is generally in the country of the buyer. The bank that advises the L/C to the seller is called the Advising Bank which is generally in the country of the seller.

The specified bank makes the payment upon the successful presentation of the required documents by the seller within the specified time frame. Note that the bank scrutinizes the "documents" and not the "goods" for making the payment. Thus the process works both in favor of both the buyer and the seller. The seller gets assured that if documents are presented on time and in the way that they have been

信用证是银行应开证申请人，即买方的要求向卖方做出的支付承诺。在信用证业务中，买方是开证行申请人，卖方是受益人，开立信用证的银行是开证行，开证行和买方通常在同一国家,把信用证交给卖方的银行叫通知行，通知行和卖方通常在同一国家。

卖方在规定的期限内提交了信用证规定的单据后，指定的银行将付款。值得注意的是，银行在支付时仅看"单据"而不看"货物"，这对买卖双方都有利，对卖方来说，只要他及时提交了信用

requested on the L/C the payment will be made and the buyer, on the other hand, is assured that the bank will thoroughly examine these presented documents and ensure that they meet the terms and conditions stipulated in the L/C.

证规定的单据，银行保证付款；对买方来说，银行将仔细审核卖方提交的单据并保证这些单据与信用证规定相符。

8.1.2 The Characteristics of the L/C
信用证的特征

The characteristics of L/C payment mainly can be summed up in the following three aspects:

★ The L/C payment is one kind of bank credit.

The bank makes the payment by its own credit. Under the condition of the L/C payment, the bank is at the first drawee's position. UCP600 stipulated that, the opening bank carries out the payment, accepts or negotiates if the documents conform to the L/C.

★ The L/C is one kind of independent and self sufficient document which is outside the contract.

The basis of drawing up the L/C is the contract. Once the L/C passes through and starts out it has become another kind of contract which is independent and outside the contract. It isn't restricted by the contract.

★ The L/C payment is one kind of document business.

Under the L/C payment, the principle is payment for document. Therefore, the L/C service is one kind of pure documentary service.

信用证支付方式的特点主要有三个：

★ 信用证是银行信用。

银行以自己的信用做出付款保证，银行承担第一付款人的责任。根据 UCP600 的规定，如果单证相符，开证行承担付款、承兑或议付的责任。

★ 信用证是独立于合同以外的自足文件。

信用证虽以贸易合同为基础，但它一经开出，就成为独立于贸易合同之外的另一种契约，它不受合同的制约。

★ 信用证业务处理的是单据。

在信用证业务下，单据是银行付款的唯一依据，因此，信用证是一种纯粹的凭单据付款的业务。

8.1.3 The Chief Contents of the L/C
信用证的主要内容

Most credits are fairly similar in appearance and contain the following details:

★ The name and address of the exporter (beneficiary);

★ The name and address of the importer (applicant);

★ The amount of the credit;

★ The particulars to the bill of exchange;

大部分信用证内容相似，包含以下内容：

★ 出口商名称和地址（受益人）；

★ 进口商名称和地址（申请人）；

★ 信用证金额；

★ 对汇票的具体要求；

★ The terms of contract and shipment, i.e. , FOB, CIF, etc;

★ A brief description of the goods covered by the credit;

★ Shipping details, including whether transshipments and partial shipment are allowed;

★ The explanation for shipping document. In the L/C, each kind of shipping document which needs should be listed, such as commercial invoice, transportation document, insurance policy and other document;

★ The expiry date.

★ 贸易术语，即 FOB、CIF 等；

★ 货物名称的简单描述；

★ 对运输的要求，包含是否允许转运或分批装运；

★ 对单据的要求，每一项需要的单据都必须在信用证中得以列明，如商业发票、运输单据、保险单据等；

★ 信用证的到期日。

8.2 Merits and Circulation of the Letter of Credit
信用证的优点和流程

8.2.1 Advantages and Disadvantages
优点和不足

Under the mode of payment by L/C, both the exporter and the importer are protected. The importer has the assurance that the goods will conform to the agreement, and the exporter is assured that the goods will be paid for. The importer might be able to get better trade terms by using the L/C system, though this will be offset somewhat by the bank's charges. When he wants to open a Letter of Credit to cover his purchase from abroad, the importer may apply to his banker for the L/C to be opened but will only pay a deposit, thus, the importer's capital will not be tied up. In other words, the bank finances or guarantees the balance of the purchase price. As far as the exporter is concerned, he knows that the goods will be paid for by the importer's bank. The confirming bank pays the drafts drawn under the L/C and has no recourse to collect from the exporter, even if the opening bank issuing the L/C does not reimburse the confirming bank.

Therefore, from what have been mentioned above, one will readily see that a banker's L/C for the payment of the purchase price is most desirable. However, the L/C cannot absolutely eliminate the risks the businessmen are likely to

在信用证支付方式下，进出口商都得到了银行的保护。对进口商来说，银行保证货物与合同相同；对出口商来说，银行保证付款。虽然银行费用较高，但通过信用证方式支付，进口商可能会得到更好的贸易条件。当进口商向银行申请开立信用证时，他只需向银行交一笔押金，这样资金就不会被冻结，换句话说，银行为货款的余额提供了融资。对出口商来说，货款将由进口方的银行支付。信用证项下的保兑行也承担起第一付款人的责任，但它并不享有对出口商的追索权，即使开证行拒绝向其付款。

综上所述，信用证的支付方式对买卖双方都有利。然而，信用证并不能完全避免进出口商所面临的风险。因为只要出口商提交了符

encounter. Since the opening bank makes the payment according to the submission of relevant documents rather than the goods, it is likely that importers may suffer from the fraudulent acts. The beneficiary may get the payment from the bank with mock documents that do not conform to physical goods, or even with documents of no goods. In addition to the fraudulent acts, the wrong practice of the related and improper procedures, ambiguous expressions or negligence, may also bring loss to the related party.

合信用证条款的单据，开证行即付款，出口商可能提交与信用证不符的单据，而银行只看单据而不看货物，如果单证一致，银行即付款。如果出口商提交了与货物不一致的单据，甚至没有出运货物，仅仅伪造与信用证相符的单据，银行也会付款。除了这些欺诈行为，相关人员的操作不当、疏忽以及信用证中某些模棱两可的条款等都可能给进出口方带来损失。

8.2.2 Circulation of the L/C
信用证的流转和使用

There are four chief parties to a basic documentary L/C transaction: the importer (applicant), the exporter (beneficiary), the importer's bank (issuing bank) and the exporter's bank (advising bank).

After signing, with the exporter, a contract agreeing to make the payment by L/C, the importer requests his bank to issue a L/C in favor of the exporter. If it accepts the importer's application, the opening bank issues a L/C and then informs its foreign branch or correspondent to advise the beneficiary (exporter), who then examines the L/C. If it does not conform to the conditions set in the sales contract, the exporter may request an amendment. After confirming the L/C, the exporter delivers the goods to the shipping company who then issues a bill of lading. Other documents, such as invoices and insurance documents are prepared by the exporter. The next step occurs when the exporter draws a draft on the opening bank and presents it, with the L/C plus documents to his or her own bank. Usually this bank will investigate the documents and, if they are in order, it will pay the draft. The L/C and documents are sent to the opening bank. It is the bank's responsibility to examine the documents in relation to the L/C issued. If discrepancies exist, they will have to be either corrected, or replaced by new documents.If no discrepancies are found after

信用证主要涉及四个当事人：进口商（开证行申请人）、出口商（受益人）、进口地银行（开证行）和出口地银行（通知行）。

进出口商签订合同，同意使用信用证方式支付，进口商向银行提出申请，要求开立以出口商为受益人的信用证。如果银行同意，它就开出信用证，然后将信用证发给其分行或代理行，通知行将信用证交给出口商，出口商收到信用证后，应审核信用证。如发现信用证条款和合同不符的话，需要求进口商修改信用证，等进口商修改信用证并得到出口商确认后，出口商即可装运货物，从船公司取得提单并准备好商业发票、保险单等其他单据。然后出口商开出以开证行为受票人的汇票，随附信用证以及所需单据向银行交单。通常情况下，该银行会审核单据，如单证相符的话将垫付汇票并将信用证及单据寄

careful checking, the opening bank will reimburse the money to the exporter's bank (negotiating bank) in accordance with the terms of the credit. The opening bank then presents the documents to the buyer for payment or acceptance. Documents will be released to the buyer upon his payment of amount due or acceptance of the draft. With the documents, the buyer can take delivery of the goods. The circulation of L/C can be illustrated as follows (see Fig. 8.1):

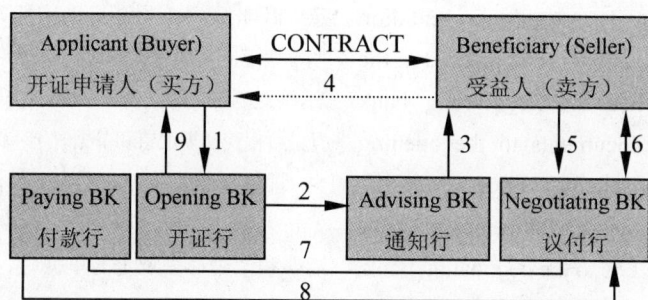

交开证行。银行有责任审核单据以确保其与信用证相符，如果发现不符点，则需更改或替换单据。如果未发现不符点，开证行将款项偿还给出口地银行（议付行）。然后将单据交给买方要求其付款或承兑，当买方付款或者承兑后，银行将单据放给买方，买方即可凭单据去提货。信用证的流转如图 8.1 所示：

```
┌──────────────────┐   CONTRACT   ┌──────────────────┐
│ Applicant (Buyer)│←············→│Beneficiary (Seller)│
│ 开证申请人（买方）│      4       │ 受益人（卖方）    │
└──────────────────┘              └──────────────────┘
    ↑   │9 1                          ↑3   │5 ↑6
┌────────┬────────┐  2   ┌──────────┬──────────────┐
│Paying BK│Opening BK│───→│Advising BK│Negotiating BK│
│付款行   │开证行    │  7 │通知行     │议付行         │
└────────┴────────┘      └──────────┴──────────────┘
     └──────────────────── 8 ──────────────────┘
```

Fig. 8.1 The Documentary Credit Cycle 跟单信用证流程

Notes：

1.The buyer makes application for a L/C with his bank and signs the opening bank's agreement form. The opening bank approves the application and issues the actual L/C document.

2. The opening bank forwards the L/C to the advising bank.

3. The advising bank delivers the L/C to the beneficiary.

4. Having examined the L/C. The beneficiary (seller) ships the goods to the buyer.

5. After that, the beneficiary prepares documents, draws a draft and presents them to his bank.

6. The negotiating bank negotiates the documents and pays funds to the beneficiary.

7. The negotiating bank forwards the documents to the paying bank.

8. The paying bank receives the documents and checks them. If the documents are in order and comply with the L/C, the paying bank credits the negotiating bank's account.

9. The opening bank notifies the buyer to make the payment for documents.

After making the payment, the buyer receives the documents and takes delivery of the goods.

【注】

1. 买方向其银行提出申请并填写开证行申请书，开证行同意并开立信用证。

2. 开证行将信用证寄交通知行。

3. 通知行将信用证转交受益人。

4. 审核信用证后，受益人发货。

5. 受益人制单、开立汇票并向其银行交单。

6. 议付行议付单据并付款给受益人。

7. 议付行将单据寄给行付款行。

8. 付款行审核单据，如单证相符，付款行偿付给议付行。

9. 开证行通知买方付款。

买方付款并取得货运单据后，即可提货。

8.3 Types of Documentary Credit 跟单信用证的种类

8.3.1 Sight & Usance Letters of Credit
即期和远期信用证

Sight L/C also means "L/C available by draft at sight" or "L/C by sight draft". Under a sight L/C, the negotiating bank makes the payment immediately upon the presentation of the sight draft and shipping documents as stipulated in the L/C by the seller. Similarly when the negotiating bank delivers the sight draft and the documents to the opening bank, the latter also makes reimbursement at once.

When the seller presents a time draft together with the shipping documents stipulated in the L/C to the negotiating bank, the latter doesn't make the payment immediately. He hands over the draft and the documents to the opening bank. The opening bank doesn't pay the money immediately either. He just accepts the draft and returns it to the seller. He makes payment when the time draft falls due. This kind of L/C is called usance L/C.

即期信用证与"凭即期汇票付款的信用证"或"即期汇票信用证"的意思相同。当卖方按信用证规定把即期汇票连同装船单据向议付行提示后，后者立刻付款。同样，议付行向开证行提交即期汇票和单据时，后者也立即付款。

当卖方向议付行提示远期汇票和信用证里规定的单据时，后者不立即付款，而是把单据和汇票转递给开证行，开证行见票也不立即付款，而仅仅承兑汇票，然后将之退给卖方，汇票到期时开证行才付款。这种信用证就叫远期信用证。

8.3.2 Confirmed & Unconfirmed Letters of Credit
保兑和不保兑信用证

The security provided by an irrevocable L/C may be enhanced if the bank in the exporter's country (advising bank) is requested by the issuing bank to add its "confirmation", thus making it a confirmed L/C. the exporter, then, has a confirmed irrevocable L/C and he is then double guaranteed against payment by both the confirming and issuing bank.

If an L/C is not confirmed, it is an unconfirmed credit, where the point of payment is the overseas issuing bank, although the advising bank would usually be prepared to negotiate the bill of exchange.

保兑信用证是指一家银行开出的不可撤销信用证由另一家银行加以保证兑付。在信用证上加以保兑的银行叫做保兑行。信用证经另一家银行保兑后，出口人就取得了两家银行的付款保证。

不保兑信用证是指未经另一家银行加具保兑的信用证，由开证行单独承担付款保证责任。

8.3.3   Revocable & Irrevocable Credit
可撤销和不可撤销信用证

A revocable documentary credit gives the buyer and/or issuing bank the ability to amend or cancel the credit at any time right up to the moment of intended payment without approval by, or notice to, the seller. Revocable credits are, therefore, of great advantage to the buyer.

An irrevocable credit means that once the credit is issued it cannot be cancelled or amended before the expiry date without the agreement of the beneficiary. Under such a credit, the exporter can rely on payment being made as soon as he has shipped the goods and produced the shipping documents called for in accordance with the terms of the credit.

可撤销信用证是指开证行在议付前，对所开出的信用证不必征得受益人或有关当事人的同意，有权随时修改或撤销信用证。这种信用证对进口人非常有利。

不可撤销信用证是指信用证一经开出，在有效期内，未经受益人及有关当事人的同意，开证行不得片面修改和撤销，只要受益人提交的单据符合信用证规定，开证行必须履行付款义务。

8.3.4   Transferable Credit
可转让信用证

A transferable credit is one where the original beneficiary transfers all or part of the proceeds of an existing credit to another party (typically the ultimate supplier of the goods). It is normally used by middlemen as a financing tool.

可转让信用证是指原信用证的受益人将全部或部分信用证的款项转让给另一方（通常为供货方），中间商一般将其作为融资工具。

8.3.5   Standby Credit
备用信用证

A standby credit is also called the guarantee L/C, which is a guaranty issued by the opening bank on behalf of the applicant declaring that the bank will undertake certain obligations. That's to say, the opening bank guarantees that when the applicant fails to fulfill its obligations that have to be done, the beneficiary can make a bill of exchange on the opening bank according to the stipulations of the standby L/C or present the opening bank the statements or evidence which can testify the applicant's failure to fulfill his obligations to take out the payment.

备用信用证又称担保信用证，开证行根据开证申请人的申请对受益人开立的承诺承担某项义务的凭证。即开证行保证在开证申请人未能履行其义务时，受益人只要凭备用信用证向开证行开具汇票，并提交开证申请人未履行义务的声明或证明文件，即可取得开证行的偿付。

8.3.6 Revolving Credit
循环信用证

A revolving credit notifies the seller that when a shipment has been made and documents presented and paid, the credit automatically becomes re-available in its original form and another shipment can be made and so on. The L/C can be used again and again under the same terms and without issuance of another L/C until the stipulated times of use and the stipulated total amount have been reached. It can avoid the repetition of the opening procedure and limitation and simplifies formalities and reduces expenses.

循环信用证是指信用证的金额被全部或部分使用后，其金额又恢复到原金额，可再次使用，直到达到规定的金额或时间为止。循环信用证既可避免多次开证手续上的重复及开证额度的限制，又可节省开证费用和押金。

8.3.7 Back-to-Back Credit
背对背信用证

In a back-to-back Letter of Credit, two Letters of Credit are involved. One is in favor of the exporter who is not the actual supplier of goods; the other is opened by the exporter in favor of the actual supplier. The back-to-back credit will show a smaller amount for the value of the goods, the difference being the profit the exporter makes. The tenor is often reduced by a few days to arrange for the substitution of invoices.

一份背对背信用证涉及两张信用证，一张信用证的受益人是出口商，但他不是真正的供货方；另一张信用证是出口商通过自己的银行开给真正的供货商，并以其为受益人。背对背信用证将显示少于货物价值的金额，其差额当作出口商的利润。付款期限通常会缩短几天以供出口商更换发票。

8.3.8 Red Clause Credit
红条款信用证

A red clause documentary credit is similar to a normal L/C except that it contains a clause (originally typed or printed in red) authorizing the negotiating bank to make clean advance to the exporter before presenting any document that may be required within the terms of the L/C. It is a form of financing provided by the buyer to the seller. By it, the beneficiary may take advantage of the importer's credit standing.

红条款信用证与普通信用证相似，但含有授权议付行在受益人提交信用证规定的单据之前提前付款给受益人的条款（最初用红字打印）。红条款信用证是买方给卖方融资的一种手段。通过它受益人可以从进口人的资信中获益。

Case Study

Being all eyes to launch your happy journey.

FROM: INDUSTRIAL BANK OF JAPAN LIMITED, TOKYO

TO: BANK OF CHINA, SHANGHAI

SEQUENCE OF TOTAL: 27: 1/1

FORM OF DOC. CREDIT: 40A: IRREVOCABLE

DOC. CREDIT NO.: 20: ILC136107800

DATE OF ISSUE: 31C: 121015

DATE IN PLACE OF EXP.: 31D: 121215 IN THE COUNTRY OF BENEFICIARY

APPLICANT: 50: ABC COMPANY, 1-3 MACHI KU STREET, OSAKA, JAPAN

BENEFICIARY: 59: SHANGHAI DA SHENG CO., LTD. UNIT C 2/F JINGMAO TOWER, SHANGHAI, CHINA

CURRENCY CODE, AMOUNT: 32B: US$2,1240.00

AVAILABLE WITH / BY … 41D: ANY BANK BY NEGOTIATION

DRAFTS AT…: 42C: SIGHT FOR 100PCT INVOICE VALUE

DRAWEE: 42D: THE INDUSTRIAL BANK OF JAPAN, HEAD OFFICE

PARTIAL SHIPMENT: 43P: ALLOWED

TRANSSHIPMENT: 43T: NOT ALLOWED

LOAD/DISPATCH/TAKING: 44A: CHINESE PORTS

TRANSPORTATION TO…: 44B: OSAKA/TOKYO

LATEST DATE OF SHIPMENT: 44C: 121130

DESCRIPT GOODS/SERVICE: 45A: 4,000 PCS "DIAMOND" BRAND CLOCK ART NO. 791 AT US$5.31 PER PIECE CIF OSAKA/TOKYO PACKED IN NEW CARTONS

DOCUMENTS REQUIRED: 46A:

IN 3 FOLD UNLESS OTHERWISE STIPULATED:

1. SIGNED COMMERCIAL INVOICE;

2. SIGNED PACKING LIST;

3. CERTIFICATE OF CHINESE ORIGIN;

4. BENEFICIARY'S CERTIFICATE STATING THAT ONE SET OF ORIGINAL SHIPPING DOCUMENTS INCLUDING ORIGINAL "FORM A" HAS BEEN SENT DIRECTLY TO THE APPLICANT;

5. *COPY OF TELEX FROM APPLICANT TO SUPPLIERS APPROVING THE SHIPPING SAMPLE;

6. INSURANCE POLICY OR CERTIFICATE ENDORSED IN BLANK FOR 110 PCT OF CIF VALUE, COVERING WPA RISK AND WAR RISK;

7. 2/3 PLUS ONE COPY OF CLEAN "ON BOARD" OCEAN BILLS OF LADING, MADE OUT TO ORDER AND BLANK ENDORSED MARKED "FREIGHT PREPAID AND NOTIFY APPLICANT".

ADDITIONAL CONDITION: 47A:

ALL DRAFTS DRAWN HEREUNDER MUST BE MARKED "DRAWN UNDER INDUSTRIAL BANK OF JAPAN, LTD., HEAD OFFICE, CREDIT NO. ILC136107800 DATED OCT. 15th, 2012" AND THE AMOUNT OF SUCH DRAFTS MUST BE ENDORSED ON THE REVERSE OF THIS CREDIT.

T/T REIMBURSEMENT IS NOT ACCEPTABLE

DETAILS OF CHARGES 71 B: ALL BANKING CHARGES OUTSIDE JAPAN ARE FOR THE BENEFICIARY'S ACCOUNT.

PRESENTATION PERIOD 48: DOCUMENTS MUST BE PRESENTED WITHIN 10 DAYS AFTER THE DATE OF ISSUANCE OF THE SHIPPING DOCUMENTS BUT WITHIN THE VALIDITY OF THE CREDIT.

CONFIRMATION 49: WITHOUT

SPECIAL INSTRUCTION TO THE ADVISING BANK: ALL DOCUMENTS INCLUDING BENEFICIARY'S DRAFTS MUST BE SENT BY COURIER SERVICE DIRECTLY TO OUR HEAD OFFICE. MARUNOUCHI, CHIYODAU, TOKYO, JAPAN 100, ATTN. INTERNATIONAL BUSINESS DEPT. IMPORT SECTION, IN ONE LOT. UPON OUR RECEIPT OF THE DRAFTS AND DOCUMENTS, WE SHALL MAKE PAYMENT AS INSTRUCTED BY YOU.

SEND. TO REC, INFO. 72: ACKNOWLEDGE RECEIPT

TRAILER ORDER

Profound Insight:

1. 本信用证的种类为(至少 4 种):

2. 该信用证的有效期、交单期分别为:

3. 如果已装船提单的签发日为 11 月 15 日,则受益人最迟应在几月几日向银行交单?

4. 该信用证项下,汇票的种类是什么?谁是汇票的付款人?

5. 受益人应提交的单据种类及其份数为如下:

Exercises

I. 术语配对

1. Applicant	A. 可转让信用证
2. Usance L/C	B. 通知行
3. Advising Bank	C. 不可撤销信用证
4. Negotiating Bank	D. 预支信用证/红字条款信用证
5. Issuing Bank	E. 开证申请人
6. Transferable Credit	F. 对背信用证
7. Revolving Credit	G. 延期付款信用证
8. Irrevocable L/C	E. 开证行
9. Red Provision L/C	F. 远期信用证
10. Unconfirmed L/C	G. 不保兑信用证
11. Deferred Payment L/C	H. 议付行
12. Back-to-Back Credit	I. 循环信用证

II. 填空

1. 信用证的主要当事人有_____、_____、_____、_____、_____、_____、_____等。

2. 信用证支付方式的特点为：信用证是_____、
   是_____、
   是_____。

3. 易货贸易和来料加工贸易多用_____信用证；两国不能直接办理进出口贸易时，往往采用_____信用证；分批交货时，多采用_____信用证；开证行资信较差时，可采用_____信用证；在投标、赊销中一般可选用_____信用证。

4. 如信用证未规定最迟交单期，则从_____日起_____天内交单。

5. 根据 UCP 600，信用证若未注明是否可撤销，则默认其为_____。
   银行审单的合理时间是_____天。

6. Re-arrange the order of the following methods of payment according to the risk level both for the seller on the left and the buyer on the right.

Exporter/Seller	Methods of payment	Importer/Buyer
Low risk		High risk

A. Documentary sight bill   Documents against Payment (D/P Bill).

B. Shipment on Open Account   Payment by the importer/buyer after delivery of goods by telegraphic transfer or international cheque.

C. Prepayment   Remittance from the importer/buyer prior to shipment by the exporter/seller by telegraphic transfer or international cheque.

D. Documentary term bill   Documents against Acceptance (D/A Bill).

E. Documentary credit   Issuance of sight or term documentary L/C with payment by draft drawn under the L/C.

III. 单项选择题

1. 信用证上若未注明汇票的付款人，根据 UCP 600，汇票的付款人应是(   )。

   A. 开证申请人   B. 开证行   C. 议付行   D. 出口人

2. 开证行或付款行如发现单据和信用证不符，应在不迟于收到单据的次日起(   )个营业日内通知议付行表示拒绝接受单据。

   A. 7   B. 6   C. 5   D. 3

3. 根据 UCP 600，信用证的第一付款人是(   )。

   A. 进口人   B. 开证行   C. 议付行   D. 通知行

4. 下述(   )是指信用证的开证申请人。

   A. Beneficiary   B. Accreditor   C. in favor of XXX   D. Issuer

5. 属于银行信用的国际贸易支付方式是(   )。

   A. 汇付   B. 托收   C. 信用证   D. 票汇

6. 一张有效的信用证，必须规定一个(   )。

   A. 装运期   B. 有效期   C. 交单期   D. 议付期

7. 如果信用证上规定：Beneficiary's Draft Drawn at Sight on us. 则汇票的付款人是(   )。

   A. Issuing Bank   B. Accountee   C. Beneficiary   D. Negotiating Bank

8. In a L/C transaction, the bank pays the seller against (   ) which agree(s) with (   ).

    A. documents; the credit

    C. documents; the contract

    B. merchandise; the contract

    D. merchandise; the buyer ordered

9. 信用证若未注明汇票的付款人，根据 UCP600，汇票的付款人应是(   )。

    A. 开证申请人   B. 开证行   C. 议付行   D. 出口人

10. Documentary collections are very suitable in cases where the exporter is reluctant to supply the goods on a(n) (   ) basis, but not need the degree of security provided by a documentary credit.

    A. documentary credit

    C. guarantee

    B. Open Account

    D. consignment

IV. 判断题

(   ) 1. An issuing bank must always reimburse the advising bank if the latter pays the credit.

(   ) 2. As a back-to-back L/C is used, it is the responsibility of the second applicant (i.e. the exporter) to reimburse the bank for payments made under it, regardless of whether or not he himself is paid under the first credit.

(   ) 3. A transferable credit can be transferred by the original beneficiary to several other (second) beneficiaries for more than once.

(   ) 4. The credit is legally independent of the underlying transaction.

(   ) 5. The beneficiary must do the following to be paid; he must present documents which conform to the credit, and must present them on or before the expiry date.

(   ) 6. So far, documentary credits are the most ideal method of payment to provide security for both buyers and sellers. Therefore, in whatever conditions, L/C should the first consideration in the method of payment for transactions.

(   ) 7. When a Letter of Credit is confirmed, all of the risks are then borne by the confirming bank free of charge.

(   ) 8. Banks deal in documents and not goods, therefore, they are only concerned that documents presented appear on their faces to comply with the terms and conditions of the documentary credits.

(   ) 9. After issuance of the L/C, the issuing bank may refuse payment if the applicant becomes bankrupt.

(   ) 10. In terms of documentary discrepancies, any discrepancies, however minor, should be asked to amend.

V. Case Analysis 案例分析

1. Reading the business letter and try to finish the exercises.

Dear Sirs,

Referring to our letter of enquiry dated September 26, we have received your Proforma Invoice No. 7659 and now wish to place an initial order for 5,000 Tapes Type No. EM127D. The order number is 8873.

We have instructed our bank, the General Commercial Bank of Venezuela to open an irrevocable documentary L/C in your favor. The amount is US$8,800. This credit will be confirmed soon by our bank's correspondent in London. You are authorized to draw a 60 days' draft on our bank against this credit for the amount of your invoice. Your draft must be accompanied by a complete set of shipping documents, consisting of:

> A full set of clean shipped Bill of Lading
> Commercial Invoice in 5 copies
> The Insurance Certificate in 3 copies

Our bank will accept your 60 days' draft on them for the amount of your invoice including the cost of freight and insurance, as agreed. Your bill will therefore be at 60 d/s for the full CIF invoice value. The credit is valid until February 20th next year.

Yours faithfully,

请指出信中所提及的内容：
（1）开证行：
（2）The type of L/C required：
（3）汇票的类型是(至少 3 种)：
（4）The validity：

2. 浙江 A 公司与美国 B 公司签订了一份国际货物买卖合同，由 A 公司向 B 公司销售一批工艺品，双方在合同中约定采用信用证方式付款。合同订立后，B 公司依约开来信用证。该信用证规定，货物最迟装运期至 8 月 15 日，提单是受益人 A 公司应向银行提交的单据之一，信用证到期日为 8 月 30 日，信用证未规定交单期。A 公司于 8 月 8 日将货物装船并取得提单，提单的日期为 8 月 9 日。8 月 28 日 A 公司向银行交单议付。问：A 公司能否顺利得到货款？为什么？

3. 我国 A 公司对意大利 B 公司出口 100 公吨货物，1000 美元/公吨，总金额为 10 万美元，收到的 SWIFT 信用证规定：有效期为 2012 年 6 月 2 日，不允许分批装运，没有规定禁止数量增减，交单地为 A 公司所在地的 K 银行，没有规定交单期，最迟装运日期为 2012 年 5 月 12 日。由于各种原因，A 公司在 5 月 10 日只装运了 98 公吨货物。A 公司在规定的交单期内向银行交单，汇票金额为 9.8 万美元。5 月 25 日，K 银行通知 A 公司，开证行提出以下两个不符点予以拒付：(1)数量与信用证不符；(2)受益人证明缺少受益人盖章签字。请问开证行的拒付理由是否成立？作为 A 公司的外贸业务员，该如何处理这个问题？

4. 我国某出口企业收到国外开来不可撤销信用证 1 份，由设在我国境内的某外资银行通知并加以保兑。我出口企业在货物装运后，正拟将有关单据交银行议付时，忽接该外资银行通知，由于开证银行已宣布破产，该行不承担对该信用证的议付或付款责任，但可接受我出口公司委托向买方直接收取货款的业务。对此，你认为我方应如何处理为好？

5. 某国 A 公司与我方 B 公司洽谈一笔交易，其他条款均已取得一致意见，但我方坚持以不可撤销的即期信用证支付，对方坚持 D/P 即期，为达成交易，双方各作让步，最后以 L/C 即期与 D/P 即期各 50%定约。试问货物出运单据和汇票如何处理？

CHAPTER 9

Inspection, Claims, Force Majeure & Arbitration
检验、索赔、不可抗力和仲裁

Focus

In this chapter, you will learn:

◇ Inspection;

◇ Claims;

◇ Force Majeure;

◇ Arbitration.

9.1   Inspection 检验

9.1.1   What Is Inspection?
什么是检验？

Inspection of goods in international trade refers to the examination of commodities stipulated in import & export contracts. According to laws and regulations, inspection certificates are usually issued by the authorized agencies to report on the quality, quantity, weight, packing, sanitation and safety of the inspected goods. Inspection is an important part of international trade, which is the extension of the quality clause of the contract and the warranty of it as well.

According to Article 36 of United Nations Convention on Contracts for the International Sale of Goods, the seller is liable in accordance with the contract and this Convention for any lack of conformity which exists at the time when the risk passes to the buyer, even though the lack of conformity becomes apparent only after that time. And in Article 38, it states: The buyer must examine the goods, or cause them to be examined, within as short a period as is practicable in the circumstances; If the contract involves carriage of the goods, examination may be deferred until after the goods have arrived at their destination;

Article 157 Contract Law of PRC stipulates that the buyer shall inspect the object within the agreed inspection period after receiving the object. In case there is no such period agreed upon in the contract, the inspection shall be made in time.

国际贸易中的商品检验是指对进出口合同中所规定的货物进行检验。根据规定，商品检验通常由有资格的检验机构对商品的品质、数量、重量、包装卫生和安全性等进行检验并出具证书。商检已成为国际贸易中不可缺少的环节，它是合同中品质条款的延续，也是品质条款的保证。

《联合国国际货物销售合同公约》第36条规定，卖方应按照本公约的规定，对风险移转到买方时所存在的任何不符合合同的情形负有责任，即使这种不符合合同的情形在该时间后方显现。在第38条中，又规定：买方必须在按实际情况可行的最短时间内检验货物或由他人检验货物，如果合同涉及到运输，检验可推迟到货物到达目的地后进行。

《中华人民共和国合同法》第157条规定，买方收到货物后必须在合同规定的时间内检验，如果合同中未规定检验时间，买方应及时对货物进行检验。

9.1.2   Inspection Agencies
检验机构

There are normally three types of inspection agencies: state commodity inspection agency; notary public runs by

检验机构大体可分为三种：官方检验机构、行业协会的公证

professional associations and the manufacturer or the buyer.

General Administration of Quality Supervision, Inspection and Quarantine of the People's Republic of China (AQSIQ) is the official inspection authority in China. According to the Law of the People's Republic of China on Import and Export Commodity Inspection, AQSIQ is in charge of the inspection of the imported and exported commodities throughout the whole country, the local Entry-exit Inspection and Quarantine Bureaus are in charge of the local inspection of the imported and exported commodities.

人以及制造商或买方。

中国国家质量监督检验检疫总局是中国官方检验机构，根据《中华人民共和国进出口商品检验法》，国家质量监督检验检疫总局主管全国进出口商品检验工作，国家质量总局设在各地的出入境检验检疫局管理其所辖地区内的进出口商品检验工作。

Ⅰ Inspection Standards
检验标准

The inspection standard is the measures and rules adopted for the inspected commodity and inspection process, which are the criteria to appraise and identify if the inspected commodity comply with the related regulations and requirements. The most popular international standards are set up by the International Organization for Standardization (ISO), International Electrotechnical Commission (IEC), International Telecommunication Union (ITU) . However, some national standards from developed countries are also famous and widely accepted. For example, the American National Standards Institute (ANSI), Deutsches Institut für Normung e.V. (DIN; in English, the German Institute for Standardization) and Japanese Industrial Standards (JIS).

检验标准是指检验机构从事检验工作在实体和程序方面所遵循的尺度和准则，是评定检验对象是否符合规定要求的准则。国际上比较有名的标准由以下组织制定：国际标准化组织、国际电工委员会、国际电信联盟等。但有些发达国家的标准也较著名并被认可，如美国国家标准、德国国家标准和日本工业标准等。

Ⅱ Inspection Certificates
检验证书

An inspection certificate is a kind of testifying documents in a written form issued and signed by the inspection agency after the inspection and appraisal of the imported and exported goods. Certificates of inspection usually fall into the following categories:

★ Inspection Certificate of Quality;

★ Inspection Certificate of Weight/Quantity;

★ Inspection Certificate of Packing;

检验证书是检验机构对进出口商品进行检验、鉴定后签发的书面证明文件。检验证书主要有以下几类：

★ 品质检验证书；

★ 重量/数量检验证书；

★ 包装检验证书；

★   Veterinary Inspection Certificate;

★   Inspection Certificate of Disinfection;

★   Inspection Certificate of Origin;

★   Inspection Certificate of Value;

★   Inspection Certificate Fumigation;

★   Inspection Certificate on Tank/Hold.

The major functions of inspection can be summed up as follows:

★   Document for customs declaration;

★   Document for bank negotiations;

★   Evidence for claims.

★   兽医检验证书;

★   消毒检验证书;

★   产地检验证书;

★   价值检验证书;

★   熏蒸证书;

★   船舱检验证书。

检验证书主要有以下作用:

★   是海关验关放行的依据;

★   是办理货款结算的依据;

★   是办理索赔和理赔的依据。

Ⅲ   Inspection Clauses in a Contract
合同中的检验条款

In an import or export contract, the most important clause is the time and place of inspection. There are three normal practices:

★   Inspection at the port/place of shipment on shipping quality and weight or quantity;

★   Inspection at the port/ of destination on landed quality and weight or quantity;

★   Inspection at the port/place of shipment and re-inspection at the port/place of destination on shipping weight and landed quality.

The third one is widely accepted in import & export contracts.

The following is one example of inspection clause in a contract:

"It is mutually agreed that the Certificate of Quality and Weight (Quantity) issued by the surveyor at the place of shipment shall be part of the documents to be presented for negotiation under the relevant L/C. The buyers shall have the right to re-inspect the quality and weight (quantity) of the cargo. The re-inspection fee shall be borne by the buyers."

在进出口合同的检验条款中，最重要的是检验时间和地点的规定，一般有三种做法:

★   在装运港/地检验，即以离岸品质和重量或数量为准;

★   在目的港/地检验，即以到岸品质、重量或数量为准;

★   在装运港/地检验，进口港/地复验，即"离岸重量、到岸品质"。

第三种是国际贸易中最常用的一种规定方式。

以下是合同中检验条款的例子:

"买卖双方同意以装运地检验机构签发的质量和重量(数量)检验证书作为信用证项下议付所提交的单据的一部分。买方有权力对货物的质量和重量(数量)进行复验，复验费由买方承担。"

9.2　Claims 索赔

9.2.1　What Are Claims?
什么是索赔？

A claim is a legal action by the party that suffers losses to ask for compensation against the defaulting party in a contract. Most claims are caused by the breach of contracts either by the seller or the buyer. When one party fails to fulfill its obligations in the contract and causes damages to the other party, the party that suffers losses will ask for compensation.

索赔是合同中遭受损害的一方在争议发生后向违约的一方提出赔偿的行为。大部分索赔是因为买方或者卖方违约引起的，当一方不能履行其在合同中的义务，给另一方带来损失时，遭受损失的一方有权提出索赔。

9.2.2　Kinds and Settlement of Claims
索赔的类型和理赔

There are three kinds of claims:

★　A claim against the insurer for loss of insured goods;

★　A claim against the carrier for damage of the shipped commodity;

★　A claim between the importer & exporter for discrepancies of the contract.

Most claims are caused by the third kind and mostly about time of delivery, quality and quantity of goods. If evidences and surveying documents for claims are valid, settlement of claims can be replacement of the damaged goods, compensation or a penalty, which usually represents a certain percentage within 5% of the total value of the contract.

Settlement of a claim in international trade means that the party breaking the contract declares that he will accept and handle the claim. According to relative laws, the time limit for a claim is two years.

However, it should be mentioned that after compensation, both parties can consider whether the original contract should be cancelled or prolonged to be fulfilled within a delayed date.

索赔有三种类型：

★　被保险货物受损，向保险公司提出索赔；

★　货物在运输途中受损，向承运人提出索赔；

★　买卖双方因一方违约而索赔。

大多索赔属于第三种，大多因为装运时间、货物品质和数量等问题引起，如果有足够的证据和有效的鉴定报告，索赔人可以得到赔偿，赔偿的方式有调换受损货物、赔偿或者罚金等，罚金一般占合同金额的5%左右。

理赔是指违约方对受损方提出的索赔要求进行处理，根据相关法律规定，索赔的期限为两年。

然而，一方对另一方进行赔偿后，双方可以就是否取消原来的合同还是推迟履行合同进行协商，就某种意义上来说，索赔和

In a sense, compensation does not mean termination of the obligations of both parties in the original contract.

Here is an example of claim clause in an contract:

"Any claim by the buyer regarding the goods shipped should be filed with in…days after the arrival of the goods at the port of destination specified in the relative Bill of Lading and/or transport document and supported by a survey report issued by a surveyor approved by the Seller."

理赔并不代表原合同的终止。

以下是合同中索赔条款的例子：

"买方对装运货物的任何索赔，必须于货物到达提单及/或运输单据所订目的港之日起 XX 天内提出，并需提供卖方同意的公证机构出具的检验报告。"

9.3　Force Majeure 不可抗力

9.3.1　What Is Force Majeure?
什么是不可抗力？

Force Majeure is commonly used in international trade contracts which free both parties from liability or obligation when an extraordinary event or circumstance, which is beyond the control of both parties, such as war, strike, riot, crime, act of God or nature (e.g. flooding, earthquake, volcano), prevents one or both parties from fulfilling their obligations under the contract.

According to Article 79 of United Nations Convention on Contracts for the International Sale of Goods, a party is not liable for a failure to perform any of his obligations if he proves that the failure was due to an impediment beyond his control and that he could not reasonably be expected to have taken the impediment into account at the time of the conclusion of the contract or to have avoided or overcome it or its consequences.

However, when there is a Force Majeure event, the party that quotes the Force Majeure clause should notice the other party promptly and present the Certificate of Force Majeure. In China Certificate of Force Majeure is issued by China Council for the Promotion of Inter national Trade (CCPIT).

不可抗力在国际贸易合约中普遍使用，在发生超出双方能力控制的特殊事件或情形下，例如战争、罢工、暴乱、犯罪、天灾(如洪水、地震、火山爆发)，一方或双方不能履行合约时，不可抗力可以使双方免于责任。

根据《联合国国际货物销售公约》第 79 条，一方当事人不能履行义务，如果他能证明此种不履行义务是由于某种非他能所能控制的障碍，而且对于这种障碍没有理由预期他在订立合同时能考虑到或能避免或能克服它及它的后果，则可免除责任。

然而，发生人力不可抗力事件时，当事人必须立即通知另一方并提交证明，在我国，该证明由中国国际贸易促进委员会出具。

9.3.2　Force Majeure Clauses in a Contract
合同中的不可抗力条款

Because of Force Majeure, contracts can be terminated or postponed when agreed by both parties. In import & export contracts, both parties normally agree to indicate the Force Majeure clause in three ways:

★ Stipulate the force majeure clause in a general way;

★ Stipulate the force majeure clause in a listing the contents way;

★ Stipulate the force majeure clause in a comprehensive way.

The third kind is widely accepted in contracts in China. The following is an example:

If the shipment of the contracted goods is prevented or delayed in whole or in part by reason of war, earthquake, flood, fire, storm, heavy snow, the seller shall not be liable for non-shipment or late shipment of the goods of this contract. However, the seller shall notify the buyer by fax or email and furnish the latter within 15 days by registered airmail with a certificate issued by the China Council for the Promotion of International Trade attesting such an event or events.

发生不可抗力事故后，双方可以协商终止合同或者推迟履行合同。在进出口合同中，一般有三种规定方法：

★　概括式规定；

★　列举式规定；

★　综合式规定。

我国进出口业务中，大多采用第三种规定方式，例如：

如果因为战争、地震、洪水、火灾、暴风雨、大雪等原因，致使卖方不能全部或部分装运或延迟装运合同货物，卖方对于这种不能装运或延迟装运本合同货物不负有责任。但卖方必须用传真或电子邮件通知买方并必须在15天内用航空挂号信件向买方提交由中国国际贸易促进委员会出具的证明此类事故的证明书。

9.4　Arbitration 仲裁

9.4.1　What is Arbitration?
什么是仲裁？

Disputes or claims can be resolved by parties concerned or submitted to a third party for arbitration. There are several ways to resolve a dispute or a claim:

★ Consultation;

★ Conciliation;

★ Arbitration;

★ Litigation.

贸易纠纷和索赔可以由当事人协商解决，也可以交由第三方仲裁。解决纠纷的方法有以下几种：

★　友好协商；

★　调解；

★　仲裁；

★　诉讼。

Arbitration is a process in which the two parties, before or after the disputes arise, reach a written agreement that they will submit the disputes which cannot be settled through amicable negotiation to a third party for arbitration. The arbitral award is final and binding on both parties.

Arbitration has its advantages:

★ When the dispute is highly technical, arbitrators with a background of expertise can be appointed;

★ Arbitration is often faster and cheaper than litigation in court;

★ Arbitration is highly confidential and arbitrators will keep commercial secrets for both the buyer and the seller;

★ Award is final and binding.

仲裁是买卖双方在争议发生之前或发生之后，签订书面协议，自愿将其不能通过友好协商解决的争议提交双方所同意的第三者予以裁决，仲裁裁决具有终局性，对双方当事人都有约束力。

仲裁具有以下优势：

★ 当纠纷涉及到技术性问题时，可以选择有相关专业背景的仲裁员；

★ 仲裁比诉讼快，费用也较便宜；

★ 仲裁有极强的保密性，仲裁员有为双方当事人保密的义务；

★ 仲裁裁决具有终局性，对双方都有约束力。

9.4.2　Arbitration Institutions
仲裁机构

In China, the arbitration institution of international trade is China International Economic and Trade Arbitration Commission located in Beijing. There are usually two types of arbitration agencies: permanent arbitration agency and temporary arbitration tribunal. Arbitration can take place either in the seller or buyer's country, or in a third country. The general procedures of a arbitration are as follows:

Submitting dispute to arbitration→Appointing arbitrators →Hearing a case→Issuing an award.

Other famous international arbitration institutions are:

★ American Arbitration Association (AAA);

★ The London Court of International Arbitration (LCIA);

★ The Arbitration Institute of the Stockholm Chamber of Commerce (SCC).

在我国，中国国际经济贸易仲裁委员会是国际贸易仲裁的机构，其总部在北京。仲裁机构有常设仲裁机构和临时仲裁庭两种，仲裁可以在卖方所在国、买方所在国或者第三国举行，仲裁程序如下：

提出仲裁申请→组成仲裁庭→审理案件→做出裁决。

国际上比较有名的仲裁机构有：

★ 美国仲裁协会；

★ 伦敦国际仲裁中心；

★ 瑞典斯德哥尔摩仲裁院。

9.4.3 Arbitration Clauses in a Contract
合同中的仲裁条款

Typical arbitration clause in an international trade contract is:

"Any dispute arising from or in connection with this contract shall be submitted to China International Economic and Trade Arbitration Commission for arbitration which shall be conducted in accordance with the Commission's arbitration rules in effect at the time of applying for arbitration. The arbitral award is final and binding upon both parties."

It should be mentioned that the party that loses the arbitration should pay for the arbitration fee. Since arbitration is final and binding, both parties cannot go further to court for a lawsuit. However, if the losing party refuses to accept the award of the arbitration, the winning party can go to court for carrying out the award.

以下是合同中比较典型的仲裁条款：

"凡因本合同引起的或与本合同有关的任何争议，均应提交中国国际经济贸易仲裁委员会，按照申请仲裁时该会现行有效的仲裁规则进行仲裁。仲裁裁决是终局的，对双方均有约束力。"

需要注意的是，仲裁的费用一般由败诉方承担，因为仲裁的裁决是终局性的，对双方当事人都有约束力，双方必须遵照执行，不得再向法院起诉。然而，如果败诉方不接受裁决，胜诉方可向有关法院申请执行。

Case Study

One company in Ningbo signed a contract in April with an American buyer for export of 1,000 dozen T-Shirts CIF New York and the latest time of shipment was end June. When the company was ready for delivery of the goods, the T-Shirts in stock were burnt accidentally by a fire. The Ningbo company informed the American side of the Force Majeure, which the American company did not accept and stuck to the stipulated time of shipment. The Ningbo company managed to ship out the goods in August, but the American side asked for compensation on late delivery.

Questions:

1. Should the Ningbo company compensate or is it a Force Majeure? Why?

2. Is the American company justified in asking for compensation? Why?

Exercises

I. 术语翻译

检验		证书	
索赔		违约	
赔偿		罚金	
不可抗力		责任	
仲裁		诉讼	
特别法庭		裁决	

II. 英译汉

1. It is mutually agreed that the Certificate of Quality and Weight (Quantity) issued by the China Exit and Entry Inspection and Quarantine Bureau at the port of shipment shall be regarded as final and binding upon both parties.

2. Should the buyer for its own sake fail to open a Letter of Credit within the time stipulated in the contract, the buyer shall pay a penalty to the seller. The penalty shall be charged at the rate XX% of the amount of L/C for every XX days if delay in opening the L/C, however the penalty shall not exceed XX% of the total value of the L/C which the buyer should have opened.

3. If the shipment of the contracted goods is prevented or delayed in whole or in part due to force majeure, the seller shall not be liable for non-shipment or late shipment of the goods of this contract. However, the seller shall notify the buyer by speed post with a certificate issued by the China Council for the Promotion of International Trade attesting such a event or events.

4. All disputes arising from or in connection with this contract shall be settled amicably through friendly negotiation. In case no settlement can be reached through negotiation, the case shall then be submitted to…for arbitration in accordance with its arbitration rules. The arbitral award is final and binding upon both parties.

III. 单项选择

1. 我国现时主管商品检验检疫工作的最高行政执法机关是(　　　)。
   A. 有关单位自行设立的检验检疫机构　　　B. 国家商检局
   C. 卫生部卫生检疫局　　　　　　　　　　D. 国家质量监督检验检疫总局
2. 国际贸易中广泛采用的规定检验时间和地点的方法是(　　　)。
   A. 在装运港检验　　　　　　　　　　　　B. 装运地检验和目的地复验
   C. 装运港检验重量和目的港检验品质　　　D. 在目的港检验
3. 国际货物贸易中出现的索赔，通常是(　　　)。
   A. 贸易索赔　　　　B. 运输索赔　　　　C. 保险索赔　　　　D. 全是
4. 适用于一般商品买卖合同的索赔条款是(　　　)。
   A. 定金法则　　　　B. 违约金条款　　　　C. 预付款条款　　　D. 异议与索赔条款

5. 按一般惯例，违约金数额不超过货物总金额的(　　　　)。

    A. 5%   B. 10%   C. 15%   D. 20%

6. 罚金的数额通常取决于(　　　　)。

    A. 违约时间的长短   B. 违约的严重程度

    C. 违约事件的起因   D. 当时当地的政府

7. 如合同中未规定索赔期或品质保证期，则按《联合国国际货物销售合同公约》的规定，买方最长的索赔时效为收到货物之日起不超过(　　　　)。

    A. 60 天   B. 180 天   C. 1 年   D. 2 年

8. 按照国际惯例，索赔都有一定期限，超过期限的索赔为(　　　　)。

    A. 无效   B. 有效

    C. 双方协商后确定   D. 由理赔方确定

9. 发生不可抗力的法律后果是(　　　　)。

    A. 解除合同   B. 延迟履行合同

    C. 解除合同或延迟履行合同   D. 既不解除合同，也不延迟履行合同

10. 在我国进出口合同中，对于不可抗力事件范围的规定，一般都采用(　　　　)。

    A. 分类式规定   B. 概括式规定   C. 列举式规定   D. 综合式规定

11. 我国出具不可抗力事故证明的机构为(　　　　)。

    A. 商会   B. 仲裁机构

    C. 商检局   D. 中国国际贸易促进委员会

12. 不可抗力条款是一项(　　　　)。

    A. 维护卖方权益的条款   B. 维护买方权益的条款

    C. 免责条款   D. 无法免责条款

13. 不可抗力条款适用于(　　　　)。

    A. 卖方   B. 买方   C. 买卖双方   D. 第三方

14. 解决争端的方式有(　　　　)。

    A. 调解   B. 仲裁   C. 诉讼   D. 全选

15. 1958 年联合国在纽约召开国际商事仲裁会议，签订了(　　　　)。

    A. 《国际贸易法委员会仲裁规则》   B. 《国际商事仲裁示范法》

    C. 《承认及执行外国仲裁裁决公约》   D. 《仲裁合作协议》

16. 国际上为解决执行外国仲裁裁决制定的公约是(　　　　)。

    A. 《海牙规则》   B. 《汉堡规则》

    C. 《维斯比规则》   D. 《1958 年纽约公约》

17. 既有自愿性的一面，又有强制性一面的争议解决方式是(　　　　)。

    A. 协商   B. 调解   C. 仲裁   D. 诉讼

18. 仲裁地点应首先选择在(　　　　)。

    A. 本国   B. 对方国   C. 第三国   D. 本国和对方国

19. 仲裁费用的承担者通常为(　　　　)。

    A. 申请仲裁方   B. 胜诉方   C. 败诉方   D. 双方各半

20. 对仲裁裁决具有强制执行的机构是(　　　　)。

    A. 仲裁庭   B. 贸促会   C. 国际商会   D. 法院

IV. 判断题

(   ) 1. All the inspection certificates are issued by various government agencies in the world.

(   ) 2. Inspection at the port of shipment and re-inspection at the port of destination is the most popular clause in contracts.

(   ) 3. Disputes in international trade can only be resolved by a claim.

(   ) 4. According to relative laws, the time limit for a claim is one year.

(   ) 5. Generally, a penalty is within 5% of the total value of the contract.

(   ) 6. Compensation means termination of the obligations of both parties in the original contract.

(   ) 7. Listing the contents of Force Majeure clause is a common way in an import & export contract.

(   ) 8. In China, Certificate of Force Majeure is issued by General Administration of Quality Supervision, Inspection and Quarantine of the People's Republic of China (AQSIQ).

(   ) 9. Arbitration can take place either in the seller or buyer's country, not in a third country.

(   ) 10. Arbitration is not final and binding, both parties can go further to court for a lawsuit.

V. 案例分析

我国某公司与比利时某企业以 CIF Antwerp(安特卫普)订立了一项农产品出口合同。订约时，我方已经知道该批货物要转销英国。货到比利时后，立即转运英国，其后，比利时某企业凭借英国企业在其所在地伦敦签发的检验证书，起诉我方公司。

问题：你认为我公司该如何应对起诉？并简述理由。

CHAPTER 10

Business Negotiation & Contract Conclusion
交易的磋商和合同的签订

In this chapter, you will learn:

✧ Forms & contents of business negotiation;

✧ Procedure of business negotiation;

✧ Conclusion of a contract;

✧ Forms & contents of a contract.

10.1   Forms & Contents of Business Negotiation
交易磋商的形式和内容

10.1.1   Forms of Business Negotiation
交易磋商的形式

Business negotiation is a bargain process between the potential parties (seller and buyer) to a contract in order to reach an agreement on price, quantity, quality and other terms and conditions of a sale.

International business negotiation usually takes two forms: verbal (oral) and written. When it is carried out verbally, traders talk about the terms and conditions with each other in person or by telephone. When business negotiation is done by writing, communications by letter, by cable, by telex or by e-mail are the usual means traders use. Sometimes both types, communications in a written form and an oral form, are used interchangeably in one single transaction.

交易磋商是指签约双方为了在价格、数量、品质和其他条款上达成协议而进行的商务谈判的过程。

交易磋商有两种形式：口头和书面。口头谈判时，贸易商面对面或通过电话谈判。书面谈判主要通过信函、电报、电传或电子邮件等形式完成。有时，一笔交易的磋商可能既要口头谈判又要书面联系。

10.1.2   Contents of Business Negotiation
交易磋商的内容

Business negotiation includes discussion on both specific and general components. Specific terms and conditions refer to name of commodity, quality, quantity, packing, price, shipment and insurance. General terms and conditions (or format terms) refer to common terms and conditions applicable to all contracts. They usually cover such aspects as the prevention and settlement of disputes, inspection of commodity, claim for reimbursement, Force Majeure, arbitration, etc.

With preset general terms and conditions, the buyers and the sellers are to negotiate those "blank terms".

交易磋商的内容可分为两部分：具体交易条件和一般交易条件。具体交易条件是指货物的品名、品质、数量、包装、价格、运输和保险条款等。一般交易条件是对每笔交易都适用条款，包括争议的预防和解决、商品检验、索偿、不可抗力、仲裁等。

买卖双方一般会事先拟定一般交易条件，仅就"空白条款"，即具体交易条件进行谈判。

10.2   Procedure of Business Negotiation 交易磋商的程序

Business negotiation usually undergoes four stages: enquiry, offer, counter-offer and acceptance, in which offer and acceptance are not only indispensable but also the base of a contract.

交易磋商一般包含四个环节：询盘、发盘、还盘和接受。其中发盘和接受是合同成立的两个基本要素，也是交易磋商环节中必不可少的。

10.2.1 Enquiry
询盘

Enquiry (or inquiry) refers to intension from a party interested in the purchase or sale of goods specified therein, indicating particular and desirable conditions regarding price and delivery terms, etc., addressed to a prospective supplier or buyer with a view to obtaining an offer or bid. In most cases, an enquiry is made by the buyer. The enquiry made by the buyer is usually called an "invitation to offer"; the enquiry made by the seller is called "invitation to a bid". It is worthy of noting that whoever makes an enquiry is not legally liable for the buying or the selling. And the opposite party can make no reply at all. But, according to the commercial practice the receiver of an enquiry will respond without delay in the usual form of a quotation, an offer, or a bid.

An enquiry can be made to one party alone or to several clients. In this way the enquirer can make a comparison between the terms and conditions stated in different replies and thus trade beneficially with the one who has offered the best terms.

Enquiries fall into two categories: general enquiry and specific enquiry. In a general enquiry, the enquirer asks for such general information as a catalogue, price list or brochures, etc. A specific enquiry asks for more specific information as the price, quality, terms of payment, desired quantity or time of shipment of a particular item.

If the enquiry is made by the buyer, it may be expressed as follows:

★   We are interested in your…(name of the commodity), please offer…;

询盘是准备购买或出售商品的人为了获得发盘或递盘，向潜在的供货人或买主探询该商品的价格、装运等条件的行为。询盘通常由买方做出，这种询盘叫做"邀请发盘"。如果询盘由卖方做出，则称为"邀请递盘"，值得注意的是，询盘人不受法律约束，受盘方可以不对询盘做任何回应，但根据国际贸易惯例，受盘人在收到询盘后应立刻以报价、发盘或递盘的方式作出答复。

询盘可以向一个或几个交易对象同时发出，这样询盘人可以比较各交易条件以便择优成交。

询盘分两种：一般询盘和具体询盘。在一般询盘中，询盘人要求出口商提供商品的一般信息，如商品目录、报价单或产品宣传册等。在具体询盘，询盘人则要求提供某一商品的价格、品质、支付条款、起订量或装运时间等具体信息。

如果询盘由买方作出，一般使用下列句型：

★   我方对……（商品名称）感兴趣，请发盘……；

★ We are in the market for... (name of the commodity), please send us your offer on FOB basis;

★ Please quote us your keenest price for...(name of the commodity).

In case of the seller's enquiry, it goes like:

★ We are in a position to supply...(name of the commodity). If you are interested, please bid;

★ (name of the commodity) is available, please send us a bid.

★ 我方想购买……（商品名称），请报 FOB 价；

★ 请报……（商品名称）的最优惠价格。

如果卖方做出询盘，一般这样表示：

★ 我方能供应……（商品名称），如感兴趣，请递盘；

★ 可供……（商品名称），请递盘。

Case Study

Can price list, catalogues and brochures published by the seller for the purpose of advertisement and promotion be considered as firm offers?

10.2.2   Offer
发盘

Offer is a major process in business negotiation. It is a definite indication of the willingness, either in writing or orally, from one party to another to contract for selling (in the case of a selling offer) or buying (in the case of a buying offer) a specific commodity on terms set out in the offer. The party who makes the offer is called the "offerer" while the opposite party is the "offeree".

There are two kinds of offer: offer with engagement and offer without engagement.

◆   **Offer with Engagement**

An offer with engagement is also called "firm offer" or "irrevocable offer". In this kind of offer, the offerer's intention to make a contract is definitely indicated and the offerer cannot revoke or amend what he has offered during the validity of the offer. Once it is unconditionally accepted by the offeree within the validity, the transaction is completed and a contract is concluded right away. So it is binding on the offerer within its validity.

发盘是交易磋商的主要步骤。它是交易的一方向另一方提出出售(售货发盘)或购买(购货发盘)某种商品的各项交易条件,并愿意按这些条件达成交易、订立合同的一种书面或口头的肯定的表示。做出发盘的人叫做"发盘人",接受发盘的人则叫做"受盘人"。

发盘有两种：有约束力的发盘和去约束力的发盘。

◆   **有约束力的发盘**

有约束力的发票又叫做"实盘"或"不可撤销的发盘"。在这种发盘中,发盘人必须表明严肃的订约意图并且发盘的有效期内不能撤销或修改,发盘一旦被受盘人无条件接受,合同即告成立。所以,这种发盘在有效期内对发盘人有法律约束力。

An offer with engagement must satisfy the following conditions:

★ It should be addressed to one or more specific persons;

★ It should be definite;

★ It must indicate that once it is unconditionally accepted by the offeree within its validity, a contracted is established;

★ It becomes effective when it reaches the offeree.

A firm offer lapses when it exceeds its validity period or when it is rejected or counter-offered. The lapsed offer is no longer binding on the offerer.

◆ **Offer without Engagement**

An offer without engagement is also called "non-firm offer" or "free offer". What is stated in an offer without engagement, contrary to the one with engagement, is unclear, incomplete and with reservation. This kind of offer is not binding on the offerer. Such expression as "reference price", "subject to our final confirmation", etc., are often used.

◆ **Validity of an Offer with Engagement**

An offer with engagement usually contains a validity period. In this case, the offer remains valid until it lapses. Validity date of an offer imposes a binding effect upon the offerer, during which the offer can neither be revoked nor be amended by the offerer, and if the offer is accepted by the offeree, a contract is then concluded.

The validity date of an offer can be stipulated either by the indication of the latest date of acceptance, such as "The offer is subject to your reply reaching us on or before June 15th, 2012, our time", or by the indication of a period of time after receipt, as "The offer is valid for three days", the duration of an offer depends on the nature of the goods, market tendency and the volume of the transaction.

If the offer is made orally, there will be no duration for it. Unless the offeree accepts the oral offer on the spot, the offer will be invalid after negotiation.

有约束力的发盘必须满足下列条件:

★ 必须向一个或一个以上特定的人提出;

★ 内容必须确定;

★ 必须表明发盘一旦在有效期内被受盘人接受,合同即告成立的意思;

★ 发盘到达受盘人开始生效。

当发盘过了有效期、被受盘人拒绝或还盘后,发盘即告失效,失效的发盘对发盘人不再有约束力。

◆ **无约束力的发盘**

无约束力的发盘也叫做"虚盘"或"自由发盘"。与实盘相反,虚盘的内容不确定,也不完整,发盘人通常有所保留。这种发盘对发盘人无约束力,在询盘中经常出现"参考价"、"以我方最后确认为条件"等字样。

◆ **有约束力发盘的有效期**

有约束力的发盘通常有有效期,发盘到期才失效。在发盘的有效期内,发盘人受其约束,他既不能撤销也不能修改发盘内容,而且发盘一旦被受盘人接受,合同即告成立。

发盘的有效期可以用规定最迟接受时间的方法来表示,如"本发盘以你方在 2012 年 6 月 15 日前复到为有效",也可以规定一段接受的时间,如"本发盘有效期为 3 天"。发盘有效期的长短取决于货物的性质、市场行情以及交易金额的大小。

口头发盘没有有效期,除非受盘人当场接受,口头发盘在谈判后即失效。

◆   **Withdrawal and Revocation of an Offer with Engagement**

According to the "United Nations Convention on Contracts for the International Sale of Goods (CISG)", an offer becomes valid when it is received. An offer can only be withdrawn if the notice of withdrawal reaches the offeree before or at the same time as the offer. Once an offer becomes valid, it can only be revoked before the acceptance is dispatched. However, if an offer itself states that it is irrevocable, contains a validity date, or the offeree has acted in reliance on the offer, it cannot be revoked.

◆   **有约束力发盘的撤回和撤销**

根据《联合国国际货物销售合同公约》，发盘在到达受盘人时生效。撤回通知早于或与发盘同时到达发盘人的情况下，发盘才可撤。一旦发盘生效，只有在发盘通知发出前才可撤销。然而，如果发盘本身说明是不可撤销的，或载明了发盘的有效期，或受盘人已本着对该发盘的信赖行事，则该发盘不可撤销。

Case Study

Of the two following offers, which is a firm offer, which is a non-firm offer? Why?

Letter 1

Dear Sirs,

We thank you for your inquiry of March 11th.

We are making you an offer for 50,000 pieces of Silk Blouses at US$86.00 per piece FOB Ningbo for shipment in Sept./Oct., 2012. Payment by irrevocable L/C at sight is required. This offer is subject to your reply reaching us on or before Aug. 15, our time.

Please note that we have quoted our best price and are unable to entertain any counter-offer.

We look forward to your early reply.

Yours faithfully,

Letter 2

Dear Sirs,

Thank you for your letter dated April 5th, in which you express your interest in our Men's Pajamas.

At your request, we take pleasure in making you the following offer, subject to our final confirmation:

Commodity:	Men's Pajamas
Quantity:	2,000 dozen
Size:	L/XL/XXL
Color:	white, blue, red
Price:	At US$96.00 per piece CIF Montreal
Payment:	By irrevocable L/C in our favor payable by draft at sight to reach the sellers one month before shipment and remain valid for negotiation in China till the 15th. day after shipment.

Our stock is light with heavy demand. Therefore, your early decision is necessary.

Faithfully yours,

10.2.3 Counter-offer
还盘

A counter-offer is a reply to an offer made by the offeree to the offeror, accepting some terms and changing other terms. A counter-offer is, in fact, a partial rejection to the original offer. So, it is a new offer and at the same time, the original offer lapses. The offeree may not agree on the price, packing or payment terms made by the offeror and state his own terms instead. Such alterations indicate that business has to be negotiated on the renewed basis. The original offeror has now become the offeree and he has the right to accept or refuse the counter-offer. In the later case, he may make another counter-offer of his own. This process may go on for many a round till the transaction is concluded or called off. The following is a formal counter-offer:

Dear Mr. Smith,

Re: Your Offer for Silk Blouses

Thank you for your letter dated June 28th, 2012, offering us 10,000 pcs of Silk Blouses at US$12.00 /pc CIF New York on usual terms.

In reply, we very much regret to inform you that our buyers here find your price too high to be acceptable. Information indicates that Indian makes are sold at a level of 20% lower than yours. We know that yours are of higher quality, but the gap is too great. So we suggest that you reduce your price to US$10.00/pc CIF New York, other terms remain unchanged.

We look forward to your reply, but in the meantime we wish to point out that the market is declining. We hope that you will make your decision at an early date.

Yours faithfully,

还盘是受盘人对发盘人发盘的回复，接受一些条款同时也更改另一些条款。还盘其实是对发盘的部分拒绝，所以它是一个新的发盘，原发盘失效。受盘人可能不能接受价格、包装或支付条款等，并提出自己的条件。这样的更改意味着双方必须在新的基础上进行谈判。原来的发盘人变成现在的受盘人，他既可接受也可拒绝此还盘，如果他拒绝这个还盘，则可做出反还盘。这样的过程可能会经历几轮，最后双方可能会达成协议，也可能谈不拢。以下是一封正式的还盘信：

敬启者：

事由：贵方真丝女衬衫的发盘

感谢贵方 2012 年 6 月 8 日 10000 件真丝女衬衫的发盘，每件 12 美元，CIF 纽约，惯常条款。

我们非常遗憾地告之，我地买方认为你方价格太高，无法接受。有资料显示，印度货的价格比你方的价格低 20%，虽然你们的质量要好一些，但差距实在是太大了。所以我们建议你方把价格降到每件 10 美元，CIF 纽约，其余条款不变。

目前市场行情正在下降，希望贵方能尽早回复。

祝   商安

10.2.4　Acceptance
接受

An acceptance is a total assent to the terms and conditions of an offer or a counter-offer, which means that the offeror and the offeree have come to an agreement on the sale. It is binding on both parties. According to "United Nations Convention on Contracts for the International Sale of Goods (CISG)", an acceptance should conform to the following conditions:

★　The acceptance must be made by the offeree who is clearly stated in the offer.

★　The acceptance must be made in the form of a statement (either verbal or written) or any other conduct. Silence and inactivity are by no means an acceptance.

★　The acceptance must be unconditional. It should be an unreserved assent to all the terms in the offer and contain no additions, modifications or limitations to the offer. But not all modifications constitute a rejection to the offer. Only material alteration, such as modifications on terms of price, payment, quality, quantity, delivery etc. will be deemed as a rejection to the offer, while non-material alterations, other than the above mentions terms, constitute an effective acceptance.

★　The acceptance takes effect when it reaches the offeror and it should be made within the time of validity of the offer.

◆　**Late Acceptance**

If the offeree makes an acceptance beyond the time limit for acceptance, this kind of acceptance is called late acceptance. According to international laws, a late acceptance is a new offer and is not valid unless:

★　The offeror informs the offeree or dispatches a notice without delay that he admits its effectiveness;

★　If a late acceptance is caused by contingency during transmission, the late acceptance is effective as an acceptance unless, without delay, the offeror orally informs the offeree that he considers his offer as having lapsed or dispatches a notice to that effect.

接受是完全同意发盘或还盘内容，意味着发盘人和受盘人之间已达成交易。接受对双方都具有约束力。根据《联合国国际货物销售合同公约》的规定，有效接受必须具备以下条件：

★　接受必须由发盘中规定的受盘人做出；

★　接受必须以口头或者书面的形式作出，也可以用行为表示，但缄默或者不行为不构成接受；

★　接受必须是无条件的。它必须是对发盘所有内容无保留的同意并且没有任何附加内容、修改或限制。但并不是所有的修改都构成拒绝，只有实质性的更改，如对价格、支付、品质、数量、交货等条件的修改才构成对发盘的拒绝，一些非实质性的更改仍可构成有效接收；

★　接收的通知要在发盘的有效期内送达发盘人才能生效。

◆　**逾期接受**

如果受盘人在发盘有效期后作出接受，此类接受被称为逾期接受。根据国际法，逾期接受是新的发盘，发盘人不受其约束，但下列两种情况除外：

★　发盘人毫不延迟地用口头或书面的形式通知受盘人，承认该项逾期接受的有效性；

★　如果逾期接受是因为传递延误造成的，则该项接收仍有效，除非发盘人毫不延迟地用口头或者书面方式通知受盘人，他认为该项接收已经失效。

◆ **Withdrawal of an Acceptance**

A contract is concluded at the moment when an acceptance of an offer becomes effective in accordance with the provisions of CISC. An effective acceptance can not be withdrawn unless the withdrawal reaches the offeror before or at the same time as the acceptance would have become effective.

◆ **接受的撤回**

根据《联合国国际货物买卖公约》条款，合同在接受生效时成立，有效的接受不能撤回，但如果撤回通知在接受生效之前或同时到达发盘人，接受得以撤回。

Case Study

Judge which of the following is an acceptance or a counter-offer:

Dear Sirs,

Thank you for your offer and samples of July 8th.

We have studied your terms and samples carefully and are pleased to accept your offer on the condition that shipment be made in Aug. instead of Sept. 2008. Enclosed is our Order No. 288. We will open the L/C in your favor soon.

Yours faithfully,

Dear Sirs,

Re: Men's Socks

We thank you for your letter dated May 6th, 2008 and through your full cooperation we have been able to accept your offer on the terms and conditions stated below:

Commodity:	Men's 100% Socks
Quantity:	2,000 dozen
Unit price:	At US$3.60 per dozen CIF New York
Color:	White, black, red
Packing:	Each pair in a polybag, one dozen to a box and ten boxes to a carton.
Shipment:	To be effected from Ningbo to New York by sea in June/July, 2008.
Terms of payment:	By 100% confirmed, irrevocable L/C in your favor payable by draft at sight to reach you one month before shipment and remain valid for negotiation in China until the 15th day after shipment.

We have instructed our bank to open a Letter of Credit for the amount of this order and shall let you know as soon as it is issued.

As we are in urgent need of the goods, we hope you will make punctual shipment within the validity of the L/C. Any delay in shipment would be detrimental to our future business.

Yours faithfully,

10.3　Conclusion of a Contract 合同的成立

A contract is an agreement between competent parties stating all the terms and conditions of a sale (sales contract) or a purchase (purchase contract). In import and export trade, a contract is a legal document made by and entered into between a seller and a buyer on the basis of their offer and acceptance. The rights and obligations of both parties are definitely stipulated in the contract. The contract is binding on them all.

In the course of business negotiation, when an offer with engagement or a counter-offer is accepted, the transaction is completed and a contractual relationship between the offeror and the offeree is established.

合同是签约双方所达成的协议，它规定了所有的销售条件(销售合同)或购买条件(购货合同)。在进出口业务中，合同是买卖双方经过发盘和接受而达成的法律文件，它明确规定了双方的权利和义务，合同对双方都有约束力。

在交易磋商过程中，当一项有约束力的发盘或还盘被接受时，发盘人和还盘人之间的契约关系即告成立。

10.4　Forms & Contents of a Contract 合同的形式和内容

10.4.1　Forms of a Contract
合同的形式

There is no legal requirement for the form of a contract. Nevertheless, a written contract is widely used in international trade practice, and written contracts usually take the following forms:

法律上对合同的形式没有特别的要求。但对外贸易一般签订书面合同，书面合同有以下几种：

◆　**Sales Contract or Purchase Contract**

A sales contract is a written agreement between a seller and a buyer stating the terms and conditions for a sale. While a purchase contract is a contract stating the terms of purchase. The major difference between a sales contract and a purchase contract is that a sales contract is drawn by the seller and a purchase contract by the buyer. A contract is very formal. It consists of not only such items as the name of commodities, specifications, quantity, price, packing, marking, shipment

◆　**销售合同或购货合同**

销售合同是买卖双方就货物的销售条件而达成的书面协议，购货合同则是卖双方就货物的购买条件而达成的书面协议。两者之间的区别在于前者由卖方起草而后者由买方起草，合同非常正式，它不仅包含商品名称、规格、数量、价格、包装、唛头、运输、

and payment, but also concerning insurance, inspection, claims, arbitration and force majeure.

支付等具体条款，还包含保险、检验、索赔、仲裁和不可抗力等一般条款。

◆ Sales Confirmation or Purchase Confirmation

Like sales contract and purchase contract, a sales confirmation and a purchase confirmation are drawn by the seller and the buyer respectively. The major difference between a contract and a confirmation is that a contract is more formal and complete while a confirmation covers several main items only. But they are equally binding on the parties legally.

◆ 销售确认书或购货确认书

与销售合同和购货合同一样，销售确认书和购货确认书分别由卖方和买方起草。合同和确认书之间最大的不同在于合同更正式、完整而确认书只包含交易的主要条款。但在法律上两者具有同等效力。

◆ Agreement 协议

An agreement is the statement (oral or written) of an exchange of promises, which serves as a legally binding contract made between two or more parties. The major difference between an agreement and the contract or confirmation is that the agreement refers to both oral and written promises, while contract and confirmation stand for written promises only.

◆ 协议

协议是双方或多方之间承诺的记载（口头或书面），是法律上具有约束力的合同。协议与合同和确认书的主要区别在于前者可以是口头也可以是书面的，但合同与确认书只有书面的形式。

◆ Memorandum 备忘录

A memorandum is the detailed record of business negotiation between the two parties. The characteristic of a memorandum is equal to that of a contract, except that a memorandum does not have contractual binding force upon the parties. But if the memorandum contains all the main terms and conditions for a transaction and bears the signature of both parties, it equals to a contract.

◆ 备忘录

备忘录是双方商务谈判的详细的纪录。备忘录与合同相似，但备忘录对各方当事人无约束力。如果备忘录包含交易的主要条件并有各方签字，它等同于合同。

◆ Letter of Intent 意向书

A letter of intent is a written statement between two parties, expressing a desire and understanding to enter into a contract, but not a binding contract. It merely serves as an expression of intent and is not a legal document.

◆ 意向书

意向书表达双方签订合同的意向，它不是有约束力的合同。它的作用仅仅是表达当事人的意向而不是法律文件。

◆   **Order 订单**

A purchase order only expresses the intention of the buyer to place an order with the seller. It functions as an offer or an invitation to offer. But if the order is accepted by the seller, it constitutes a purchase contract and is legally binding on all parties.

◆   **订单**

货物订购单是买方向卖方订货的意向，相当于发盘或邀请发盘。但如果订单被卖方接受则构成购货合同，在法律上对双方都有约束力。

10.4.2 Contents of a Contract
合同的内容

According to commercial laws, a contract generally shall contain the following terms:

★   The name of the contracting parties and their domicile;

★   The date and place of the signing of the contract;

★   The type of the contract;

★   Quality clause (including goods description, quality, specifications, etc.);

★   Quantity clause (including weight, numbers, length, dimension, volume, capacity, etc.);

★   Package clause (including the mode of packing and its material);

★   Price clause (including the unit price, pricing currency and the price terms used);

★   Shipment clause (including time of shipment, port of loading and port of destination, transshipment, partial shipment and mode of transportation, such as charter, liner, railway, airline,, multimodal transportation);

★   Insurance clause (the risk to be covered, the percentage of insurance and the party effecting insurance);

★   Payment clause (the payment method and time of payment, etc.);

★   Commodity inspection clause (including the time, place and organization of inspection);

★   Claims clause;

★   Arbitration clause;

★   Force Majeure clause.

根据商业法，合同应包含以下内容：

★   签约双方的名称及所在地；

★   签约的时间和地点；

★   合同的类型；

★   品质条款（包含商品名称、品质、规格等）；

★   数量条款（包含重量、数量、长度、尺寸、容积、体积等）；

★   包装条款（包含包装方式和材料）；

★   价格条款（包含单价、计价货币、贸易术语等）；

★   运输条款（包含装运时间、装运港、目的港、转运、分批装运、运输方式，如租船、班轮、铁路、空运、多式联运等）；

★   保险条款（包括投保险别、投保加成、投保人）；

★   支付条款（支付方式及时间等）；

★   商品检验条款（包含检验的时间、地点及检验机构等）；

★   索赔条款；

★   仲裁条款；

★   不可抗力条款。

A formal contract or confirmation should be prepared in duplicate, each of which should be signed by both parties. Each party should keep a signed copy of it. Some of the contracts or confirmations commonly used in international trade are available in printed form, so that only the date, price, name of the commodity, name of the parties and similar particulars need to be filled in. The following is a specimen of a Sales Contract.

正式的合同或确认书应一式两份，双方都必须在上面签字，各方都需保留一份经双方签字的合同。国际贸易中，有些合同都事先印制好，只要填制时间、价格、品名、当事人等一些具体的内容即可。下面是一份销售合同样本。

1. 售货确认书
SALES CONFIRMATION

The Sellers: The Buyers:

2. 编号
Contract No.: _____

日期
Date: _____

地点   2
Place: _____

3.下列签字双方同意按以下条款达成交易

The undersigned Sellers and Buyers have agreed to close the transaction according to the following terms and conditions.

4. 品名及规格 COMMODITY AND SPECIFICATIONS	5. 数　量 QUANTITY	6. 单　价 UNIT PRICE	7. 金　额 AMOUNT
8. SHIPPING MARK			

9. 总值

TOTAL VALUE:

10. 包装

PACKING:

11. 目的地

DESTINATION:

12. 运输

SHIPMENT:

13. 保险

INSURANCE:

14. 付款方式

PAYMENT:

15. 检验　　　卖方须在装运期前_____日委托_____检验机构对本合同货物进行检验。

INSPECTION:　并出具检验证书，货到目的港后，由买方委托_____检验机构进行复验。

The Seller shall have the goods inspected _____ days before the shipment and have the Inspection Certificate issued by _____. The Buyer may have the goods re-inspected by _____ within _____Days after the goods' arrival at the destination.

16. 仲裁
ARBITRATION:

凡因执行本合同发生的或与本合同有关的一切争议，应由双方通过友好协商解决；如果协商不能解决，应提交中国国际贸易促进委员会对外经济仲裁委员会根据该会的仲裁程序暂行规则进行仲裁。仲裁裁决是终局的，对双方都有约束力。

All disputes arising from the execution of, or in connection with this contract, shall be settled amicably through friendly negotiation. In case no settlement can be reached through negotiation, the case shall then be submitted to the Foreign Economic & Trade Arbitration Commission of China Council for the Promotion of International Trade, Beijing, for arbitration in accordance with its provisional rules of procedure. The arbitral award is final and binding on both parties.

17. 一般条款
GENERAL TERMS:

(1) 质地、重量、尺寸、花型、颜色均允许合理差异。对合理范围内差异提出的索赔，概不受理。

Reasonable tolerance in quality, weight, measurements, designs and colors is allowed, for which no claims will be entertained.

(2) 买方对下列各点所造成的后果承担全部责任：(甲)使用买方的特定装潢、花型图案、商标等；(乙)不及时提供生产所需的规格和其他细则；(丙)不按时开信用证；(丁)信用证条款和合同不符而不及时修改信用证。

The Buyers are to assume full responsibilities for any consequences arising from (a) the use of packing, designs or brand pattern made to order; (b) late submission of specifications or any details necessary for the execution of this Sales Confirmation; (c) late establishment of L/C; (d) late amendment to L/C inconsistent with the provisions of the Sales Confirmation.

(3) 人力不可抗拒的事故造成无法交货者，卖方不负任何责任。

The Sellers are not responsible for late or non-delivery in the event of Force Majeure or any contingences beyond the Sellers' control.

(4) 凡有对装载的货物提出索赔者，必须在货到目的地后 30 天内提出。

Claims, if any, concerning the goods shipped should be filed within 30 days after arrival at destination.

(5) 买方应在收到本确认书后十天内签退一份给卖方。如在此期限内不提出任何异议，本售货确认书即生效。凭买方订单或凭买方先前之确认而缮制的售货确认书，在发出后即生效。非经双方同意，不得更改或撤销。

The Buyers should sign one copy of this Sales Confirmation and return it to the Sellers within 10 days after receipt. If nothing is proposed to the contrary within that time, this Sales Confirmation will be effective. Sales Confirmation, issued on the strength of the Buyers' order or earlier confirmation, is effective immediately on its issuance, and subject to neither modification nor cancellation, unless agreed upon by both parties.

_____   _____
　　买方(The Buyers)   卖方(The Sellers)

Exercises

I. 术语翻译

还盘	询盘
发盘	发盘人
受盘人	实盘
虚盘	一般交易条件
失效	撤销
达成交易	接受

II. 填空

1. 国际货物买卖合同中的主要交易条件包括：＿＿＿＿＿＿＿、＿＿＿＿＿＿＿、＿＿＿＿＿＿＿、
   ＿＿＿＿＿＿＿、＿＿＿＿＿＿＿。

2. 交易磋商的程序可概括为四个环节：＿＿＿＿＿＿＿、＿＿＿＿＿＿＿、＿＿＿＿＿＿＿、
   ＿＿＿＿＿＿＿。其中＿＿＿＿＿＿＿和＿＿＿＿＿＿＿是必不可少的。

3. 根据《联合国国际货物销售合同公约》规定，所谓发盘"内容十分确定"是指发盘至少包
   括三个基本要素：＿＿＿＿＿＿＿、＿＿＿＿＿＿＿、＿＿＿＿＿＿＿。

4. 《公约》规定，发盘于＿＿＿＿＿＿＿＿＿＿＿＿时生效。

5. 受盘人对发盘内容的变更有＿＿＿＿＿＿＿＿和＿＿＿＿＿＿＿＿＿＿之分，前者不能构成有
   效接受，后者是否构成有效接受取决于发盘人。

6. 晚于发盘有效期送达发盘人的接受，法律上称为＿＿＿＿＿＿＿＿的接受。

7. 关于接受的生效，英美法采用＿＿＿＿＿＿＿＿原则；大陆法采用＿＿＿＿＿＿＿＿原则；《公约》
   采用＿＿＿＿＿＿＿＿原则。

8. 根据《联合国国际货物销售合同公约》规定，受盘人可以采用＿＿＿＿＿＿＿＿的方式表示接
   受，也可以用＿＿＿＿＿＿＿＿表示。

III. 单项选择题

1. 发盘是向(　　　)提出的订立合同的建议。
   A. 一个特定的人　　　　　　　　　B. 一个或一个以上特定的人
   C. 不特定的人　　　　　　　　　　D. 法人

2. 为邀请对方向自己订货而发出的商品目录单、报价单以及一般的商业广告，是(　　　)。
   A. 发盘　　　　　　B. 还盘　　　　　　C. 邀请发盘　　　　　D. 新的发盘

3. 在国际货物买卖交易磋商中，有条件的接受(　　　)。
   A. 视对发盘所做修改的性质及发盘人的态度而决定其是否构成有效接受
   B. 构成发盘
   C. 构成还盘
   D. 构成邀请发盘

4. 中国 A 公司于 3 月 1 日对一日本外商发盘，限 10 日内复到为有效，外商于 6 日发出接受通知，A 公司于 12 日收到，事后 A 公司未表态，那么(　　　)。

　　A. 该逾期接受有效，合同成立

　　B. 该接受逾期无效，合同未成立

　　C. 经电信部门出具有关证明后方能认定是否有效

　　D. 此为还盘

5. B 公司于 1 月 15 日用电子邮件向外国一公司发盘，要求在 20 日复到有效，1 月 18 日外国公司发出表示接受的信件并附订单邮件，但 1 月 19 日我公司收到外商要求撤回接受电子邮件，根据《联合国国际货物销售合同公约》的规定，此接受(　　　)。

　　A. 不可以撤回，必须与 B 公司签订合同

　　B. 可以撤回

　　C. 经 B 公司同意方可撤回

　　D. 视为发盘

6. 以下(　　　)不是 EDI 必须包括的内容。

　　A. 纸单据和电子单据同时传递　　　　　B. 按统一的标准编制资料

　　C. 电子方式的传递方式　　　　　　　　D. 计算机应用程序之间的连接

7. "兹报西湖牌电动车 6000 辆(规格详见 2 月 10 日订单)，每辆 58 美元，FOB 宁波，标准出口包装，7 月装船，不可撤销信用证付款，限 2 月 25 日复到我方有效。"该传真属于(　　　)。

　　A. 询盘　　　　　　　B. 发盘　　　　　　　C. 还盘　　　　　　D. 接受

8. "你方 6 月 18 日电悉，若将降价 5%，则接受。"此传真属于(　　　)。

　　A. 询盘　　　　　　　B. 发盘　　　　　　　C. 还盘　　　　　　D. 接受

9. 在发盘人发出发盘后的第 3 天，发盘人即收到受盘人通过往来银行开来的不可撤销信用证，受盘人的做法属于(　　　)。

　　A. 询盘　　　B. 发盘　　　C. 还盘　　　D. 接受

10. "你方 6 月 18 日电悉，接受各项条件，另在外包装左侧刷唛头。"此传真属于(　　　)。

　　A. 询盘　　　　　　　B. 发盘　　　　　　　C. 还盘　　　　　　D. 接受

Ⅳ. 判断题

(　　　) 1. 发盘必须明确规定有效期，未规定有效期的发盘无效。

(　　　) 2. 在交易磋商过程中，发盘是由卖方作出的行为，接受是由买方作出的行为。

(　　　) 3. 按照《联合国国际货物销售合同公约》的规定，受盘人可以在发盘有效期内用开立信用证这一行为表示接受。

(　　　) 4. 向广大公众发出的商业广告不具有发盘性质，是因为接受广告信息的人不具有特定性。

(　　　) 5. In international trade, the effective formation of a sales contract must go through five links, namely, enquiry, offer, counter-offer, acceptance and conclusion of a sales contract.

(　　　) 6. It is a widely accepted rule in international trade the silence and inactivity on the part of offeree constitutes acceptance.

(   ) 7. When accepting an offer, there should be no conditions of acceptance or any material modification, addition or restriction in the acceptance. Otherwise, such as offer would be regarded as a rejection to the offer and constitutes a counter-offer.

(   ) 8. According to international trade convention, under no circumstances can an offer be revoked once it is made by the offeror.

(   ) 9. An offer containing such phrases as "subject to our final confirmation", "subject to prior sale" can only be taken as an offer without engagement and can be revoked even after it has been accepted by the offeree.

(   ) 10. When a counter-offer has been rejected by the offeror, the offeree can still accept the original offer before the time of the original offer expires.

V. 案例分析

1. 我国 A 公司向美国 B 公司传真发盘一批货物，A 公司于 2012 年 5 月 18 日发盘如下："WE TAKE PLEASURE IN MAKING YOU AN OFFER FOR 1,000 M/TS OF CRYSTAL SUGAR AT US$1,200.00 NET CIF NEW YORK FOR SHIPMENT IN JUNE/AUGUST. PAYMENT BY IRREVOCABLE L/C PAYABLE AT SIGHT IS REQUIRED. THE OFFER IS SUBJECT TO YOUR REPLY REACHING HERE ON OR BEFORE MAY 25TH, 2012, OUR TIME."

B 公司于 5 月 22 日回复："WE ACCEPT YOUR OFFER FOR 1,000 M/TS OF CRYSTAL SUGAR AT US$1,200.00 NET PER M/T CIF NEW YORK FOR SHIPMENT IN JUNE/AUGUST. PAYMENT TO BE MADE BY IRREVOCABLE L/C PAYABLE AT SIGHT PROVIDED THAT YOU FURNISH US WITH CERTIFICATE OF ORIGIN IN ADDITION TO THE USUAL DOCUMENTS AND THE GOODS SHOULD BE PACKED IN SEAWORTHY PACKING." 此时，该货物国际市场价格上涨了 20%，A 公司又与日本某公司按国际市场价签订了合同。2012 年 5 月 25 日 A 公司去电："THANK YOU FOR YOUR FAX OF MAY 22ND. WE VERY MUCH REGRET THAT OWING TO MARKET FLUCTUATION, THE GOODS HAD BEEN SOLD OUT BEFORE WE RECEIVED YOUR FAX." 双方因此为合同是否成立发生纠纷。

请问：A 公司这样做是否合理？B 公司有权要求 A 公司履行合同吗？

2. 2012 年 3 月 1 日，日本 B 公司向我国 A 公司询购童装。3 月 15 日 A 公司发盘："WE ARE PLEASED TO OFFER YOU FIRM FOR 200 DOZEN OF CHILDRED'S OVERALLS AT US$100.00 PER DOZEN CIF KOBE FOR AUGUST SHIPMENT. PAYMENT TO BE MADE BY IRREVOCABLE SIGHT L/C. THE OFFER IS SUBJECT TO YOUR REPLY REACHING HERE ON OR BEFORE MARCH 25TH 2012."

3 月 22 日收到 B 公司答复："YOUR OFFER OF MARCH 15TH HAS BEEN RECEIVED BUT THE PRICE IS TOO HIGH. BUSINESS IS POSSIBLE IF YOU REDUCE THE PRICE TO US$90.00 PER DOZEN CIF KOBE."

A 公司次日复："WE HEVE QUOTED THE KEENEST PRICE AND REGRET BEING UNABLE TO MAKE ANY REDUCTION IN PRICE."

3 月 26 日，B 公司只要求航邮样品以供参考。

3 月 29 日，A 公司寄出样品，并函告对方："THE OFFER IS SUBJECT TO YOUR REPLY REACHING HERE ON OR BEFORE APRIL 8TH."

4 月 3 日，B 公司回函表示接受发盘全部内容。4 月 10 日送达 A 公司。经办人员认为是逾期接受，未做任何表示。

7 月 6 日，A 公司收到 B 公司开来的信用证，但此时原材料价格上涨，公司已将价格调整到每打 110 美元，故于 7 月 8 日回复："YOUR ACCEPTANCE DATED APRIL 3RD DIDN'T REACH US UNTIL APRIL 10TH, WHICH OBVIOUSLY BELONGED TO LATE ACCEPTANCE. THE CONTRACT WAS NOT ESTABLISHED. WE HAVE RETURNED YOUR L/C TO THE BANK. IF YOU ARE INTERESTED, WE REOFFER AS FOLLOWS: AT US$110.00 PER DOZEN CIF KOBE FOR SEPTEMBER SHIPMENT, OTHER TERMS REMAIN UNCHANGED."

7 月 12 日 B 公司答：WE ACCEPTED YOUR OFFER ON APRIL 3RD. YET OUR ACCEPTANCE DIDN'T REACH YOU UNTIL APRIL 10TH, AND IT NORMALLY ONLY TAKES THREE DAYS. OBVIOUSLY IT WAS DELAYED IN TRANSMISSION. ACCORDING TO NO. 2 OF ARTICLE 21 OF "UNITED NATIONS CONVENTIONS ON CONTRACTS FOR THE INTERNATIONAL SALE OF GOODS", YOUR FAILURE TO INFROM US OF THE LATE ACCEPTANCE MEANS THAT THE CONTRACT HAS BEEN ESTABLISHED. PLEASE CONFIRM THAT YOU WILL EXECUTE THE CONTRACT. OTHERWISE YOU SHOULD BEAR ALL THE CONSEQUENCIES THUS OCCURRED.

请分析 B 公司的观点是否正确？

VI. 根据所给资料填制英文合同

合同号码：93-366

卖方：江南陶瓷(ceramics)进出口公司(中国杭州)

买方：日本远东商社(Far East Trading Co.)

商品名称：中国餐具

规格：货号 3376

数量：600 套

单价：成本加保险费加运费东京价每套 45 美元

总值：22500 美元

包装：适合海运纸板箱包装，每箱 1 套

保险：由卖方根据中国保险条款按发票金额 110%投保一切险和战争险

装运港：中国上海或宁波

目的港：东京

交货期：2012 年 8 月

唛头：由卖方选定

支付条款：凭不可撤销、可转让即期信用证付款。信用证须不迟于装运月份前 30 天到达卖方。

有效期应为最后装运期后 15 天在中国到期。

签订日期、地点：2012 年 5 月 8 日于中国杭州

1. 售货确认书
SALES CONFIRMATION

2. 编号
Contract No.:_____
日期
Date: _____
地点
Place: _____

The Sellers: The Buyers:

3. 下列签字双方同意按以下条款达成交易

The undersigned Sellers and Buyers have agreed to close the transaction according to the following terms and conditions.

4. 品名及规格 COMMODITY AND SPECIFICATIONS	5. 数　量 QUANTITY	6. 单　价 UNIT PRICE	7. 金　额 AMOUNT
8. SHIPPING MARK			

9. 总值
TOTAL VALUE:

10. 目的地
DESTINATION:

11. 运输
SHIPMENT:

12. 保险
INSURANCE:

13. 付款方式
PAYMENT:

CHAPTER 11

Performance of International Trade Contracts
国际贸易合同的履行

In this chapter, you will learn:
- ✧ General procedures of export transactions;
- ✧ General procedures of import transactions.

11.1 General Procedures of Export Transactions
出口合同履行的程序

In international trade, as soon as a sales contract is signed it becomes legally binding on both the seller and buyer. Each party bears its own rights and obligations. The seller should execute its basic obligations of delivering the goods or any documents relating to the goods and transferring the ownership of the goods to the buyer as stipulated in the contract. It includes getting the goods ready, arranging for the Letter of Credit, applying for the inspection of the goods before shipment, obtaining official documents such as export license, certificate of origin, etc., chartering or booking shipping space (in the case of CFR or CIF), arranging for insurance (in the case of CIF), going through customs formalities, shipping on board the goods, making documents for negotiation, settling the proceeds of the goods, collecting verification and exporting drawback.

在国际贸易中,合同一成立即对买卖双方构成法律上的约束力,双方都有其权利和义务,卖方必须按合同规定履行其交货或交单的义务,把货物的所有权转移给买方。这些环节包括:备货、安排信用证、装运前申请商品检验、申领官方单据如出口许可证和原产地证等、租船订舱(在 CFR 或 CIF 合同中)、投保(在 CIF 合同中)、出口清关、装船、制单结汇、出口收汇核销以及出口退税等。

11.1.1 Getting the Goods Ready
备货

The seller should, first of all, place an order with the manufacturer for the goods. All information about the product, including quality, specifications, quantity, packing, marking, delivery should be passed on to the manufacturer in the form of a purchase contract. The following points should be carefully noted:

★ Quality

The quality of the goods should be in strict accordance with the contract stipulations. When the sale is by description, the goods should comply with the description; when the sale is by sample, the goods should conform to the sample in quality; if the contract is based on both descriptions and sample, both quality requirements should be satisfied.

卖方需向制造商下订单,出口合同中关于商品的所有信息,如品质、规格、数量、包装、包装标志、装运时间等都必须在出口方和制造商之间的购货合同中得以体现。出口商在备货中应注意以下问题:

★ 品质

货物的品质必须完全符合合同的规定,如果是用文字说明表示品质,则货物品质必须与文字说明相符;如果是凭样品成交的,则货物必须与样品相符;如果合同规定既凭文字说明又凭样品,则所交货物品质必须符合两者。

★   Quantity

The quantity to be delivered should comply with the contract requirement. When words like "about", "approximately", "circa" or similar expressions are used to modify quantity, the actual delivered quantity of the goods can be 10% more or less than the specified quantity under UCP600. But the surplus is limited in respective amount permitted in the L/C. A tolerance of 5% more or less will be allowed provided that the amount of the drawings does not exceed the amount of the credit. This tolerance does not apply when credit specifies that the quantity should be counted on packing unit or individual items. If there is no specific requirement that whether the weight is count on gross weight or net weight in the contract or L/C, the net weight should be applied according to international practice.

★   Packing

When the contract use ambiguous words like "customary packages", "seaworthy shipment packing", the goods should be packed in the customary way or on the common understanding about the packing requirements by both parties. The seller should inspect the inner and outer packing, correct any mistakes and omissions that may cause failure of the contract. The seller should bear any losses caused by improper packing of the goods.

★   Sole ownership of the goods

The seller should also guarantee the complete ownership of the goods which are to be sold to the buyer, that is, no any third party can claim any right to the goods, such as patent, trade marks, copyright, etc.

★   数量

出口商所交货物的数量必须与合同条款一致。根据 UCP 600，如果在数量前有"约"、"大约"或相似的词语修饰，则数量可以有 10%的增减，但金额不能超过信用证的金额。UCP600 还规定，如果总支取金额不超过信用证金额，货物数量允许有 5%的增减幅度，但如果信用证规定数量是以包装单位或个数、件数来计算时，本增减幅度不适用。如果合同或信用证中未说明以毛重还是以净重计算，则按国际惯例，以净重计算。

★   包装

如果合同使用"按惯常方包装"、"适合海运的包装"等，卖方需按双方约定的包装方式包装。卖方必须仔细核对货物的内外包装及装潢，如有任何包装不良或破损情况，应及时修整，因包装不当产生的损失由卖方承担。

★   货物的所有权

卖方必须保证他完全拥有所售货物，无任何第三方对货物具有权利，如专利、商标、版权等。

购销合同

需方：　　　　　　　　　　　　　　　合同编号：

　　　　　　　　　　　　　　　　　　签约日期：

供方：　　　　　　　　　　　　　　　签约地点：

　　　　　　　　　　　　　　　　　　外销合同：

根据《中华人民共和国合同法》和有关法规，经双方协商签订本合同并信守下列条款：

一、商品

品名及规格	数量	单位	单价(含税)	金额	交货期

总金额(大写)

二、质量要求：

三、包装要求：

四、交货地点：

五、付款方式(选择其中一项或两项)

　　A. 供方凭增值税专用发票，专用税收缴款书、进仓单(送货回单或集装箱单)、购货合同向需方办理收款。

　　B. 待需方收到客户货款后，供方凭增值税专用发票、专用税收缴款书、进仓单(送货回单或集装箱单)、购货合同向需方办理收款。

六、责任条款：

　　1. 因供方的责任造成国外客户索赔的，其索赔款及因索赔发生的费用由供方承担。

　　2. 需方已安排供方出产的商品，因外销变化需要做出某些调整或变更的，其修改部分则为合同的组成部分。

七、本合同有效期从　　　年　　月　　日至　　　年　　月　　日

八、纠纷处理办法及地点：执行本合同过程中如有争议，双方同意通过协商解决；如协商未能取得一致，则由 XX 市所辖人民法院管辖。

九、本协议由双方签字盖章生效。合同一式两份，供需双方各执一份。

十、备注：

需方授权代表　　　　　　　　　　　供方授权代表

盖章　　　　　　　　　　　　　　　盖章

11.1.2　Arranging for the L/C
信用证

◆　**Rushing the Establishment of the L/C**

　　In the export trade of China, foreign clients often delay in opening the L/C within the time limit stipulated in the contract for one reason or another. The seller should urge the buyer to open the L/C so as to ensure the smooth performance of the contract. The following is a specimen letter rushing the establishment of the L/C:

Dear Sirs,

Referring to the 6,000 pieces of Ladies' Blouses under our S/C No. 678, we wish to call your attention to the fact that the date of shipment is drawing near, but we have not received the covering L/C up to now. Please do your utmost to expedite its establishment, so as to enable us to execute the order within the stipulated time.

For your information, there is a direct vessel sailing for your port around the middle of next month. If we have your L/C before the end of this month, we might catch the steamer.

In order to avoid subsequent amendments, please see to it that the L/C stipulations are in strict conformity with the terms and conditions of the contract.

We look forward to your L/C at an early date.

Yours faithfully,

◆　**Examining the L/C**

　　On receipt of the L/C, it is essential for the seller to examine the terms of the L/C. The L/C terms should be in strict conformity with S/C stipulations. In actual business, the unconformity between the L/C, S/C and national policy often occurs for the reason of the buyer's or the opening bank's negligence or mistakes, or special regulations on credits in some nations, or a few buyers' trap in the L/C. Therefore, the examination of the credit is a key step for the seller in the execution of the contract. Special care must be taken in the following points:

◆　催证

　　在出口业务中，国外客户经常因为各种各样的原因不能在合同规定的时间内开立信用证，为确保合同的顺利履行，卖方应催促买方开证，以下是一封催证信函：

敬启者：

　　有关第 678 号售货合同项下的 6000 件女衬衫，我们想提请贵方注意，装运期已临近，但到目前为止，我方还未收到相关信用证，请尽快开立信用证，以便我方在规定的时间内交货。

　　下月中旬有一艘直达轮到你处，如果贵方信用证能在本月底前到我方，则可能赶上。

　　为避免日后的修改，请务必使信用证上的条款和合同的条款完全相符。

　　敬候佳音。

祝　　商安

◆　审证

　　卖方在收到信用证后应立即对信用证进行审核以确保信用证的条款和合同的条款完全一致。在实际业务中，由于买方或开证行的疏忽或错误，有些国家对信用证的特殊规定，或一些买方刻意的行为，信用证和合同条款以及国家政策常常不符。因此审证非常重要，在审证时应注意下列问题：

★ **The political background and financial standing of the issuing bank**

If the issuing bank is domiciled in a country which has not a friendly relationship with China, this credit is not acceptable. If the issuing bank is a very small bank with poor financial standing, the credit is not acceptable either.

★ **The form of the credit**

Credit with the word "revocable" should be rejected. The undertaking clause of the issuing bank should be included. Though some kinds of credits are marked "irrevocable", the issuing bank will add some limits and reservations regarding the undertaking of the issuing bank including such clauses as "This credit is not effective until we receive the notification of import license". In this case, the seller should not ship the goods until effective advice arrives.

★ **The amount and currency of the credit**

The amount and currency of the credit should conform to that of the contract. If there is a more or less clause in the contract, the amount of the L/C should cover the more or less part. The unit price and total amount should be correct. The amount in figures and words should agree with each other.

★ **Time of shipment, presentation period and the expiry date and place**

Time of shipment refers to the time when the seller has the goods loaded on board the transporting vehicle to the destination or when the seller delivers the goods to the carrier. In fact, the issuing date of shipping documents under different transportation methods represent the date of shipment. For instance, the issuing date of a bill of lading stands for the date on which the cargo are loaded on board the named vessel.

Presentation period means the period between the validity date of the L/C and the latest date of shipment during which the beneficiary can make the documents and present the documents for negotiation. Generally, the presentation period is counted from the date of shipment and it's often stipulated as 10 to 15 days after the date of shipment.

According UCP 600, every L/C should bear an expiry date and place. Banks will reject documents which overrun the

★ **开证行的政治背景和资信状况**

如果开证行所在国家与我国没有经贸往来，则不能接受。如果开证行很小且资信差，此类信用证也不能接受。

★ **信用证的性质**

不可接受可撤销信用证，信用证内必须写明开证行保证付款的文句。虽然有些信用证上标有"不可撤销"字样，但开证银行会加上一些限定性或保留性的条款，如"本信用证在我们收到(买方获得)进口许可证的通知时生效"。在这种情况下，卖方需等信用证生效通知到了以后才能装运。

★ **信用证的金额和币别**

信用证金额应与合同一致，如合同有溢短装条款，则信用证的金额还应包含溢短装部分的金额，单价与总金额要一致，金额的大小写也必须相符。

★ **装运期，交单期，到期时间和地点**

装运期是指卖方把货物装到相应交通工具上或将货物交给承运人的时间。事实上，不同装运单据上的签发日期代表装运日期。如，提单上的签发日是指货物装上提单上载明的船只的日期。

交单期是最晚装运日和信用证的到期日之间的一段时间，受益人可以在此期间制单并交单议付。交单期通常为装运期后的10到15天。

根据 UCP600，一切信用证都必须规定到期日和到期地点，银

maturity. The place of expiry falls into three: place of beneficiary, place of applicant or at a third country. The Chinese exporters should try to have the L/C expired in China so that they may have enough time to prepare the documents for negotiation.

★　**The documents**

The types, copies of documents as well as the methods to fill out are required.

★　**Partial shipment and transshipment**

The transshipment and partial shipment clauses in the L/C should be in compliance with that in the contract. If the L/C does not forbid partial shipment and transshipment, it's understood as allowing according to UCP 600. If the L/C allows partial shipment and stipulates clearly the time and amount for each lot while shipment is not carried out in any one lot accordingly, the L/C will be invalid from this very lot.

★　**Insurance clause**

The risks and amount to be covered should agree with those in the contract. If extra risks or amount are required by the L/C, the additional charges should be for the account of the importer. Under FOB or CFR terms, no insurance documents are required.

★　**Additional conditions**

Special requests for documents, shipment, etc., are often revealed here.

★　**Banking charges**

The L/C is opened by the bank at the request of the importer. So the importer should bear all the banking charges including issuing fee, advising fee, amendment fee, etc. But some credit bear such clauses as "All banking charges outside Japan are for beneficiary's account."

行拒绝接受超过有效期的单据，到期地点有三种规定方法：在受益人国内到期、在开证申请人国内到期、在第三国到期，中国的出口商应争取信用证在中国到期以便有足够的时间制单结汇。

★　**单据**

单据的类型、份数以及填制方法等都必须审核。

★　**分批装运和转运**

信用证中关于分批装运和转运的条款必须与合同规定一致。根据 UCP600，如果信用证中未禁止分批或转运，则视为允许。如果信用证允许分批装运并规定了每批装运的时间和金额，而其中的一批未按规定装运，则信用证从该批起即告失效。

★　**保险条款**

保险的险别和金额都应与合同规定相符，如果信用证要求加保额外的险别或增加投保金额，则额外的费用由买方承担。如果是以 FOB 或 CFR 成交的，无需任何保险单据。

★　**附加条款**

对单据或者运输等的特殊要求都会在这里显示。

★　**银行费用**

信用证是银行应买方的要求开立的，所以买方应该承担所有的银行费用，如开证费、通知费、改证费等。但有些信用证要求受益人承担银行费用，如："日本国以外的所有银行费用由受益人承担"。

◆ **Asking for amendments to the L/C**

Upon examination of the L/C, the beneficiary should list out all the discrepancies and contact the applicant for the amendments to the L/C without any delay. He should always bear in mind that before the receipt of the amendments from the issuing bank advised through the same advising bank as the original L/C, he can never make the shipment, otherwise he will put himself in a very unfavourable position. The following is a specimen letter asking for amendments to the L/C:

Dear Sirs,

Thank you for your L/C No. BOC070325, but we regret to say that we have found some discrepancies. Pease amend the L/C as follows:

1. "Hangzhou Imp. & Exp. Corp." should read "Li Du Textile Imp. & Exp. Corp., Hangzhou, China";

2. Please amend "VANCOUVER TRADING CO. LTD." to read "COMMERCIAL BANK OF TORONTO";

3. Please amend "available by draft drawn on them" to read "available by draft drawn on us";

4. The total amount should be "CANADIAN DOLLARS TWENTY-FOUR THOUSAND" instead of "TWENTY THOUSAND";

5. "At 60 days' sight" should read "at sight";

6. Delete Insurance Policies or Certificates;

7. The port of destination should be "Vancouver" instead of "Toronto";

8. Transshipment should be allowed.

As the time of shipment is drawing near, please make the above amendments as soon as possible.

Yours faithfully,
Li Du Textiles Imp. & Exp. Corp.

◆ 申请改证

在审核完信用证后，受益人必须列出所有的不符点并立刻与开证申请人联系，要求修改信用证。值得注意的是，信用证的修改须由原通知行转递，受益人在收到信用证的修改通知之前不能装运货物，不然他会陷于非常不利的处境。下面是一份要求修改信用证的信函：

敬启者：

贵方 BOC070325 号信用证已收悉，谢谢。但很遗憾，信用证中有一些不符点，请修改如下：

1. "杭州进出口公司"应改为"丽都纺织品进出口公司，中国，杭州"；

2. 请将"温哥华贸易公司"改为"多伦多商业银行"；

3. 请把"向他们开立汇票"改成"向我们开立汇票"；

4. 总金额应为 24000 加元而不是 20000 加元；

5. 汇票付款期限是即期汇票而不是见票 60 天付款；

6. 删除条款"保险单或保险凭证"；

7. 目的港改为温哥华,不是多伦多;

8. 允许转运。

因装运期已临近，请尽快修改信用证。

祝　商安

丽都纺织品进出口公司

Case Study

Zhejiang ABC Company signed a sales contract with Canada Trade Company on May 5th, 2012. The contract specifies August as shipment period but does not make clear the time for the buyer to open the L/C. ABC Company did not receive the relative L/C and kept rushing Canada Trade Company for the establishment of the credit from the end of July. On Aug. 5th, the company received an e-mail from the buyer asking them to ship the goods immediately and promising to have the L/C opened in two days. The seller booked shipping space and received the credit on Aug. 10th. Upon examination, Zhejiang ABC Company found some discrepancies and wrote to Canada Trade Company on the same day asking them to amend the L/C. They promised to amend the credit immediately but ask the seller to ship the goods as scheduled. The seller shipped the goods on Aug. 13th and received the amendment to the L/C two days later. Unfortunately, the amendment still did not agree with the contract terms. How would you settle the problem if you were the exporter?

11.1.3 Applying for the Inspection of the Goods
申请商品检验

All goods required by the law or regulations or the contract to be inspected by China Import & Export Commodity Inspection Bureau should be presented to the Bureau for inspection when they are ready. For the goods that have passed the inspection, the Bureau issues an inspection certificate, which is the evidence to the customs for release.

For the goods without compulsory inspection requirements, random checks are performed by the inspection organizations in order to assure the quality of the export goods.

法律、法规或合同规定要检验的货物必须在备妥后由中国进出口商品检验局检验。对通过检验的货物，商检局出具检验证书，海关凭以放行。

无需法定检验的商品，商检机构进行随机抽检以保证出口货物的品质。

中华人民共和国出入境检验检疫
出境货物报验单

报检单位(加盖公章)　　　　　　　　　　　　　　　*编号_____

报检单位登记号：　　　　联系人：　　　电话：　　　报检日期：　　年　月　日

发货人	(中文)					
	(外文)					
收货人	(中文)					
	(外文)					

货物名称(中外文)	HS 编码	产地		数量/重量	货物总值	包装种类及数量

运输工具名称号码		贸易方式		货物存放地点	
合同号		信用证号		用途	
发货日期		输往国家(地区)		许可证/审批号	
启运地		到达口岸		生产单位注册号	

集装箱规格、数量及号码

合同、信用证订立的检验检疫条款或特殊要求	标记及号码	随附单据(划√或补填)	
		□合同	□包装性能结果单
		□信用证	□许可/审批文件
		□发票	□
		□换证凭单	□
		□装箱单	□
		□厂检单	□

需要证单名称(划√或补填)		检验检疫费	
□品质证书　　__正__副	□植物检疫证书　　__正__副	总金额(人民币元)	
□重量证书　　__正__副	□熏蒸/消毒证书　　__正__副	计费人	
□数量证书　　__正__副	□出境货物换证凭单__正__副		
□兽医卫生证书__正__副	□出境货物通关单　__正__副		
□健康证书　　__正__副		收费人	
□卫生证书　　__正__副			
□动物卫生证书__正__副			

报检人郑重声明：	领取证单	
1. 本人被授权报检。	日期	
2. 上列填写内容正确属实，货物无伪造或冒用他人的厂名、标志、认证标志，并承担货物质量责任。 　　　　　　　　签名：_____	签名	

注：有"*"号栏由出入境检验检疫机构填写。

中华人民共和国出入境检验检疫
出境货物通关单

1. 发货人			5. 标记及号码	
2. 收货人				
3. 合同号/信用证号		4. 输往国家或地区		
6. 运输工具名称及号码		7. 发货日期	8. 集装箱规格及日期	
9. 货物名称及规格	10. HS 编码	11. 申报总值	12. 数量/重量，包装数量及种类	

13. 证明

上述货物业经检验检疫，请海关予以放行

本通关单有效期至　　　　年　　月　　日

签字：　　　　　　　　　　　　　　　　　日期：　　年　月　日

14. 备注

11.1.4 Obtaining Official Documents
申请官方文件

Before arranging a contract, an exporter should learn about the export policy, rules and regulations concerning the exported goods and ensure whether he needs or should obtain the export license from the government.

Every country imposes import duties on the imported goods, the rate of which is based on the origin of goods. So the exporter should obtain certificate of origin for the goods from relevant government authorities. For finished or semi-finished products exported to developed countries, GSP Form A should be obtained.

在签订合同前，出口商必须了解本国的出口政策及法律法规并了解其出口货物是否需要出口许可证等。

任何国家都会对其进口产品征收进口关税，原产国不同，税率也不同。因此，出口商需从有关当局签发原产地证书，对出口到发达国家的工业制成品或半制成品，还需签发普惠制原产地证书格式 A。

中华人民共和国出口许可证申请表

1. 出口商：　　　　　代码： 领证人姓名：　　　　电话：	3. 出口许可证号：				
2. 发货人：　　　　　代码：	4. 出口许可证有效截止日期： 　　　　　　　　年　　月　　日				
5. 贸易方式：	8. 进口国(地区)：				
6. 合同号：	9. 付款方式：				
7. 报关口岸：	10. 运输方式：				
11. 商品名称：　　　　　　　　　　　　　　　　商品编码：					
12. 规格、等级	13. 单位	14. 数量	15. 单价(币别)	16. 总值(币别)	17. 总值折美元
18. 总　计					
19. 备　注 　　　　　　　　　申请单位盖章 申领日期：	20. 签证机构审批(初审)： 　　　　　　　经办人： 终审：				

填表说明：1. 本表应用正楷逐项填写清楚，不得涂改、遗漏，否则无效。

　　　　　2. 本表内容需打印多份许可证的，请在备注栏内注明。

　　　　　3. 本表填写一式两份。

中华人民共和国出口许可证
EXPORT LICENCE OF THE PEOPLE'S REPUBLIC OF CHINA

出口商: 编码: Exporter	出口许可证号: Export Licence No.
发货人: 编码: Consignor	出口许可证有效截止日期: Export Licence Expire Date
贸易方式: Terms of Trade	进口国（地区）: Country/Region of Importation
合同号: Contract No.	付款方式: Terms of Payment
报关口岸: Port of Clearance	运输方式: Means of Transport
商品名称: Description of Goods	商品编码: Code of Goods

规格、等级: Specifications	单位: Unit	数量: Quantity	单价: Unit Price	总值: Amount	总值折美元: Amount in USD
总 计: Total					

备 注: Supplementary Details	发证机关盖章: Issuing Authority's Stamp & Signature
	发证日期: Licence Date

普惠制原产地证书
申请书

申请单位：   证书号：

注册号：

申请人郑重申明：

　　本人被正式授权代表本企业办理和签署本申请书。

　　本申请书及普惠制原产地证格式 A 所列内容正确无误，如发现弄虚作假，冒充格式 A 所列货物，擅改证书，自愿接受签发机构的处罚并承担法律责任，现将有关情况申报如下：

生产单位		生产单位联系人电话			
商品名称(中英文)		HS 编码			
商品 FOB 总值(以美元计)		发票号			
最终销售国	证书种类画"×"	加急证书		普通证书	
拟出运日期					

贸易方式和企业性质(请在适用处画"×")

正常贸易 C	来料加工 L	补偿贸易 B	中外合资 H	中外合作 Z	外商独资 D	零售 Y	展卖 M

包装数量或毛重或其他数量	

原产地标准：

本项商品系在中国生产，完全符合该给惠国给惠方案规定，原产地情况符合以下第(　)条；

(1) "P"(完全国产，未使用任何进口原材料)；

(2) "W"(含进口成分)，其 HS 税目号为_____；

(3) "F"(对加拿大出口产品，其进口成分不超过产品出厂价值的 40%)。

本批产品系：1. 直接运输从_____到_____；

　　　　　　2. 转口运输从_____中转国(地区)_____到_____。

申请人说明：

　　　　　　　　　　　　　　　　　　　　　领证人：

　　　　　　　　　　　　　　　　　　　　　电话：

　　　　　　　　　　　　　　　　　　　　　日期：

　　现提交中国出口货物商业发票副本一份，普惠制原产地证书格式 A 一正两副，以及其他附件_____份，请予审核签证。

　　注：凡含有进口成分的商品，必须按要求提交含进口成分受惠商品成本明细单。

ORIGINAL

1. Goods consigned from (the Exporter's business name, address, country)	Reference No.
	GENERALIZED SYSTEM OF PREFERENCES **CERTIFICATE OF ORIGIN** **(Combined declaration and certificate)** **FORM A** Issued in **THE PEOPLE'S REPUBLIC OF CHINA** **(COUNTRY)**
2. Goods consigned to (the Consignee's name, address, country)	
	See Notes overleaf
3. Means of transport and route (as far as known)	4. For official use

5. Item No.	6. Marks and No. of packages	7. No. and kind of packages; description of goods	8. Origin criterion (see Notes overleaf)	9. Gross weight or other quantity	10. No. and date of invoices

11. Certification	12. Declaration by the exporter
It is hereby certified, on the basis of control carried out, that the declaration by the Exporter is correct.	The undersigned hereby declares that the above details and statements are correct; that all the goods were produced in
	---
	(country)
	and that they comply with the origin requirements specified for those goods in the Generalized System of Preferences for goods exported to
	---
	(importing country)

---	Place & date, signature of authorized signatory.
Place & date, signature & stamp of certifying authority.	

11.1.5　Effecting Insurance
投保

Under CIF or CIP terms, the exporter insures the goods before shipment at his own expenses. The insurance company will issue an insurance policy or certificate if they accept the application. One consignment under different contract numbers or covered by different credits should be insured separately under different policy numbers.

For other trade terms like CFR, the seller needs to provide shipping advice to the buyer as soon as it is available in order to enable the buyer to effect insurance before shipment.

对以 CIF 或 CIP 术语成交的合同，出口商负责投保并承担保险费，如保险公司同意承保则将签发保险单或保险凭证，不同合同或不同信用证项下的同一批货物，必须分别投保。

以其他贸易术语成交的合同如 CFR，卖方需要及时向买方发送货物装运通知以利买方及时投保。

11.1.6　Going through the Customs Formalities
出口报关

Export goods should be declared to the customs for clearance before being loaded. The exporter should fill in the customs declaration forms for export goods and submit appropriate documents such as commercial invoice, packing list, export license, inspection certificate and copy of contracts. The customs will inspect the goods and decide if the cargo can be cleared through. Once the goods are cleared, shipment can be made at any time.

出口货物必须在装船前报关。出口商必须填制出口货物报关单并提交相关单据如商业发票、装箱单、检验证书及合同副本等，海关审核决定是否予以放行，货物清关后，可以在任何时间装运。

11.1.7　Making Shipment
装运

Under CFR or CIF terms, the exporter undertakes the responsibility of chartering or booking shipping space. The seller needs to charter a whole vessel if the size of the consignment is big enough, which normally is the case with bulk goods, while liner is used for other goods.

The procedure of booking space is as follows:

★　The exporter fills out a Booking Note;

在 CFR 或 CIF 术语下，出口商负责租船订舱，如果货物量大的话，需租船，大部分货物通过班轮运输。

定舱的程序如下：

★　出口商填制出口货物托运单；

★ The shipping company or freight forwarder arranges the vessel and space and issues a shipping order;

★ The exporter sends the goods to CY (Container Yard) or CFS (Container Freight Station) as instructed;

★ The exporter applies for customs clearance;

★ The captain or mate issues a mate's receipt after the shipment is loaded on board;

★ The exporter exchanges the mate's receipt for Bill of Lading.

★ 船公司或货运代理安排仓位并签发装发货单；

★ 出口商将货物送到集装箱堆场或集装箱中转站；

★ 出口商申请出口清关；

★ 货物装上船后，船长或大副签发大副收据；

★ 出口商将大副收据换取海运提单。

11.1.8　Making Documents for Negotiation
制单结汇

Documents play a vitally important role in L/C settlement. So the first thing to do for the seller after shipment is to make all the documents required by the L/C properly and punctually. The documents required mainly include the following:

★ Finance documents: bill of exchange, cheque;

★ Commercial documents: invoice, packing list, etc.;

★ Transportation documents: B/L, Railway Bill, etc.;

★ Insurance documents: insurance policy, insurance certificate, etc.;

★ Official documents: C/O (Certificate of Origin), GSP Form A, E/L (Export License), certificate of inspection, etc.;

★ Other documents: beneficiary's declaration, shipping advice, etc.

The principle for documentation is: correctness, completeness, punctuality, conciseness and clarity. All the documents presented should be in strict compliance with the L/C terms and with each other. The seller should submit the documents to banks for negotiation within the presentation period and the expiry date of the L/C.

在信用证支付方式下，单据起着非常重要的作用。因此，出口商在装运货物后应立即将信用证要求的单据备妥，信用证下所需单据主要包含以下几类：

★ 金融单据：汇票、支票；

★ 商业单据：发票、装箱单等；

★ 运输单据：提单、铁路运单等；

★ 保险单据：保险单、保险凭证等；

★ 官方单据：原产地证书、普惠制原产地证书格式 A、检验证书等；

★ 其他单据：受益人证明、装运通知等。

制单的要求是：正确、完整、准时、简明和清楚。提交的所有单据必须做到单证相符、单单相符。卖方必须在交单期和信用证的有效期内向银行交单议付。

Case Study

In April 12th, 2012, a bank in Hong Kong, China established a Letter of Credit to the amount of US$16,000.00 for shipment in August, the date of expiry was Sept. 15th, 2012. The L/C stipulated in the additional clause that all the documents must bear the L/C No.

On Sept. 10th, 2012, the beneficiary presented the documents with all the documents bearing the L/C No. except the packing list. The negotiating bank did not find the discrepancy and sent the documents to the issuing bank for reimbursement. On the same day, the reimbursing bank, i.e. the New York branch of the issuing bank credited the negotiating bank's account with US$16,000.00. However, four days later, the issuing bank telexed its refusal of payment, claiming "nonconformity" between the document and the L/C.

Questions:

1. Is the issuing bank's refusal of payment reasonable? Why?

2. What is the crux of the case? Which party should be virtually responsible for the discrepancies in the documents?

3. In making the international settlements, banks only accept documents which are free from any discrepancy but must be in conformity with each other. Is this an international practice?

11.1.9 Settling the Proceeds of the Goods 结算货款

Three ways are employed to settle the proceeds of the goods under negotiable L/C practice in China: settlement on receipt, periodical settlement and bill purchase.

★ **Settlement on Receipt**

After examination of the documents presented by the beneficiary, if the negotiating bank can find no discrepancy, he will send the documents to foreign paying bank (normally the issuing bank) for payment. Upon receipt of the credit note from the paying bank, the negotiating bank will convert foreign exchange into RMB at the prevailing exchange rate and credit the amount into the beneficiary's account.

★ **Periodical Settlement**

The negotiating bank set out a fixed date of settlement according to an estimation of the payment date from the paying bank.

在我国，出口结汇主要有三种方式：收妥结汇、定期结汇和押汇。

★ 收妥结汇

议付行收到出口商的单据后，经审核无误，将单据寄到国外付款行（一般为开证行）索取货款。在收到该行的贷记通知书时，议付行按照当日的外汇牌价，将货款折合成人民币拨入出口商账户。

★ 定期结汇

议付行根据向国外付款行索偿所需时间，预先确定一个固定的结汇日期。

★　**Bill Purchased**

The negotiating bank buys the bill of exchange and the whole set of negotiation documents from the beneficiary on the condition that the documents contain no mistakes. The amount to be paid to the beneficiary equals to the face value less than the interest and fees from the negotiating date to the estimated paying date. The negotiating bank becomes the owner of the bill of exchange with the whole set of documents and claims payment from the paying bank. This is to provide the beneficiary with better cash flow.

★　押汇

议付行在审单无误的情况下从受益人手中买入汇票及整套单据，其所付金额为汇票票面金额扣除从议付日到估计收到票款之日的利息。议付行买入汇票后即成为汇票持有人，可凭票向付款行索取票款。这是为了给出口商提供资金融通的便利。

11.1.10　Collection Verification
收汇核销

In China, the system of collection verification is designed to follow the foreign currency income of every export transaction to assure its safe income. The procedures for collection verification are:

★　Apply for the blank Foreign Currency Verification and Cancellation Form from the Foreign Currency Administration Bureau before shipment;

★　Fill out the form with necessary information;

★　Submit the form with other documents for customs declaration;

★　Upon receipt of the payment, verify the collection with the Foreign Currency Administration Bureau.

中国的收汇核销制度是为了跟踪每一笔出口交易，确保安全收汇。收汇核销程序如下：

★　装运前向外汇管理局申领空白的出口收汇核销单；

★　填写相关内容；

★　出口报关时，与其他单据一起交给海关；

★　收到货款后，向外管局核销。

11.1.11　Export Drawback
出口退税

In order to encourage export, Chinese government grants export drawback to exporters at different rates according to the variety of goods. Only goods which have been imposed tax can enjoy export drawback after being exported. The tax department is responsible for the export drawback. The exporter can apply to the department with the relevant documents after collection verification.

为了鼓励出口，中国政府按不同的产品给予不同的退税。只有征过税的商品才能在出口后得以退税，税务局负责出口退税工作，出口商应在收汇核销后办理出口退税事宜。

11.2　General Procedures of Import Transactions
进口合同的履行

The performance of an import contract includes the following procedures: applying for the import license or foreign exchange, arranging for the establishment of the L/C, effecting shipment, arranging insurance, paying against the documents, clearing import customs, taking delivery of the goods, having the goods inspected and lodging a claim if any.

进口合同的履行包含以下环节：申领进口许可证或外汇、申请开立信用证、装运货物、安排保险、付款赎单、进口报关、提货、报检以及索赔等。

11.2.1　Applying for the Import License or Foreign Exchange
申请进口许可证或外汇

In order to regulate domestic market, many countries use import license and foreign exchange authorization system. China is of no exception. The importer should first apply for the import license or foreign exchange from the relevant authorities by filling out in the application forms together with the proforma invoice issued by the exporter. Therefore, the importers will not open the L/C until the relevant licenses and foreign currencies are obtained. The purpose is to control the inflow of foreign goods to protect domestic industries, or to maintain the trade balance,etc.

为了规范国内市场，很多国家都实行申领进口许可证和外汇制度，中国也不例外。进口商必须填写相关申请书，连同出口商的形式发票向相关部门申请进口许可证或外汇。因此，进口商必须在获得进口许可证和外汇后才能申请开立信用证。此举的目的在于控制进口商品的数量以保护国内工业、保持贸易平衡等。

11.2.2　Arranging for the Establishment and Amendment of the L/C
安排开证和改证

Under the L/C practice, the importer should take the initiative in opening the L/C within the time limit stipulated in the contract. An application form should be filled in by the importer to request his bank to establish a documentary credit in favor of the exporter.

If the bank agrees to open the L/C for the importer, a certain percentage of the credit amount as margin from the applicant will be required.

如以信用证方式支付，进口商应主动在合同规定的时间内申请开立信用证，进口商需填写开证申请书向银行申请开立以出口商为受益人的信用证。

如果银行同意开立信用证，进口商需支付信用证金额的一定比例作为押金。

Usually the exporter will be advised of the opening of the credit well before shipment so that he can have enough time to examine the details contained in the credit. If any discrepancies with the contract terms are found, the exporter will inform the importer of the discrepancies. The importer should instruct the issuing bank to amend the credit accordingly without delay. The amendment to the L/C should be advised through the same bank as the original L/C.

信用证必须在装运前到达出口方以便其有足够的时间审核，如果出口商发现信用证条款与合同不符，他将通知进口商，进口商必须立即指示其银行进行修改，信用证的修改通知书须由原通知行转递。

开立不可撤销跟单信用证申请书
APPLICATION FOR IRREVOCABLE DOCUMENTARY CREDIT

Date 日期 _____

To: 致:

Please issue by SWIFT an Irrevocable Letter of Credit as follows:
请通过 SWIFT 方式开立如下不可撤销跟单信用证:

Advising Bank (if blank, at your option) 通知行	Credit No.信用证号码
	Expiry Date and Place 到期日和到期地点
Applicant （full name & detailed address）申请人（全称和详细地址）	Beneficiary (with full name and address) 受益人（全称和详细地址）
Amount (in figures & words) 金额（大、小写）	Credit available with 此证可由 □any bank 任何银行 □issuing bank 开证行 By □ sight payment 即期付款 □acceptance 承兑 □ negotiation 议付 □ deferred payment 延期付款
Partial shipments 分批装运 □ allowed 允许 □ not allowed 不允许 Transshipment 转运 □ allowed 允许 □ not allowed 不允许	Draft at_____ for_____ % of invoice value 汇票付款期限_____，发票金额的_____ % Drawn on 付款人 _____
Shipment from 装运从	For transportation to 运至 Latest shipment date 最迟装运日

Documents required: (marked with "✕") 所需单据（用"✕"标明）：

Signed Commercial Invoice in _____ copies indicating L/C No. and Contract No.

经签字的商业发票一式_____份，标明信用证号和合同号

Full set of clean on board Ocean Bill of Lading □ made out to order and □ blank endorsed,

marked □ freight prepaid / □ to collect □ showing freight amount and notifying _____

全套清洁已装船海运提单做成 □空白抬头 □空白背书，注明"运费 □ 已付/ □ 到付"，

□标明运费金额，并通知_____

Air Waybills consigned to applicant marked "freight □ prepaid / □to collect" notifying

_____

空运单据收货人为开证申请人，注明"运费□已付/□待付"，并通知

_____

Full set of Insurance Policy / Certificate for _____ % of the invoice value, blank endorsed, showing claims

payable in China in the currency of the draft, covering

□ ocean marine transportation □ air transportation

□ overland transportation, All risks and War risks and

_____

全套保险单/保险凭证，按发票金额的 _____%投保，空白背书，注明赔付地在中国，以汇票币种支

付，覆盖□海运 □空运 □陆运，承保一切险，战争险和

_____

Packing List in _____ copies indicating quantity, gross and net weight of each package.

装运单一式_____份，注明每一包装的数量、毛重和净重。

Certificate of Quantity / Weight in _____ copies issued by_____

数量 / 重量证明一式_____份，由_____出具

Certificate of Quality in_____copies issued by_____ 品质证一式 ____ 份，由_____出具。

Certificate of Origin in_____ copies issued by _____

产地证一式_____份，由_____出具

Beneficiary's Certified copy of fax / telex dispatched to the applicant within _____day(s) after shipment

advising □L/C No., □name of vessel, □flight No. □shipping date ,

□name of goods, quantity, □weight and value of goods.

受益人传真/电传方式通知申请人装船证明副本。该证明须在装船后_____天内发出，并注明

□信用证号、□船名、□航班号、□装运日、

□货物的名称、□货物的数量、□重量和货物价值。

Other documents, if any 其他单据

Description of goods or services 货物或服务描述

Additional instructions: 附加条款

All banking charges outside the Issuing Bank are for account of Beneficiary.

开证行以外的所有银行费用由受益人承担。

Documents must be presented within _____ days after date of issuance of the transport document but within the validity of the credit.

所需单据须在运输单据签发日后_____天内提交，但不得超过信用证有效期。

Third party as shipper is not acceptable. 第三方为托运人不可接受。

Both quantity and Credit amount _____ % more or less are allowed.

数量及信用证金额允许有_____%的增减。

Other terms and conditions, if any 其他条款

申请人盖章

11.2.3 Effecting Shipment
安排运输

Under FOB term, the importer is responsible for arranging shipment. The exporter should inform the importer of the time the goods get ready to enable him to book shipping space. Special care should be taken to the time the seller can make delivery and the time the buyer arranges to load on board the vessel he has booked. They should match with each other to avoid extra charges such as demurrage fees, etc.

In usual practice, the buyer authorizes the seller to arrange shipment with the carrier designated by him locally and pays for the freight for FOB transactions.

FOB 贸易术语下，进口商负责运输事宜，但出口商必须将货物备妥的时间告诉进口商以便其订舱。应该注意的是，卖方交货的时间和买方装船的时间要衔接好以免产生一些如滞期费等的额外费用。

在实际业务中，买方通常会委托卖方将货交到其指定的承运人那里并付运费。

11.2.4　Arranging Insurance
投保

Under the terms of CFR, FOB, FCA or CPT, the buyer should arrange insurance by himself. People's Insurance Company of China is the compulsory insurer for China's imports and exports. The buyer should apply to the insurance company before time of shipment for insurance by filling out the application form that contains the following details:

★　Description of the goods;

★　Name of the vessel;

★　B/L No.;

★　Package numbers;

★　Risks and amount to be covered;

★　ETA and ETD;

★　Port of loading and port of destination.

Once the goods are insured, the insurance company will bear all risks that occur within the set conditions.

For transactions under CFR and CPT, special attention should be paid by the seller to send shipping advice to the buyer to enable him to effect insurance before shipment. Otherwise, the seller should bear any losses thus occur.

The importers doing large volume of business often use open policies. An open policy provides coverages for all goods shipped by the insured while the policy is in effect. The imports & exports of the insured are automatically covered with pre-agreement of the insurer.

在 CFR、FOB、FCA 或 CPT 贸易术语下，买方负责保险。在中国，所有的进出口货物都必须由中国人民保险公司承保。买方需在货物装运前填写投保单，向保险公司办理保险手续，投保单内容如下：

★　货物名称；

★　船名；

★　提单号；

★　件数；

★　投保金额和险别；

★　预计到达时间和预计离港时间；

★　装运港和目的港。

货物一旦被保险，保险公司就承担保险责任范围内的一切风险。

如果是以 CFR 和 CPT 成交的，卖方一定要及时给买方发出装运通知以便其在装运前办理保险手续，否则，卖方将承担一切由此引起的损失。

进口量大时，进口商通常采用预约保险的方法。按约定，在预约保险单的有效期内，保险公司对被保险人所进口的货物自动承保。

中国人民保险公司杭州分公司
国外运输险投保单

兹将我处出口物资依照信用证规定拟向你处投保国外运输险计开：

被保险人	（中文）	过户	
	（英文）		

标记或发票号码	件数	物资名称	保险金额

运输工具(及运载工具)		约于　年　月　日启运	赔款偿付地点
运输路程	自　经　到	转载地点	

要保险别：	投保单位签章
	年　月　日

SHIPPING ADVICE

Dear Sirs,

Re: Invoice No. XXXX, L/C No. XXXX

We hereby inform you that the goods under the above mentioned credit have been shipped. The details of shipment are as follows:

Commodity: Quantity:

Ocean Vessel: Bill of Lading No.:

Container /Seal No.:   E.T.D.:

E.T.A.:

We hereby certify that the above content is true and correct.

(Signature)

11.2.5 Paying against the Documents
付款赎单

Under L/C practice, the shipper will draw on the paying bank and present all the documents required to the negotiating bank soon after shipment. The paying bank will pay for the documents if the bank confirms that all documents are in strict conformity with the L/C. Then the bank will notify the applicant to make payment and get the documents. If the applicant can find no discrepancies upon further examination, he should make payment in the pre-agreed manner.

If the paying bank finds discrepancies in the documents, he will contact the applicant within 5 working days for decision. The decisions are:

★ Refuse to pay;

★ Pay partially for those which comply;

★ Make payment after inspection;

★ Pay against a letter of indemnity from the seller;

★ Pay while reserving the right to claim for compensation.

在信用证支付方式下，出口商在出运货物后，向付款行开出汇票并将全套单据交给议付行。付款行收到单据后即审单，如果单证相符的话，付款行付款，然后通知开证申请人付款赎单。开证申请人审核无误后必须即按约定的方式付款。

如果付款行发现单据有不符点，他需在 5 个工作日内通知开证申请人。开证行申请人可以有以下几个选择：

★ 拒付；

★ 仅付相符部分货款；

★ 验货后再付款；

★ 凭卖方担保书付款；

★ 付款，但保留对卖方索赔的权利。

11.2.6 Having the Goods Inspected
报检

When the vessel carrying the goods arrives at the destination, the shipping company will inform the importer or his agent. The importer should apply for the inspection or quarantine for the imported goods. The whole set of documents including the contract, commercial invoice, B/L, packing list, and the arrival notice should be submitted to the Commodity Inspection Bureau at port of discharge to apply for inspection. The goods cannot be released, put into production, sold until they pass the inspection.

当载货船只到达目的港后，船公司将通知进口商或其代理人。进口商需向检验机构申请对货物进行检验检疫。报检时需向卸货港的商检局提交合同、商业发票、提单、装箱单、到货通知等单据。货物只有通过检验后才能清关、生产、出售等。

11.2.7   Clearing the Import Customs
进口清关

Like exported goods, the imported goods must be cleared through the customs, too. The importer or its authorized agent (freight forwarder or professional customs broker) should submit the necessary documents like The Customs Declaration Form for Import Goods, commercial invoice, B/L, inspection certificate and Import License, etc. The customs officer will check the goods against the documents to see whether they match each other. The check can be taken in the warehouse or at a location within the customs' domain of supervision. Bulk or dangerous cargoes can be checked alongside the ship.

和出口一样，进口货物也需清关。进口商或其代理（货运代理、专业报关经纪人）需向海关提交相关单据如进口货物报关单、商业发票、提单、检验证书、进口许可证等。海关将验货以确保货物和单据相符，海关验货可以在仓库或者在其监管范围内的地点。散装货或危险品可以在船边验货。

11.2.8   Taking Delivery of the Goods
提货

After the goods are cleared and import duties are imposed, the importer can now take delivery of the goods from the carrier according to the set procedure against shipping documents, especially the bill of lading, which represents the ownership of the goods.

在办理了进口报关、交纳了进口关税后，进口商可以凭装运单据，特别是提单(物权凭证)，向承运人提货。

11.2.9   Lodging a Claim (If Any)
索赔

After inspection, if problems such as short delivery, inferior quality or wrong shipment are found and attributed to the exporter, the importer should lodge claims against the exporter. If the loss or damage is due to the negligence of the carrier, the claim should be made against the carrier. If the loss or damage has been caused by risks that are covered by insurance, the claim should be made against the underwriter.

Claims should be filed within the time limit stipulated in the contract. The following documents should be presented to support the claim:

验货后，如进口商发现出口商短交、货物质量低劣或发错货等，他可以向出口商提出索赔。如果损失是由承运人的责任造成的，则需向承运人提出索赔。如果损失是在保险公司的承保范围内的，则向保险公司提出索赔。

索赔需在合同规定的时间内进行，还需提交以下单据作为证明材料：

★	Claim breakdown list;		★	索赔清单;
★	Inspection certificate;		★	检验报告;
★	Copy of B/L;		★	提单副本
★	Commercial invoice;		★	商业发票;
★	Packing list;		★	装箱单;
★	Insurance policy.		★	保险单。

The following is a specimen letter lodging a claim:　　　　**以下是一封索赔信:**

Dear Sirs,

S.S. "Blue Sky" – Rice

Referring to our letter of March 10th, 2012, in connection with the rice under Contract No. AB123 shipped per S.S. "Blue Sky". After the goods were discharged at Shanghai, we found that there is a short-weight of 1,236 m/ts and therefore we are now lodging claims with you as follows:

Claim No.	Claim for	Amount
DA01	short-weight	US$1,200.00
DA02	quality	US$1,500.00
	Total amount	US$2,700.00

In order to support our claims, we are sending you herewith one copy each of Inspection Certificate Nos. SCIB101 and SCIB102 together with our Statement of Claims which amount to US$2,700.

Please give our claim your most favorable consideration and let us have your settlement at an early date.

Yours faithfully,

敬启者:

事由: "Blue Sky"船——大米

请参阅我方 2012 年 3 月 10 日的信函,有关第 AB123 号合同项下的大米已经由 "Blue Sky" 轮装运。货物在上海港卸下后,我们发现重量少了 1 236 公吨,特向贵方提出索赔如下:

索赔号	索赔原因	索赔金额
DA01	短重	US$1,200.00
DA02	质量问题	US$1,500.00
总计		US$2,700.00

我们随函附上商检证明第 SCIB10 和 SCIB102 号以及我们的索赔清单,计 2 700 美元整。

请考虑我方索赔并尽早答复。

祝　商安

Exercises

I. 术语翻译

议付	分批装运
交单期	货物所有权
工作日	保函
预约保险	外汇核销
出口报关	出口退税
装运单据	违约

II. 填空

1. 在国际贸易中，_____负责审核信用证的真伪，_____审核信用证的条款。
2. 对信用证进行修改的申请必须通过_____交给开证行，而信用证的修改通知书必须通过_____传递给受益人。
3. 货物装运后，托运人用_____向船公司换取提单。
4. 我国出口结汇的方法有三种：_____、_____、_____。
5. 如果信用证的修改通知包含数项内容，受益人必须_____或_____。
6. 在 CFR 条件下，卖方必须及时向买方发出_____，以便买方在装运前办理保险。
7. 如信用证上未规定交单期，按 UCP600，受益人必须在装运后_____天内向银行交单。
8. 如信用证上装运期和有效期是同一天，该信用证被称为_____信用证。

III. 单项选择题

1. 出口报关的时间应是(　　　)。
   A. 备货前　　　　　　B. 装船前　　　　　C. 装船后　　　　　D. 货到目的地后
2. 一份 CIF 合同下，合同和信用证均未规定投保何种险别，交单时保险单上显示投保了平安险，该商品为玻璃杯，其他单据与信用证相符。因此(　　　)。
   A. 银行将拒收单据　　　　　　　　　B. 买方将拒收单据
   C. 买方应接受单据　　　　　　　　　D. 银行应接受单据
3. 审核信用证的依据是(　　　)。
   A. 合同及 UCP600 的规定　　　　　　B. 一整套单据
   C. 开证申请书　　　　　　　　　　　D. 商业发票
4. 如果合同只规定了最后装运期而未规定信用证的开立时间，那么买方应在合理时间内开证。按惯例，信用证的开立时间为(　　　)。

A. 装船期开始的第一天   B. 投保日期的次日

C. 签订买卖合同的次日   D. 装运前 15—30 天开抵卖方

5. 除非信用证另有规定，在所支付的款项不超过信用证金额的条件下，货物数量允许有( )的增减。但信用证规定的数量以包装件数或以个数计数时，此项增减幅度则不适用。

 A. 10%   B. 5%   C. 3%   D. 2%

6. 买方按时( )是卖方履行合同的前提。

 A. 租船定舱 B. 开立信用证 C. 投保   D. 支付货款

7. 进口企业审核单据时，处于中心位置的单据是( )。

 A. 进口许可证 B. 商业发票 C. 商品检验证书 D. 进口报关单

8. 向出口方提出索赔时，以下索赔依据中不必出具的是( )。

 A. 提单   B. 装箱单   C. 发票   D. 保险单

9. 信用证方式下付款，审核进口货物单据的部门是( )。

 A. 进口企业   B. 开证银行和进口企业

 C. 开证银行   D. 开证银行、进口企业和保险公司

10. 在进出口贸易中，信用证的开证申请书由( )开立。

 A. 出口方 B. 进口方 C. 出口方银行 D. 进口方银行

IV. 判断题

( ) 1. In import & export trade, the basic obligation for the seller is to provide the buyer with the goods which comply with the requirements in the contract.

( ) 2. The mate's receipt is a temporary receipt issued by the shipping company to the shipper as a proof that the consignment has been loaded onto the ship.

( ) 3. For T/T before shipment, the B/L, commercial invoice and packing list should be sent to the buyer through the bank for payment.

( ) 4. If the seller fails to make shipment within the time of validity of the inspection certificate, he can request that the validity of the inspection certificate be extended automatically.

( ) 5. The importer may refuse to pay if there are any discrepancies in the negotiation documents.

( ) 6. In credit operation, the bank deals with documents and not with the goods. Any discrepancies may cause refusal to payment.

( ) 7. If the L/C states the latest shipment date as Apr. 30th and expiry date May 15th. The beneficiary shipped the goods on Apr. 12th and submitted the document to the negotiating bank on May 6th. The bank should pay out according to UCP 600.

( ) 8. A clean B/L shows that the goods on board are in good condition.

( ) 9. The expiry date in an L/C is the date for the seller to receive payment.

( ) 10. For unacceptable clauses in an L/C, the seller should contact the issuing bank directly for amendment.

V. 案例分析

1. 我某公司与欧洲某客户达成一笔圣诞礼品的出口交易。合同规定以 CIF 为交货条件，交货期为 2012 年 3 月 31 日以前，但合同未规定信用证的开证日期。卖方于 3 月初开始向买方催促，经过多次催促，买方信用证于 3 月 25 日到达卖方，由于收到信用证的时间较晚，我方于 4 月 5 日才将货物装运完毕，当我方向银行提交单据时，遭到银行拒付。请问：(1)银行的拒付是否有理？(2)此案中，我方有哪些失误？

2. 我国某公司收到国外买方开来的即期不可撤销信用证，证中规定装运期不得晚于 2012 年 2 月 15 日，我方因舱位紧缺，无法如期装运，于 2 月 6 日电请买方将装运期和有效期同时延展 15 天。2 月 10 日我方接买方来电同意我方要求。接电后，我方立即安排装运，于 2 月 20 日装船完毕并于 23 日备齐整套单据向银行交单议付，但银行拒绝收单。请问：银行拒收是否合理？为什么？

3. 我国某进口商与斯里兰卡某出口商在签订的合同中约定以 FOB Colombo 价格条件购买波纹绸，合同价款共计 100 万美元。但在产品接受出口检验时被发现其中混有不合格产品，约占 19%，卖方未处理即装船出口。因为合同中规定不合格率不得超过 10%，故我方收到货物后要求卖方给予降价处理。请问：(1)买方这样做是否符合公约规定？(2)我方要卖方赔偿，该准备哪些单据？

CHAPTER 12

Trade Forms
贸易方式

Focus

In this chapter, you will learn:

- ✧ Agency;
- ✧ Distribution;
- ✧ Consignment;
- ✧ Tenders;
- ✧ Auction.

International trade forms refer to the common practices and channels between countries for the flow of commodities or services. It includes the specific forms of import & export transaction or various ways of transaction. Unilateral import & export are the commonly used business methods. In the current international trade there are various ways of trade forms such as agency, distribution, consignment, tenders, barter-trade, compensation trade, technology transfer, technology licensing and joint venture, etc.

对外贸易方式是指对外贸易经营的方式，包括进出口交易的具体形式或所使用的各种具有不同特点的交易方法。单边进口和单边出口是市场间普遍采用的经营方式。当前国际贸易中，贸易方式多种多样，如代理、经销、寄售、招标和投标、易货贸易、补偿贸易、技术转让、技术许可和合资等。

12.1　Agency　代理

In commercial circles, agency is usually contracted between the two parties, a principal and an agent, the latter being authorized to act under the control and on behalf of the former on a commission basis in business transactions with a third party. In foreign trade, a seller in the name of a principal may authorize an agent abroad to push his goods and complete business. When an order is placed, a sales contract is generally concluded between the seller and the buyer, and the agent is given by the principal a certain amount of commission in reward for his work done in accordance with the agency agreement between them. In this respect the agent is a commission agent, who, in reality, merely live on commission basis without bearing any losses.

代理是指代理人根据委托人的授权，代表委托人与第三人订立合同或实施其他法律行为。在对外贸易中，卖方可以以委托人的身份授权其在国外的代理代销商品。当买卖双方订立合同后，卖方通常会根据其与代理之间的代理协议，给代理一定的佣金作为报酬，这种代理叫佣金代理，他只赚取佣金而不负责盈亏。

12.1.1　Commission Agent
佣金代理

A commission agent is an agent specializing in buying or selling goods for a principal in another country for a commission. Such agents always execute the orders given by a principal to buy or to sell goods on payment of a fee or a commission based on the value of the deal. In international

佣金代理专为另一国的委托人买卖货物而获取佣金。这种代理执行委托人的指令销售或者购买商品，并按照交易的金额提取佣金。国际贸易有的进口代理和出口

trade practice, there are import & export agents. Export agents make arrangements for exporting the goods. They arrange transport, obtain insurance cover and see that all the documents are complete and in order while import agents make all the arrangements to receive goods for importing firms.

代理两种。出口代理代表出口商销售货物,他们安排货物运输、保险、制单等事宜,而进口代理则为进口商提供购货服务。

12.1.2　General Agent
　　　　总代理

A general agent is an agent who is authorized to do all the acts related to the principal's business, which may include negotiating contracts, establishing credit, arranging for shipping and setting up overseas offices and outlets.

总代理可以作为委托人的全权代表从事销售活动,如交易磋商、开立信用证、安排装运以及建立海外分支机构或经销店等。

12.1.3　Sole Agent
　　　　独家代理

Sole agency is also called exclusive agency. He is entitled to an exclusive right to sell the designated goods for the principal in a specified area within a stated period of time. Once a sole agent is appointed, the principal is no longer in a position to sell directly or indirectly the same kind of goods to any other buyers in that specified area within the validity of the sole agency agreement. In this sense, it is understood that if there is any sales of the goods made through others in that area the sole agent is entitled to a commission though the business is not canvassed through him. And, equally, before the termination of the sole agency agreement the sole agent is obliged not to sell any similar or competitive goods from other sources in that particular area.

独家代理在特定地区和一定期限内,对指定的商品享有专营权。一旦签订了独家代理协议,委托人在协议的有效期内,不得在以上范围内自行或通过其他代理人进行销售,并且委托人自己不能越过独家代理直接向该地区投入指定商品。也就是说,若委托人要与指定地区的买主直接交易,他仍要向独家代理支付约定的佣金。同样,在协议的有效期内,独家代理人在该地区也不能销售类似或者是其他竞争对手的商品。

独家代理协议

Exclusive Agency Agreement

本协议于_____年___月___日在_____(地点)由有关双方在平等互利的基础上达成，按双方同意的下列条件发展业务关系：

This agreement is made and entered into by and between the parties concerned on _____ (Date) in _____ (Place) on the basis of equality and mutual benefit to develop business on terms and conditions mutually agreed upon as follows:

1. 协议双方 The Parties Concerned

甲方：_____	乙方：_____
Party A：_____	Party B：_____
地址：_____	地址：_____
Add：_____	Add：_____
电话：_____	电话：_____
Tel：_____	Tel：_____
传真：_____	传真：_____
Fax：_____	Fax：_____

2. 委任 Appointment

甲方指定乙方为其独家代理，为第三条所列商品从第四条所列区域的顾客中招揽订单，乙方接受上述委任。

Party A hereby appoints Party B as its Exclusive Agent to solicit orders for the commodity stipulated in Article 3 from customers in the territory stipulated in Article 4, and Party B accepts and assumes such an appointment.

3. 代理商品 Commodity

4. 代理区域 Territory

仅限于_____(比如：中国)

In _____ (for example: China) only.

5. 最低业务量 Minimum turnover

乙方同意，在本协议有效期内从上述代理区域内的顾客处招揽的上述商品的订单价值不低于_____美元。

Party B shall undertake to solicit orders for the above commodity from customers in the above territory during the effective period of this agreement for not less than US$_____.

6. 价格与支付 Price and Payment

每一笔交易的货物价格应由乙方与买主通过谈判确定，并须经甲方最后确认。

付款使用保兑的、不可撤销的信用证，由买方开出，以甲方为受益人。信用证须在装运日期前_____天到达甲方。

The price for each individual transaction shall be fixed through negotiations between Party B and the buyer, and subject to Party A's final confirmation.

Payment shall be made by confirmed, irrevocable L/C opened by the buyer in favor of Party A, which shall reach Party A _____ days before the date of shipment.

7. 独家代理权 Exclusive Right

基于本协议授予的独家代理权，甲方不得直接或间接地通过乙方以外的渠道向中国顾客销售或出口第三条所列商品，乙方不得在中国经销、分销或促销与上述商品相竞争或类似的产品，也不得招揽或接受以到中国以外地区销售为目的的订单，在本协议有效期内，甲方应将其收到的来自中国其他商家的有关代理产品的询价或订单转交给乙方。

In consideration of the exclusive rights granted herein, Party A shall not, directly or indirectly, sell or export the commodity stipulated in Article 4 to customers in China through channels other than Party B; Party B shall not sell, distribute or promote the sales of any products competitive with or similar to the above commodity in China and shall not solicit or accept orders for the purpose of selling them outside China. Party A shall refer to Party B any enquiries or orders for the commodity in question received by Party A from other firms in China during the validity of this agreement.

8. 商情报告 Market Report

为使甲方充分了解现行市场情况，乙方承担至少每季度一次或在必要时随时向甲方提供市场报告，内容包括与本协议代理商品的进口与销售有关的地方规章的变动、当地市场发展趋势以及买方对甲方按协议供应的货物的品质、包装、价格等方面的意见。乙方还承担向甲方提供其他供应商类似商品的报价和广告资料。

In order to keep Party A well-informed of the prevailing market conditions, Party B should undertake to supply Party A, at least once a quarter or at any time when necessary, with market reports concerning changes of the local regulations in connection with the import and sales of the commodity covered by this agreement, local market tendency and the buyer's comments on quality, packing, price, etc. of the goods supplied by Party A under this agreement. Party B shall also supply Party A with quotations and advertising materials on similar products of other suppliers.

9. 广告及费用 Advertising and Expenses

乙方负担本协议有效期内在中国销售代理商品做广告宣传的一切费用，并向甲方提交所用于广告的声像资料，供甲方事先核准。

Party A shall bear all the expenses for advertising and publicity in connection with the commodity in China within the validity of this agreement, and shall submit to Party A all the audio and video materials intended for advertising for prior approval.

10. 佣金 Commission

对乙方直接获取并经甲方确认接受的订单,甲方按净发票售价向乙方支付___%的佣金。佣金在甲方收到每笔订单的全部货款后_____天内向乙方支付。

Party A shall pay Party B a commission of_____% on the net invoiced selling price on all orders directly obtained by Party B and accepted by Party A. Within _____days from the date Party A receives the full payment for each order, Party A shall pay the commission to Party B.

11. 政府部门间的交易 Transactions between Governmental Bodies

在甲、乙双方政府部门之间达成的交易不受本协议条款的限制,此类交易的金额也不应计入第五条规定的最低业务量。

Transactions concluded between governmental bodies of Party A and Party B shall not be restricted by the terms and conditions of this agreement, nor shall the amount of such transactions be counted as part of the turnover stipulated in Article 5.

12. 工业产权 Industrial Property Rights

在本协议有效期内,为销售有关洗衣机,乙方可以使用甲方拥有的商标,并承认使用于或包含于洗衣机中的任何专利商标、版权或其他工业产权为甲方独家拥有。一旦发现侵权,乙方应立即通知甲方并协助甲方采取措施保护甲方权益。

Party B may use the trade-marks owned by Party A for the sale of the Washing Machines covered herein within the validity of this agreement, and shall acknowledge that all patents, trademarks, copyrights or any other industrial property rights used or embodied in the Washing Machines shall remain to be the sole properties of Party A. Should any infringements be found, Party B shall promptly notify and assist Party A to take steps to protect the latter's rights.

13. 协议有效期 Validity of Agreement

本协议经有关双方如期签署后生效,有效期为_____年,从_____年___月___日至_____年___月___日。除非作出相反通知,本协议期满后将延长_____个月。

This agreement, when duly signed by the both parties concerned, shall remain effect for _____ months from _____ (date) to _____ (date), and it shall be extended for another _____ months upon expiration unless notice in writing is given to the contrary.

14. 协议的终止 Termination

在本协议有效期内,如果一方被发现违背协议条款,另一方有权终止协议。

During the validity of this agreement, if either of the two parties is found to have violated the stipulations herein, the other party has the right to terminate this agreement.

15. 不可抗力 Force Majeure

由于水灾、火灾、地震、干旱、战争或协议一方无法预见、控制、避免和克服的其他事件导致不能或暂时不能全部或部分履行本协议，该方不负责任。但是，受不可抗力事件影响的一方须尽快将发生的事件通知另一方，并在不可抗力事件发生 15 天内将有关机构出具的不可抗力事件的证明寄交对方。

Either party shall not be responsible for failure or delay to perform all or any part of this agreement due to flood, fire, earthquake, draught, war or any other events which could not be predicted, controlled, avoided or overcome by the relative party. However, the party affected by the event of Force Majeure shall inform the other party of its occurrence in writing as soon as possible and thereafter send a certificate of the event issued by the relevant authorities to the other party within 15 days after its occurrence.

16. 仲裁 Arbitration

凡因本合同引起的或与本合同有关的任何争议，均应提交中国国际经济贸易仲裁委员会华南分会，按照申请仲裁时该会实施的仲裁规则进行仲裁。仲裁裁决是终局的，对双方均有约束力。

Any dispute arising from or in connection with this contract shall be submitted to China International Economic and Trade Arbitration Commission, South China Sub-Commission for arbitration, which shall be conducted in accordance with the Commission's arbitration rules in effect at the time of applying for arbitration. The arbitral award is final and binding upon both parties.

甲方: _____   乙方: _____

(签字)   (签字)

Party A: _____   Party B: _____

       (Signature)   (Signature)

12.2 Distribution 经销

Unlike agents, distributors buy goods from the principals on their own account and take title to them and resell them to their customers in their territory. Thus, there is no contractual relationship between the principal and the ultimate consumers. The distributor takes his remuneration from the margin between the prices at which he buys the products and the prices at which he sells them to the customers. Since the distributor is an independent contractor, he assumes far more risks and obligations than an agent does.

Two kinds of distributors are generally used:

★ Sole or exclusive distributor, which means the only distributor in a territory;

★ Non-exclusive distributor. There may be several non-exclusive distributors appointed by the principal or supplier in one territory.

与代理商不同,经销商要先买下货物,拥有他们,然后再卖给他们负责经销区域内的客户。因此,最终客户和委托人之间没有直接的契约关系。经销商买下商品后再将商品卖出以赚取差价。因为经销商买断了货物,因此他比代理承担更多的风险和义务。

经销有两种方式:

★ 独家经销,又称包销,在某一地区享受独家专营权;

★ 一般经销,供货商或者委托人可以在某一地区选择几家经销商经销同一商品。

独家经销协议
Exclusive Distribution Agreement

合同号:

No.:

日期:

Date:

为在平等互利的基础上发展贸易,有关方按下列条件签订本协议:

This Agreement is entered into between the parties concerned on the basis of equality and mutual benefit to develop business on the terms and conditions mutually agreed upon as follows:

1. 订约人

Contracting Parties

供货人(以下称甲方)

Supplier: (hereinafter called "Party A")

销售代理人(以下称乙方)

Agent: (hereinafter called "Party B")

甲方委托乙方为销售代理人，推销下列商品。

Party A hereby appoints Party B to act as his selling agent to sell the commodity mentioned below.

2. 商品名称和数量或金额

Commodity and Quality or Amount

双方约定在协议有效期内，销售不少于_____的商品。

It is mutually agreed that Party B shall undertake to sell not less than _____ of the aforesaid commodity in the duration of this agreement.

3. 经销地区

Territory

只限在_____

In _____ only.

4. 订单的确认

Confirmation of Orders

本协议所规定商品的数量、价格及装运等，应在每笔交易中确认，其细目应在双方签订的销售协议书中作出规定。

The quantities, prices and shipments of the commodities stated in this Agreement shall be confirmed in each transaction, the particulars of which are to be specified in the Sales Confirmation signed by the two parties hereto.

5. 付款

Payment

订单确认之后，乙方须按照有关确认书所规定的时间开立以甲方为受益人的保兑的、不可撤销的即期信用证。一方开出信用证后，应立即通知甲方，以便甲方准备交货。

After confirmation of the order, Party B shall arrange to open a confirmed, irrevocable L/C available by draft at sight in favour of Party A within the time stipulated in the relevant S/C. Party B shall also notify Party A immediately after L/C is opened so that Party A can arrange shipment.

6. 市场情况报告

Reports on Market Conditions

乙方每三个月向甲方提供一次有关当时市场情况和用户意见的详细报告。同时，乙方应随时向甲方提供其他供应商的类似商品样品及其价格、销售情况和广告资料。

Party B shall forward once every three months to Party A the detailed reports on current market conditions and of consumers' comments. Meanwhile, Party B shall, from time to time, send to Party A samples of similar commodities offered by other suppliers, together with their prices, sales information and advertising materials.

7. 宣传广告费用

Advertising and Publicity Expenses

在本协议有效期内，乙方在上述经销地区所进行的广告宣传的一切费用，由乙方自理。乙方须事先向甲方提供宣传广告的图案及文字说明，由甲方审阅同意。

Party B shall bear all the expenses for advertising and publicity within the aforementioned territory in the duration of this Agreement and submit to Party A all patterns and/or drawings and description for prior approval.

8. 协议有效期
Validity of Agreement

本协议经双方签字后生效，有效期为_____天，自_____至_____。若一方希望延长本协议，则需在本协议期满前一个月书面通知另一方，经双方协商决定。若协议一方未履行协议条款，另一方有权终止协议。

The Agreement, after its being signed by the parties concerned, shall remain in force for _____ days from _____ to _____. If either party wishes to extend this agreement, he shall notice, in writing, the other party one month prior to its expiration. The matter shall be decided by the agreement and by consent of the parties hereto. Should either party fail to implement the terms and conditions herein, the other party is entitled to terminate this Agreement.

9. 仲裁
Arbitration

在协议履行过程中，如产生争议，双方应友好协商解决。若通过友好协商达不成协议，则提交中国国际贸易促进委员会对外贸易仲裁委员会，根据该会仲裁程序暂行规定进行仲裁。该委员会的决定是终局的，对双方均具有约束力。仲裁费用，除另有规定外，由败诉一方承担。

All disputes arising from the execution of this Agreement shall be settled through friendly negotiation. In case no settlement can be reached, the case in dispute shall then be submitted to the Foreign Trade Arbitration Commission of the China Council for the Promotion of International Trade for arbitration in accordance with its provisional rules of procedure. The award shall be regarded as final and binding on both parties. Arbitration fees shall be borne by the losing party unless otherwise stipulated.

10. 其他条款
Other Terms and Conditions

(1) 甲方不得向经销地区的其他买主供应本协议所规定的商品。如有询价，当转达给乙方洽办。若有买主希望从甲方直接订购，甲方可以供货，但甲方须将有关销售确认书副本寄给乙方，并按所达成交易的金额发票给予乙方_____%的佣金。

Party A shall not supply the contracted commodity to any other buyer(s) in the above mentioned territory. Direct enquiries, if any, will be referred to Party B. However, should any other buyers wish to deal with Party A directly, Party A may do so. But Party A shall send to Party B a copy of Sales Confirmation and give Party B _____% commission on the basis of the net invoice value of the transaction(s) concluded.

(2) 若乙方在_____月内未能向甲方提供至少_____订货，甲方不承担本协议的义务。

Should Party B fail to pass on his orders to Party A in a period of _____ months for a minimum of _____, Party A shall not bind himself to this Agreement.

(3) 对双方政府间的贸易，甲方有权按其政府的授权进行有关的直接贸易，而不受本协议约束。乙方不得干涉此种直接贸易，也无权向甲方提出任何补偿或佣金要求。

For any business transacted between governments of both parties, Party A may handle such direct dealings as authorized by Party A's government without binding himself to this Agreement. Party B shall not interfere in such direct dealings, nor shall Party B bring forward any demand for compensation there from.

(4) 本协议受签约双方所签订的销售确认书条款的制约。

This Agreement shall be subject to the terms and conditions in the Sales Confirmation signed by both parties hereto.

本协议于＿＿＿年＿＿月＿＿日在＿＿＿＿签订，正本两份，甲乙双方各执一份。

This Agreement is signed on ＿＿＿＿＿＿＿ at ＿＿＿＿ and is in two originals; each party holds one.

甲方   乙方
(签字)   (签字)
Party A   Party B
(signature)   (signature)

12.3　Consignment 寄售

Consignment is the delivery of goods from the exporter (the consignor) to the agent (consignee) under an agreement that the agent sells the goods for account of the exporter. The consignor retains title to the goods until they are sold. The consignee sells the goods for commission and remits the net proceeds to the consignor.

Usually, the overseas consignee is advised of the goods sent to him by means of a proforma invoice. This gives him some ideas of the price the exporter hopes to realize when the goods are sold. Any expenses incurred, such as warehousing, insurance or selling expenses, are for the consignor's account. When the goods are sold, the consignee will render a sales report which shows the gross proceeds, the expenses incurred and the consignee's commission, etc.

The following is an example of a consignment contract:

寄售是一种委托销售地的代销商代为销售的贸易方式。在货物售出之前，其所有权归寄售人拥有。代销商卖出货物后扣除佣金等费用，将余款汇交寄售人。

在寄售方式下，寄售人通常会事先寄交代销商形式发票，代销商可以从形式发票上得知出口商想要出售的价格。在寄售中发生的一切费用，如仓储费、保险费以及销售费等都由出口商承担。当货物售出后，代销商向出口商提交销售报告，上面显示销售总收入、费用以及其应收的佣金等。

下面是寄售合同的样本：

寄售合同

Consignment Contract

Contract No.: _____

Place: _____

Date: _____

_____ Corporation (hereinafter referred to as Party A) and _____ Company in USA (hereinafter referred to as Party B), have, through friendly negotiations, agreed to sell _____ in China on consignment basis, subject to the terms and conditions as stipulated below.

_____公司(以下简称甲方)与美国_____公司(以下简称乙方),通过友好协商,双方同意在中国寄售_____, 协议条款如下:

(1) Name of Commodity 商品名称:

(2) Quantity 数量:

(3) Specifications 规格:

(4) Unit Price 单价:

(5) Total Value 总金额:

(6) Time of Shipment 装运时间:

(7) Destination 目的地:

(8) Insurance 保险:

(9) Documents: immediately after the shipment is effected, Party B shall notify Party A by cable of the shipped quantity, number of cases, and the Bill of Lading number, and airmail to Party A the clean on board B/L and Commercial Invoice in quintuplicate.

单据:乙方发货后,应及时电告发货数量、件数、提单号,同时将提单、发票各一式 5 份寄给甲方。

1. Terms and conditions 寄售条件:

A. Terms of Consignment: _____ days starting from the goods' arrival at the destination.

寄售期限:货物到达目的地后开始计算,以_____天为一寄售期。

B. The locations, methods and prices for selling shall be decided by Party A according to the situation, and Party B will not intervene. However, Party B may make proposals in the respect. Both parties shall exchange information in a timely way, study together, and settle any problems that may arise during the consignment period while Party B shall facilitate sales in every possible way.

销售地点、销售方式和价格等由甲方根据情况决定,乙方不得干涉,但乙方可以提出积极的建议。对于销售中出现的问题,双方应及时交换情况,共同研究解决方法,同时乙方应给予甲方一切有助于销售的便利。

C. If any advertising or promotion should be undertaken in any sales location, Party A will make proposals and Party B shall bear the expenses.

对各销售点的广告宣传，由甲方提出建议，乙方负担费用。

D. If any breakage of containers is found at the goods' arrival for which Party B is responsible, or any deterioration of quality occurs during the period of consignment, Party B shall make compensation at the contracted prices or replace the substandard goods with fresh goods according to Party A's certificate.

货物到达时，属于乙方责任的破损，或在寄售期内发生的变质等，凭甲方的证明按合同价格计算，由乙方给予补偿或退还。

E. During the period of this consignment, if Party A requires an increased quantity of the said commodity, Party B shall cooperate with Party A in order to expand sales.

在本批货寄售期内，如甲方对适销品种需要追加数量和金额时，乙方应予配合，以利于扩大销售。

2. Terms of payment 付款方式:

A. Party A shall, within _____ days after the expiration of the period of consignment, remit the total amount to Party B at the contract unit prices according to the varieties and quantities actually sold.

在寄售期结束后_____天内，甲方根据实际销售的品种、数量，按合同规定的单价计算金额给乙方。

B. For unsold goods, Party A shall make a list to Party B. The two parties shall decide through mutual consultations, whether to return the unsold goods to Party B or automatically transfer them to the next consignment contract.

对未销出的货物，甲方应列清单提供乙方，经双方协商退还乙方或自动转入下期销售合同。

C. The price of the portion of the shipment suffering quality deterioration or breakage shall be deducted from the total amount to be remitted, with the exception of those already disposed of or settled. However, Party A must furnish Party B with detailed invoice of deductions.

对货物破损、变质的部分，除在寄售期内已做处理和解决外，应按合同价格计算在汇款总额中扣除，但甲方应提供乙方扣除货款的详细发票。

3. This contract is made out in the original in Chinese and English, each party keeps one of them and both versions are equally valid.

本合同以中英文书就，双方各执中、英文正本一份，两种文本具有同等效力。

Party A   **Party B**

_____ Corporation   _____ Corporation

12.4   Tenders 招标和投标

A tender is an offer or proposal to purchase a specified quantity of commodity. Tender, as one special trade form, is widely used in international trade nowadays, especially for government construction projects and purchase of goods in large quantity. In tender, the price of goods or service is not quoted by the seller, but decided by choosing the most advantageous one from the offers of bidders.

Generally, a tender involves the procedures as invitation for bids, submission of tenders, bid opening, tender discussion and tender decision, establishment of contract and execution of contract.

招标是招标人发出招标公告，提出准备买进商品品种数量和有关条件等。招标，作为一种特殊的交易方式，如今已在国际贸易中，特别是在政府工程承包和大宗采购中得到了广泛的应用。在投标中，货物或服务的价格不由卖方开报，而是由卖方从投标方的报价中选出最有利的价格。

招标一般包含七个步骤：招标、投标、开标、评审、评标和决标、签订合同和履行合同。

12.5   Auction 拍卖

Auction is a public sale of merchandise held at a certain place, where would-be buyers or the bidder making the highest offer or bid becomes the buyer. Auctions are commonly used for selling nonstandard commodities of those that cannot be stored for long, such as tea, tobacco, wool, fur and timber. Auction procedures are different from those used in doing general export business. In general, auction may go through such stages as preparation, auctioning and conclusion of sales.

拍卖是在一定的地点，将货物向买主公开展示，由其相互出价竞购，最后由拍卖人把货物卖给出价最高的竞拍者。拍卖的商品大多是一些品质不易标准化或难以久存的商品，如茶叶、烟叶、羊毛、裘皮、木材等。拍卖与一般的出口不同，一般包含准备阶段、拍卖阶段和成交阶段。

Exercises

I. 术语翻译

独家代理	招标
经销	投标
寄售	拍卖

II. 问答题

1. 什么是经销？经销协议中涉及的当事人之间的是什么关系？
2. 什么是代理？代理的类型和作用是什么？
3. 什么是寄售？寄售方式和正常出口销售有什么不同？
4. 何为招标和投标？投标人在投标时应注意什么？
5. 何为拍卖？它有哪些特点？

III. 案例分析

1. 美国某公司和香港 A 公司签订一份独家代理协议，指定香港公司为独家代理。在订立协议时，美国公司正在试验改现有产品的性能。不久，美国公司试验成功，并把这项改进后的同类产品指定香港另一家公司作独家代理。问：美国公司有无这种权利？为什么？

2. 某公司研制出一种产品，为打开产品的销路，公司决定将产品运往俄罗斯，采用寄售方式出售商品。在代售方出售商品后，我方收到对方的结算清单，其中包括商品在寄售前所花费有关费用的收据。问：寄售方式下，商品寄售前的有关费用应由谁承担？为什么？

3. 某公司拟通过招标、投标方式选定工程队，为该机构建造办公大楼。该机构在发出的招标书中规定，投标人在投标时要提供合同金额的 10% 的履约保证金。经筛选，A 工程队中标，取得为该机构办公大楼的承建权。取得承建权后，A 工程队却因种种原因不履行合约，并向该机构提出退回全部保证金的要求，遭到拒绝。问：该机构的拒绝退款是否有理？为什么？